LANDMARK COLLECTOR'S LIBRARY

North Wales & Chester
In The Civil War

Norman Tucker, F. R Hist. S.

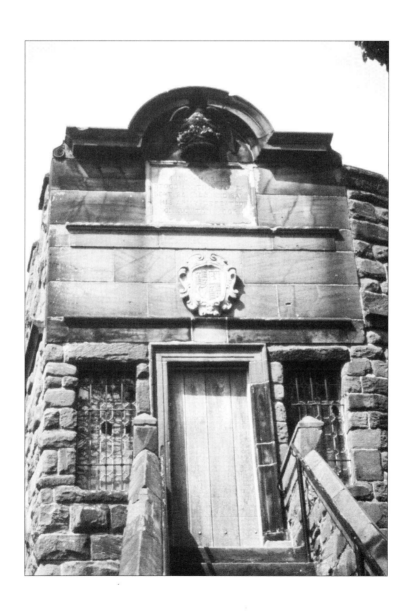

Royalist Officers Of North Wales 1642-1660

Norman Tucker

Virtually at the time of going to press with this book, the author's considerably amended copy of the above first edition was located and kindly made available by Ivor Wynne Jones.

Over 300 additional names with details had been added and extensive additional biographical notes added to the existing text. Very few were corrections.

It is proposed, subject to demand, to issue a limited print run, revised 2nd edition on a first come, first served basis. A maximum of 1,000 copies will be published, with a subscribers' list. Books will be numbered.

The text will incorporate a quantity of illustrations such as memorials to, and homes of specific officers similar to those used in this book.

To order, photocopy the order form below, phone or use one of the other electronic means listed. We will send further details in due course with a specification of the book, price etc. *No money is required now.*

For collectors of the works of Norman Tucker: please note that this will include a Preface on the author by Ivor Wynne Jones and the book will be the Official Memorial Edition.

Please send me details of Royalist Officers in North Wales 2nd Edition

Name: ....

Address: ....

....

Postcode: ....   Telephone: ....

QUICK ORDERLINE: Ring 01335 347349

Or send to:
Landmark Publishing Ltd
Ashbourne Hall, Cokayne Avenue, Ashbourne, Derbyshire DE6 1EJ
Tel: 01335 347349 Fax: 01335 347303
e-mail: landmark@claranet web site: www.landmarkpublishing.co.uk

Welsh Office
Helen Maurice-Jones
Clovercroft, Burton Road, Rossett,
Wrexham, LL12 0AR
Tel: 07779115236

Previous page: King Charles Tower, formerly the Phoenix Tower, on the town wall at Chester
Opposite page: Caernarfon Castle

North Wales & Chester
In The Civil War

Norman Tucker, F. R Hist. S.

Landmark Publishing

Published by

Ashbourne Hall, Cokayne Ave
Ashbourne, Derbyshire DE6 1EJ England
Tel: (01335) 347349 Fax: (01335) 347303
e-mail: landmark@clara.net
web site: www.landmarkpublishing.co.uk

2nd edition

ISBN 1 84306 028 0

Printed by Bath Press

Design & reproduction by Simon Hartshorne

Cover captions:

Front cover: Rhuddlan Castle, showing the Gatehouse
Back cover: The rear of Beaumaris Castle looking towards Snowdonia

CONTENTS

Phillips The Civil War in Wales & the Marches. J Roland Phillips (1874).

A. & M Ancient and Modern Denbigh. J. Williams (1856).

Hyde Hall A Description of Caernarvonshire (1809-1811). E. Hyde Hall. Caernarvonshire Historical Society. Record Series. No. 2.

Hall A History of Nantwich. J. Hall (1883).

Chester. Vol. XXV The Siege of Chester by the late Canon Rupert Morris, D.D., F.S.A. edited by P. H. Lawson, A.R.I.B.A. Chester and North Wales Archaeological and History Society *Journal,* No. XXV (1923).

Taylor Historic Notices of the Borough and County Town of Flint. H. Taylor (1883).

Newcome An account of the Castle and Town of Ruthin. R. Newcome. (1829). An account of the Castle and Town of Denbigh.

Hemingway A History of the City of Chester. J. Hemingway (1831).

C.W.P. Calendar of Wynn (of Gwydir) Papers. National Library of Wales (1926).

D.N.B. Dictionary of National Biography.

Mahler The History of Chirk Castle and Chirkland. Margaret Mahler (1912).

O.P. The Ottley Papers. Shropshire Archaeological Society.

Cal. S.P.D. Calendar of State Papers Domestic.

Parry Royal Visits and Progresses to Wales. E. Parry (1850).

Arch. Camb. Archaeologia Cambrensis.

Caerns. H.S. Tr. Caernarvonshire Historical Society Transactions.

Denb. H.S. Tr. Denbighshire Historical Society Transactions.

Flints. H.S. Pub. Flintshire Historical Society Publications.

Palmer (Wrexham Church) A History of the Parish Church of Wrexham. A. N. Palmer.

Palmer (13) Townships The History of the 13 townships of the old parish of Wrexham. A. N. Palmer.

UNV. OF N.W. University of North Wales.

N.L.W. National Library of Wales.

Aberconwy A History of the Antiquities of the Town of Aberconwy. Rev. Robert Williams (1835).

FOREWORD

A task of this nature inevitably places a writer under obligation to others. Some authorities have passed on, leaving their labours to speak on their behalf. I have reaped the benefit of the research done by J. Roland Phillips, John Williams of Denbigh, and Archdeacon Richard Newcome whose books are now difficult to obtain. *The Siege of Chester* by the late Canon Rupert Morris contains helpful references to North Wales affairs.

Among living authors the greatest authorities on this period in Wales are Professor A. H. Dodd and Sir Frederick Rees. I should be lacking in gratitude as well as in courtesy if I did not acknowledge my indebtedness to Professor Dodd, not merely for his authoritative works on which I have drawn freely, but for his unfailing kindness whenever I have had occasion to consult him.

The Librarian of the University of North Wales, Mr. Emyr Gwynne Jones, has graciously allowed me access to manuscripts and reference books. Professor Glyn Roberts has been equally courteous in giving me the benefit of his wisdom. The Caernarvonshire County Archivist, Mr. W. Ogwen Williams, has cheerfully assisted me when I have had occasion to examine ancient records. I have been helped, too, by Mr. E. D. Jones, keeper of manuscripts at the National Library of Wales, and Mr. M. Bevan Evans, County Archivist for Flintshire. The laborious task of fair-copying my typescript has been willingly performed by my wife.

In undertaking this book I have been urged not merely by a desire to draw attention to North Wales's participation in the Civil War, but also by a wish to pay tribute, belated and inadequate though it is, to many brave men whose sacrifices and sufferings have been well-nigh forgotten.

Norman Tucker

1

Though the part North Wales played in the Great Rebellion was not conspicuous it was of consider-able consequence. With a typically apt phrase that Civil War gossip, Arthur Trevor (half-brother to Sir Marcus Trevor of Brynkinallt) described Wales as 'the nursery of the King's infantry'. The parliamen-tary commander-in-chief in Cheshire, Sir William Brereton, regarded Wales as the magazine whence 'all his Majesty's provisions of victualls and men doe proceed'.[1]

If the King lacked sturdy pikemen or musketeers for his hard-pressed foot it was to North Wales the royal eyes instinctively turned. Should Rupert desire footmen for his famous Bluecoats he came to North Wales to recruit. This discomfited prince slept in Ruthin Castle on August 22, 1644, after riding this way to replenish his ranks depleted at Marston Moor. It was the men of North Wales who stormed the barricades at Brentford and helped Rupert to capture Birmingham. It is significant that King Charles, after raising his standard at Nottingham, marched to Shrewsbury, well knowing that he could count on the loyalists in North Wales to swell his ranks. The two visits the King paid to Wrexham early in the campaign indicate the importance he attached to the area.

Whether a survey of the defensive works of North Wales was made at the outset is not known but it is improbable. Provided no landing was attempted by Irish rebels – and there were several alarums – no one anticipated that the tranquil countryside would be disturbed by strife. The issue – so it seemed – would be settled in far-off England. The rebels (every Cavalier was convinced) would never withstand the fiery charges of Rupert's slashing horsemen. People were of one mind – that 'one battle would settle it'.

The Parliament depended on the Militia Acts to supply their army with fighting men; the King operated through the Commission of Array. Which system was more efficacious depended on the sentiment which prevailed in an area or on the influence of the leading families.

Flintshire and Denbighshire – at least, east Denbighshire – being nearer the English border were the counties most actively interested in the trend of national events. Though Parliamentary sentiment was not unknown in south Caernarvonshire and round about Wrexham it was not assertive, North Wales as a whole was regarded as Royalist territory. The loyal baronet of Lleweni represented the shire of Denbigh in the Short Parliament, but Sir Thomas Salusbury stood down at the next election rather than compete with his opulent uncle, Sir Thomas Myddelton of Chirk Castle, who used his wealth and his influence on behalf of the Parliament as soon as he was elected. Simon Thelwall of Plas-y-Ward who represented the borough followed suit and later obtained a commission as colonel of horse.

The area possessed a few professional soldiers such as Colonel Robert Ellice of Gwasnewydd who served under Gustavus Adolphus; Lieut.-Colonel Thomas Davies of Gwysaney who fought in the campaigns of the Thirty Years War; and possibly Sir John Owen of Clenennau, but the majority of the officers were amateur warriors.

The Bishops' Wars provided a mild experiment in calling out local levies. Statistics of the musters are illuminating as they show how recruiting accelerated when the Civil War broke out. In 1640, Denbigh county raised 200 footmen, Caernarvonshire contributing 160 and Flintshire 80.[2] It was required that there should be 'one drum and drummer for every 100 men'. Each man received 8d. per day during the exercising of the troops. The order that 'a good choice is to be made from the trained

[1] *Chester. Vol. XXV.* p.42. [2] *C.W.P.* 1664.

bands of men able-bodied and of meet years' indicates that the totals quoted did not exhaust the resources of each county. All men between sixteen and sixty were liable for military service in an emergency. Arms and armour would be stored in a magazine, usually in the county town where there was a castle. The strongholds which were to feature in the Civil War were:

Flintshire: Hawarden, Flint, Rhuddlan.
Denbighshire: Holt, Chirk, Ruthin, Denbigh.
Caernarvonshire: Conwy, Caernarfon.
Merionethshire: Harlech.
Anglesey: Beaumaris.

Farther off lay Aberystwyth Castle, Montgomery Castle, and Powys Castle—termed Red Castle. Near Beaumaris at Aberlleiniog was a small fortalice known as 'Lady Cheadle's Fort'. Powys Castle was the seat of Lord Powys, and Chirk was the palatial home of Sir Thomas Myddelton. The remaining castles were in a ruinous state, roofs leaking, wood rotting, ramparts crumbling yet with substantial walls which presented a formidable obstacle.

By this time North Wales had a definite road system though hard surfaces were not known until the coming of the turnpikes a century later. Ogilby in his road map of 1675 shows the main route from Chester passing through Denbigh, Henllan, Llannefydd, Betws-yn-Rhos and Dolwen to what is now termed 'Glan Conway Corner', and so to the ferry. He adds: 'Another Road is from Chester to Flint and Holywell then Over Rhylan Marsh through Abergely to Conway.' This was the route traversed by Lord Byron's emaciated warriors after the fall of Chester; they were allowed five days to cover the distance to Conwy.[3] Ogilby's map marks a gallows on Denbigh Green, Speed depicts one outside Flint; at Beaumaris, the name of Gallows Point is a reminder of a county town's function in the olden days. A few fishing-boats and barks engaged in coastal trade were to be found at Conwy, Beaumaris and Caernarfon.

The market towns were:

Flintshire: Flint, Rhuddlan.
Denbighshire: Denbigh, Ruthin, Llangollen, Wrexham.
Caernarvonshire: Conwy, Bangor, Caernarfon, Pwllheli, Nevin.

Clusters of villages (usually centred on a parish church or at road junctions), farms, and the houses of the gentry, gave animation to a countryside which contained many lonely stretches where woodland, moor and hillside were more conspicuous than cultivated fields. There were no great centres, and industries were restricted to coal and lead mining in Flintshire and limestone and slate quarrying elsewhere. Trade derived chiefly from the sale of woollens and cattle. The old order of life prevailed in these rural areas and it is doubtful whether the humble countrymen were stirred by the religious and political issues which fanned the flame of fanaticism in London. When war was declared, loyalty to the squire probably was more potent than fealty to a remote King. It took several years' strife and the sight of Parliamentary raiding parties driving off flocks and herds to arouse real passion and full realization of the grim horrors of war.

During the early stages of the Civil War, Welsh activity centred on the border fortress towns of Chester and Shrewsbury. The levies of Flint and Denbigh counties frequently fought on Cheshire or Shropshire battlefields. Gradual incursions from across the border caused apprehension in Royalist circles, particularly after the Parliamentarian triumph at Marston Moor. After Lord Byron's defeat at the battle of Montgomery in September 1644, the Puritan party became more confident. The whole

---

[3] *Chester. Vol. XXV.* p. 193.

aspect of the war altered and North Wales Cavaliers began to adopt an attitude of defence. The campaign in South Wales bore little relation to that in the North.

It was the protracted siege of Chester which had the greatest influence on affairs in North Wales. Though Denbighshire and Flintshire had experienced an ever-increasing number of raids by Parliamentarians engaged in the siege, it was only after 'the Loyal City' capitulated in February 1646, that a wholesale Parliamentary advance was undertaken.

The petitions sent to the King in Yorkshire before the outbreak of hostilities indicate that – thanks to the inspiration of Richard Lloyd, the King's attorney general for North Wales – the gentry were pledged to support the royal cause and were already making their preparations. The squires who supplied the Deputy Lieutenants, the Justices of the Peace, and the Commissioners of Array, fired by patriotic ardour, laboured to provide Charles with money, munitions and men. It is doubtful whether one of them foresaw to what interminable length the war was to drag its dreary way.

After this lapse of time it is impossible to comprehend the extent to which the passions of the participants were stirred by their conflicting religious convictions. Yet some diluted sentiment has survived, sufficient to cause many persons to range themselves with one side or the other. The Royalist sees Parliamentarians as rebels, knaves and hypocrites; the Puritan considers the King's party cruel, profligate and irreligious.

The obvious truth is that there were good and bad in both camps. In both armies were to be found the scum of humanity which war so frequently brings to the surface, and their evil deeds live after them. There were also high-souled gentlemen who, while abhorring the task of slaying fellow-countrymen, believed so vehemently in the cause they espoused that they gave their wealth and risked their lives to uphold that which they held to be right. For this war differed from those fought for revenge, or gain, or the lust of power, inasmuch as each side strove for an ideal; the one upholding the Crown and the Church, the other struggling for individual freedom and religious liberty.

It seemed a clear-cut issue at the start. As the months passed the war-skein became so entangled that not even the leaders could perceive what pattern was likely to emerge. The Scots took first one side and then the other. Presbyterians strove with Anglicans and then turned aside to clash with Independents. Republicans, Levellers, and Fifth Monarchy Men contributed to the confusion, and in the end the Parliament had to contend with the army which it had created. If some men stumbled is it to be wondered at? Verily they saw through a glass darkly.

To men of simple faith the issue was less involved. Sir Thomas Salusbury asserted that he could not serve the Lord unless he served 'the Lord's annointed'. His kinsman, Colonel William Salesbury (sic), when he learnt that despite his gallant resistence, Denbigh Castle was doomed, could write: 'For the condition of our King and his kingdoms, if God has soe disposed, blessed be his name and welcome be his will.'

The occupation of churches was not always wanton desecration; it must, at times, have been a military necessity. Royalists attacking Nantwich turned Acton Church into a fort. If, as tradition has it, Mytton stabled his horses in Llangwstenin (old) church, it might have been because the weather was inclement and no other shelter was available. The worst sin the Parliamentarians committed at Northop was, apparently, to steal the curate's surplice. Captain Harry Birch at the time of the Brereton raid in November 1643, wrote:

'I myself coming into the church of Hawarden the morning after they were there, found the Common Prayer-Book scattered up and down the chancel, and some well read man, without doubt, conceiving that the Common Prayers had been in the beginning of a poor innocent old church bible, tore out almost all Genesis .... In windows where there was oriental glass they broke in pieces only the faces .... They had pulled the rails down about the table, and very honestly reared them to the wall (it was well they were in

Llangwstenin Church, where Major-General Mytton is supposed to have stabled his horses

a coal country, where fuel was plentiful) and brought down the table to the midst of the church.'[4]

To the Puritans a table placed against the east wall of the chancel represented an 'altar': hence this gesture of disapprobation.

At variance with the popular conception of iconoclastic Roundheads is the sentiment expressed by a certain 'S.R.' who wrote from Caernarfon on the day after its governor, Lord Byron, surrendered to Major-General Mytton:

'I must tell you they are here, for the matter of religion, most ignorant and brutish people, who know very little of God; and it is heartily to be wished that some honest and godly-painful ministers would come to preach the Gospel to them. Indeed, there are some prelates and prelatical clergy in Carnarvon very malignant, and such as the people are like to profit little by, except they will study to preach Jesus Christ more than, for ought I can hear, they have done. The country-towns hereabouts have been quite without all manner of preaching almost. But blessed be God, we are in a fair way to reduce these parts to the obedience of the Parliament who, I doubt not, will take care to send a powerful ministry so soon as North Wales is totally reduced.'[5]

The victors regarded the task of evangelising the vanquished as a serious obligation. In 1649 they formed a Commission for the Propagation of the Gospel in Wales, a body which functioned actively if not always happily for a number of years. Its members included supporters with commissions

[4] *Phillips*. Vol. 2. p. 114. [5] *Phillips*. Vol. 2. p. 309.

prominent in less peaceful circles; names which strike a note of irony.

Professor A. H. Dodd writes: 'Until it received its *coup de grace* in 1653 the Propagation remained the real government of Wales.'[6]

By practical demonstration preachers like Vavasour Powell proved they could wield the broadsword as effectively as the sword of the spirit. Vavasour was wounded in the attack on Beaumaris in 1648. Others like Cornet Jeffrey Parry of Rhydolion were ready to go to prison for their religious convictions. Wrexham district produced a number of earnest Puritans. Many were undoubtedly influenced by Morgan Llwyd the preacher-mystic. Among the men who prayed as well as fought were Captain William Wynne, a commissioner under the Act for the better propagation and preaching of the Gospel in Wales, Captain Gerald Barbour, a friend of the Rev. Philip Henry who described him as a 'saint of the Lord', and the valiant Captain Edward Taylor of Pickhill who unhorsed the redoubtable Sir John Owen. Wrexham, in fact, proved to be (in Dr. Thomas Richards' words) a hotbed of Puritanism and 'bred a numerous crop of cornets and captains'.[7]

Such is the complicated composition of the human personality that saints and sinners intermingled on the Propagation of the Gospel Committee. Here are the names of some who served in North Wales:

COLONEL JOHN JONES, the regicide
SIR JOHN TREVOR, Bart.
CAPTAIN RICHARD PRICE
COLONEL GEORGE TWISTLETON
COLONEL JOHN CARTER
LIEUT.-COLONEL THOMAS MASON
CAPTAIN THOMAS BALL
CAPTAIN HUGH COURTNEY
CAPTAIN EDWARD TAYLOR
CAPTAIN ROGER SONTLEY
CAPTAIN WILLIAM WYNNE
CAPTAIN LUKE LLOYD
CAPTAIN ANDREW ELLIS (who was married to the daughter of Lord Saye and Sele)[8]

An incongruous convocation to spread abroad the doctrine of the Prince of Peace!

[6] *Studies in Stuart Wales*. p 148. [7] *Flints. H.S. Publ*. No 13. p.53. [8] *Studies in Stuart Wales*. p. 152.

2

During the Civil War there was a complete lack of uniformity of apparel until the formation of the New Model army by the Parliament in 1645. Foot soldiers then adopted the red tunic which was ever after to be the hallmark of the British infantryman. Even so, the colour of their breeches was not specified provided the garments were grey or a similar 'sad' colour. Surprisingly few relics of the arms and armour have survived in this area. While the Office of Works were restoring Conwy Castle in 1955 several cannon-balls of small calibre were found.[9] They were probably fired by Parliamentary batteries during the siege of 1646. In the Grosvenor Museum, Chester, is a jack-boot the leather of which is of a thickness which makes one marvel it was ever worn. Several basket-hilted broadswords are doubtless souvenirs of the fight on Rowton Moor.

Armour was favoured for a short time at the outbreak of hostilities. Gradually it fell into disuse, men preferring to risk wounds rather than suffer the discomfort its wearing entailed. Headpieces were unbearably heavy and were often replaced by broad-brimmed hats. The term 'helmet' was never used. 'Headpiece' was the accepted term though this was usually abbreviated to 'pot'. A cuirass was alluded to as a 'breast-and-back'. Buff-coats were favoured by the cavalry, the thick leather being expected to turn a sword cut. They were usually sleeveless to give the sword arm greater freedom, thus permitting the doublet's sleeves to be seen. Fighting units were divided into four main groups: horse, dragoons, foot and ordnance.

Mounted men were termed 'horse'. As the senior branch the troopers were well paid (when paid) and better equipped than the foot. They played the determining part in an action which was usually settled by a cavalry charge. The chief weapon was the broadsword. Holster-pistols and carbines were sometimes carried but their use does not seem to have been encouraged. Occasionally a small poll-axe was favoured by the Cavaliers. The normal unit was a troop of 120. A trooper provided his own mount on the understanding that he was recompensed in the event of its death or injury.

The title 'dragoon' has changed with the passing years. Then it signified mounted infantry. The men were trained to fight as foot, were armed with muskets, and used their nags (an animal inferior to the cavalry charger) merely as a means of transport.

The rough nature of much of the North Wales terrain made mounted infantry desirable. Sir Richard Lloyd of Esclus commanded a dragoon regiment, Sir Thomas Hanmer of Hanmer raised two companies of dragoons, and Lieutenant-Colonel Thomas Davies of Gwysaney was ordered to combine dragoons with infantry in his regiment of 500 Flintshire men.

Referred to as 'foot', the infantry were divided into two groups: pikemen, who wore protective armour and carried pikes of 16 or 18 foot length; and musketeers, termed 'shot'. At the start the latter were equipped with the cumbersome matchlock which had to be supported on a rest and fired by the application of a smouldering 'match'. The cord of this, several feet in length, was held between the second, third and fourth fingers of the left hand. At night the glow betrayed movements as did the rattle of cartridge-cases which swung from the bandoleers. Risk of explosion was great. The matchlock was replaced by the flintlock as speedily as possible. The ball used weighed an ounce; some were as heavy as 12 to the pound.

Sir Charles Firth[10] quotes Lupton as placing the effective range at 400 yards, but comments: 'the

[9] *More have since been discovered in the castle well.* [10] *Cromwell's Army.* p. 89.

musket was effective at a longer distance than was generally supposed.' Firing was inaccurate. When Nantwich experienced a night attack by Lord Capell's forces several hours' shooting resulted in the death of one calf.

Field-pieces were used in many battles but they did not play an important part except in siege warfare. Siege-pieces such as cannon and culverin required a large team of oxen and could only be moved when the road surface was dry. There was no standard of calibre; the weight of shot was approximate. A cannon-ball was usually termed a bullet. The names of ordnance sound strange:

CULVERIN: 18 to 20 lb.
DEMI-CULVERIN: 9 to 10 lb.
SAKER: 6 lb.
MINION: 31/2lb.
DRAKE: 3 lb. or less.
FALCONET: 2 lb.
ROBINET: 1 lb.

In the grounds of Gloddaeth Hall lies an ancient cannon pitted with rust. It is seven feet long and has a bore of 5$^{1}/2$ inches – a culverin's measurement. How it came there is a mystery but it was probably used for battering Conwy in 1646. Raised ground at Llandudno Junction facing the castle still goes by the name of Cae Battery (Battery Field). Stone balls fired from mortars during the siege

The culverin at Gloddaeth Hall, now St David's College

have been unearthed at Denbigh and Chester. 'The heaviest piece habitually used in the field was the culverin,' writes Sir Charles Firth. It 'carried point blank about 400 paces, and had an extreme range of 2,100 [11] paces. It required eight horses to draw it.' [12]

An infantry regiment was normally 1,200 strong; a dragoon regiment 1,000, but the figures were governed by circumstances. Though Colonel Roger Mostyn raised 1,500 men for the King at the outbreak of war, by 1644 his numbers had dwindled to 300. 'After a few months fighting,' comments Sir Charles Firth, 'the Royalist army was full of colonels whose regiments were no stronger than a troop or a company.' [13]

When a regiment sustained heavy losses it was the King's practice instead of bringing it up to strength to issue a new commission to another colonel to form a fresh regiment.

Regiments bore no number but went by their colonel's name. Frequently they wore his colours. Thus, Sir Thomas Fairfax's soldiers had a blue uniform, so had Prince Rupert's Bluecoats. There were also the King's Red Regiment and the Duke of Newcastle's Whitecoats. John Hampden's men wore green.[14] The Earl of Essex's regiment had orange, and this shade, in compliment to the commander-in-chief, was adopted by the Parliament as their badge. Each company carried its own colours to assist in rallying its men during the fog of battle smoke. The old practice of a regiment using its colonel's livery on its facings, and being known by his name, is perpetuated in the Green Howards. Payment of the fighting men was notoriously irregular. The Parliament, with London's financial resources at their disposal, were more consistent in their payments but the result was far from satisfactory. Once General Mytton's own men opened fire on him at Wrexham because they were exasperated at their pay being sadly in arrears. Brereton complained that the Lancashire horse were unreasonable and would not fight unless properly paid.

A document in the Chirk Castle collection throws light on the payments made to the garrison in 1646 after the Royalists had forsaken their trust and Myddelton had regained his majestic home. Infantry, stationed at Chirk, received: lieutenant 14s. per week, ensign (second lieutenant) 10s. 6d., sergeant 5s. 3d., corporal and drummer 3s.[15] This is considerably less than the standard rate quoted by Sir Charles Firth in *Cromwell's Army* which places a lieutenant of foot at 4s. a day and an ensign at 3s.[16] In the instance of the garrison a deduction might, of course, have been made for subsistence. But rates of pay varied.

One of the vexed questions of the war was how troops could be paid. Charles's debt to his amateur soldiers is too great to be computed. Squires like Roger Mostyn, William Price, William Wynne of Melai, Hugh Wynne of Bodysgallen are known to have raised their own regiments at their own expense and it is quite probable that most of the other gentry also bore the cost even though the fact has not been recorded. When such professional soldiers as Sir John Owen, Colonel Robert Ellice or Lieutenant-Colonel Thomas Davies were ordered to form regiments, it is possible that payment came from the royal war chest. As time passed and this source became depleted, non-payment of the wages of royalist soldiers (despite levies on various counties and towns, and 'free quartering') caused increasing dissatisfaction, and doubtless was the indirect cause of much of the plundering. It will be noticed that when Chirk Castle was captured, the King ordered Colonel Ellice to dispose of the plunder to provide funds for the new regiment of foot he was to raise. After the Anglesey rebellion of 1648 the gentry responsible for the disturbance were fined a sum sufficient to cover the wages of the officers and common soldiers who had to be called out to suppress it.

'Free quarter' is now little more than an empty phrase. During the Civil War it carried an ominous ring. Householders were compelled to board soldiers on the promise of future payment. Sir Charles Firth writes: 'It did not mean that food and lodging was provided gratis, but that payment for them was deferred.' [17]

[11] *Rev. William Harrison,* Elizabeth arms England *(1587), gives the range at 4,000 yards.* [12] Cromwell's Army, *p. 150.* [13] *Ibid. p. 26.* [14] Oliver Cromwell. *John Buchan. p. 153.* [15] Mahler. *p. 18g.* [16] Cromwell's Army. *p. 188.* [17] Cromwell's Army. *p. 218.*

Chirk Castle, the home of Sir Thomas Myddleton

War-calloused warriors who did not trouble to differentiate between friend and foe proved unwelcome guests. The bitterness engendered may be imagined.

In piecing together the story of the early years of the war it is inevitable that the emphasis rests on the King's party. The Cavaliers were, in the first place, the dominant party. Records of their activities, such as their petition to Charles at York, have survived to testify to their ardour. Much of the correspondence which has been preserved comes from Royalist pens–possibly because the other writers considered it safer to commit their recorded opinions to the flames. An impression is thus created that the squirarchy of North Wales were Royalists almost to a man, but this was not the case. In South Caernarvonshire men like Thomas Madryn (the sheriff), Thomas Glynne of Glynllifon, John Bodwrda, William Lloyd of Plashen (who later gave his life for the Parliamentary cause), and even Sir William Williams of Vaenol, had leanings towards the Puritan party but, their habitations being set in a Royalist neighbourhood, they were compelled by circumstances to become Commissioners of Array. In east Denbighshire the Parliament's supporters were not all drawn from the ranks of yeomen farmers and prosperous tradesmen. One of the Broughtons of Marchwiel is said to have strayed from the Royal path followed by so many of his kindred. Major Francis Manley of Erbistock, wounded fighting for the King, had a younger brother, John, who became a major in the opposite camp and acquired considerable influence. Strangest of all, the King's most doughty warrior, Colonel William Salesbury, had as his heir, Captain Owen Salesbury, who fought for the Parliament; an apostasy his stubborn parent never forgave. They died unreconciled.

The conduct of the troops changed as the struggle intensified. There is no indication of cruelty at the start; and not a great deal of disorderliness. In fact, when, during the winter of 1642-3, the troops of Colonel Roger Mostyn got out of hand and looted the Chester house of the Parliamentary commander, the civic authorities were so shocked by this unseemly behaviour that they endeavoured to make restitution. Three years later the event would probably not have elicited comment. The character of the earliest troops was doubtless reflected in their conduct. The soldiers would be mainly volunteers inspired by a principle or stimulated by desire for adventure, or else they were men whose masters required such service. Later, when the supply of volunteers failed to swell the ranks adequately on either side, both parties resorted to conscription. So involved did the war become that it is said that many of the best infantry in the New Model Army were ex-Royalist foot who had obtained their freedom by undertaking to serve their new masters, a decision made easier by the promise of attractive pay.

Idealism, indeed, appears to have been one of the first casualties in this conflict which was ostensibly fought for an ideal.

Beamaris Castle from Castle Field

3

1642 The First Civil War

To obtain a correct background for the events of the Civil War it is necessary to bear in mind two military occasions which absorbed public attention during 1639 and 1641. First came Charles's futile and humiliating expeditions against the Scots. One benefit indubitably accrued! The mismanagement of the campaigns brought home the unpleasant truth that English amateurs after so many years of peace were ill-prepared for military adventures. The campaigns, however, served the purpose of a dress rehearsal as organisation was necessary to call out the militia.

The general of horse who commanded at Newcastle was no other than Lord Conway, owner of Conwy Castle, that nebulous personage who hovers like a spectre over the more material figures of Archbishop Williams and John Owen. Later Lord Conway was transferred to Ireland as general of horse but was recalled to London where he watched the King's interests in the House of Lords. He was prime mover in a conspiracy to raise London for the royal cause, and on its discovery was placed in durance by the Parliament.

Charles, in a letter to Archbishop Williams, explained that Lord Conway could not fortify and provision Conwy Castle 'being imprisoned by some of our rebellious subjects'. [18]

In the late autumn of 1641 the country was horrified by news of massacres of Protestants in Ireland. Already regiments had been serving in that country under Lord Strafford's rule, but the Parliament resolved to dispatch in addition 10,000 foot and 2,000 horse to put down the revolt. Once war broke out in England they became a forgotten army until their reappearance tipped the scale in the King's favour. The opportune arrival of the fleet bearing these ragged veterans had a decisive effect on the issue in North Wales.

During the summer of 1642 the rumblings of the coming storm grew ominous. King Charles had quitted intransigent London for Yorkshire. After the Scottish campaign the arms of the disbanded militia were stored in the fortress-port of Hull. The King, desirous of securing these to arm his volunteers, rode at the head of 300 Cavaliers to demand their surrender. The governor, Sir John Hotham, shut the city gates in the royal face. Frustrated and humiliated, the Stuart was forced to withdraw. The incident had far-reaching consequences. Had the royal infantry been suitably equipped at Edgehill they would have given a better account of themselves and hundreds of ill-armed Welshmen would have survived the slaughter.

The King was wroth. So, too, was Archbishop Williams in his palace at Cawood. [19] He expressed his opinion of Sir John so vehemently that Hotham's son, when it came to his ears, drew his sword and swore to cut off the prelate's head. When the Archbishop learned that young Hotham had ridden forth to execute his threat, he abandoned Cawood Castle and fled incontinently back to his native town of Conwy. As it transpired his unpremeditated act enabled him to serve the royal cause far more effectively than he could have done in Yorkshire.

In North Wales the leading Royalists – inspired by Richard Lloyd of Esclus – penned petitions to the King professing their loyalty and imploring his Majesty to take up arms against the Parliamentary disturbers of the peace.

The Flintshire petition, which bore the signature of the octogenarian knight, Sir Roger Mostyn,

[18] *Hacket*, quoted by Williams, *Aberconwy*, p. 57. [19] Near Selby, Yorkshire.

was presented to the King at York on August 4. As this was only a matter of three weeks before the King raised his standard at Nottingham, it may be assumed the gentry of North Wales were in active preparation for the approaching conflict.

Wrexham was the largest town in North Wales. Unlike its neighbouring boroughs it possessed no tutelary castle but lay open and exposed. Nevertheless, it was regarded as a convenient centre for assemblies. Only a few miles away Holt Bridge led to the Puritan stronghold, Nantwich, the proximity of which possibly accounted for the strong Parliamentary sentiment which stubbornly persisted in this district.

It was Wrexham which was selected for the meeting of the gentry of Denbighshire and Flintshire that August when they unanimously resolved to raise a regiment of volunteers for the King, and to subscribe £1,500 for the purpose. For the commanding officer they chose Sir Thomas Salusbury, second baronet of Lleweni, the paramount house of West Denbighshire. A comparatively young married man, with a son eight years old, Sir Thomas had served in the Short Parliament but was better known as an Oxford scholar, with a predilection for poetry. From a letter he wrote at the time it is obvious he was an idealist who regarded the campaign as tantamount to a crusade to uphold the divine right of kings.

According to Judge Bulstrode Whitelock, young Roger Mostyn raised 1,500 men for the King in 12 hours. If this applies to a separate regiment it signifies that these two counties alone contributed over two thousand of the Welshmen who followed the King to Edgehill.

In Caernarvonshire Colonel John Owen, who returned to his native county to recruit a regiment of volunteers, met with less response, and could not muster sufficient men to join in the march from Shrewsbury which ended at Edgehill. And this despite the lure that the regiment would form a life-guard for the Prince of Wales, the saturnine twelve-year-old destined to attain notoriety as the Merrie Monarch.

When the King sojourned at Shrewsbury he presented to the town two pieces of ordnance for its defence. Considering these insufficient, the Shrewsbury Royalists applied to the King for his good offices with the gentlemen of Caernarvonshire to procure them the loan of additional artillery. On December 31 his Majesty at Oxford addressed a letter to John Griffith esq., and others of that county desiring them to lend him 'such pieces of artillery as may be of use to our towne of Shrewsbury; undertaking to return them att the end of the service, unless in the interim it shall be agreed between you and the said towne to buy and sell the said peeces'. [20] Many cart-loads of arms were brought to Shrewsbury out of Flintshire and Denbighshire.[21]

King Charles visited North Wales on several occasions. In 1645 he slept at Chirk Castle and also at Denbigh Castle. He was twice at Wrexham. On September 27, 1642, he addressed the populace from the old shire hall – later burnt. On October 7, he returned and was the guest at Bryn-y-Ffynnon, the town house of Richard Lloyd, whom he knighted.[22]

Events in North Wales must necessarily have been influenced by the stand taken by the loyal city of Chester. Though there were many changes in the garrison during the war the core appears to have been consistently provided by the regiments of Colonel Hugh Wynne and Colonel Roger Mostyn.

Surprisingly little has been preserved about the part played by North Wales troops in the battle of Edgehill. Charles and his amateur army set forth from Shrewsbury on October 12, intent on capturing London. The Earl of Essex with a larger force marched north to intercept him. So deficient was the scout-craft of both sides that the armies passed each other without being aware of their proximity. Thus, when contact was made, Charles had his back to his capital and Essex faced the city he intended to protect.

It is common knowledge that the King's success was jeopardised by Rupert's irresponsible charge – in which he was followed by Sir John Byron who commanded the reserve of horse. As a result the

---

[20] Owen and Blakeway. *Hist. of Shrewsbury*. 1. p. 432. [21] Ibid. p. 429. [22] *D.N.B.*

Royalist foot were left unprotected. For several hours they were at push of pike. The Welsh under Salusbury formed the second line of defence. In the gathering gloom the bewildered, ill-armed men of Flint and Denbigh crowded together to face the flashing broadswords of Balfour's cavalry until, in the chill October twilight, the field was strewn with slashed corpses, soon to be tumbled into communal graves. There are no casualty lists. Perhaps those turf tombs account for the absence of some well known North Wales names from the annals of the Civil War. The Welsh unfortunates do not appear to have made a good showing. A Robert Evans, referring to Colonel Salusbury, wrote that his fellow countrymen were '1,200 poor Welsh vermin, the offscowering of the nation'.

It seems clear that Sir Thomas Salusbury was engaged in the battle. The King marched to Oxford which he entered on October 29, and soon after this Sir Thomas was awarded the degree of D.C.L. by the university. [23] This infers that he went there with the King.

A couple of weeks after Edgehill the Welsh infantry of Salusbury's regiment redeemed their reputation. When the King's march on London was checked at Brentford, the barricades which had defied Rupert's horsemen were stormed by the men of Denbighshire–who incidentally plundered the town by way of recompense.

Warburton writes: 'Rupert soon indulged himself and his favourite regiment, the Prince of Wales' by making a bold dash at Brentford capturing on his way the advanced post at Sir Richard Gwynn's and charging into the streets of Brentford.' [24]

Deterred by the menace of the London trained bands assembled on Turnham Green, the King retired to Oxford and his forces went into winter quarters. The university city, overcrowded, would have no accommodation for soldiers not required to man the defences. Colonel Salusbury's decimated regiment made their way back to the more congenial confines of North Wales.

With Christmas came the hope of compromise. A 'bare and poor truce' (to quote Archbishop Williams) was arranged in Cheshire but it was shortlived. The good prelate regarded the issue lightheartedly at this time for a letter written from his home at Penrhyn shows that he was 'engaged in so many visits and feasts at Tom Bulkeley's [Baron Hill] and Sir William Williams' [Vaenol] that it will be nine, ten or twelve days at the least before he can leave these parts'. [25]

Edgehill survivors must have straggled home with tales of the fight but no written record appears to have been preserved. The rigours of the campaign may have proved too severe for the constitution of the poet-soldier, Sir Thomas Salusbury, for by the following August he was dead. No further reference occurs to the regiment of which he was colonel. At Mostyn Hall is a silver medallion inscribed *R. Mostyn*. According to family tradition it was picked up on the battlefield and is accepted as proof of Roger's presence at Edgehill.

No warlike activity is indicated in North Wales but doubtless the drilling of trained-bands, the manufacture of powder, and the collection of weapons went on under the inspiring leadership of Sir Richard Lloyd, Attorney General for North Wales. His Wrexham home was admirably placed for preserving contact with the loyal fortress towns of Shrewsbury and Chester.

The outstanding organisers for the King at this period were Archbishop Williams in the west and Sir Richard Lloyd in east Denbighshire. Sir Richard evidently found Esclus Hall too remote, for he acquired as his town house the famous Bryn-y-ffynnon which had hitherto belonged to John Jones of Maes-y-garnedd, who later attained questionable fame as 'the regicide'. Whether Sir Richard purchased Bryn-y-ffynnon or took possession under the exigencies of war is uncertain. His tombstone in Wrexham parish church proclaims that he was 'a loyal and devoted subject and servant of the Royal Martyr, Charles I, whom he received at Bryn-y-Ffynnon in this town in the year 1642'.

Charles's first visit to Wrexham on September 27 during his journey from Chester to Shrewsbury

---

[23] *D.N.B.* [24] Quoting Clarendon, III 327. This advanced post was probably Sir Richard Wynn's house at "Brainford" at it was termed (Vide. *C.W.P.*). [25] *C.W.P.* 1719. *Note.* Charles's letters sent to the Commissioners of Array for Caernarvonshire are printed in full in an appendix to the Rev. P. B. Williams' *Guide to Caernarvonshire.* 1821.

must have been a memorable occasion. High Street would doubtless be packed with people. According to tradition the King addressed the inhabitants of the counties of Denbigh and Flint from a window of the ancient Shire Hall.

It is apparent that by this time the local volunteers had reached Shrewsbury. This is implied in Charles's opening words:

'I am willing to take all occasions to visit all my good subjects, in which number I have cause to reckon you of these two counties, and having lately had a good expression of your loyalty and affection to me by those levies, which at your charge have been sent me from your part (which forwardness of yours I shall always remember to your advantage) and to let you know how I have been dealt with by a powerful malignant party in this Kingdom, whose designs are no less than to destroy my person and crown, the laws of the land, and the present government both of Church and state.'

After denouncing the subtlety and cunning practices of the Parliamentary leaders the King continued:

'I am robbed and spoiled of my towns, forts, castles, and goods; my navy forcibly taken from me and employed against me; all my revenue stopped and seized upon; and at this time a powerful army is marching against me. I wish this were all. They have yet laboured further to alienate the affections of my good people.'

Charles concluded:

'My confidence is in the protection of Almighty God and the affections of my good people. And that you may clearly see what my resolutions are I shall cause my voluntary protestation lately taken, to be read to you. And I desire that the Sheriffs of these two counties will dispose copies of that, and what I now deliver unto you, having no other way to make it public.'*

In an atmosphere of uncertainty and anxiety the good folk of North Wales waited to see what the new year would bring forth.

Wrexham Church and the white-painted property predate the King's visit of 1642

*Printed in full in Phillips vol 2. pp. 20-22

1643

The dawn of 1643 saw the people of North Wales looking outward over the invisible wall of the border, less concerned with domestic affairs than in devising support for the cause in England. It was not until autumn that the seriousness of the conflict was realized. The first and obvious centre of their interest was Chester. Lying a matter of twelve miles from Wrexham where Royalist manor-houses clustered thickly it would be the first citadel to which the King's supporters would gravitate, even as it was the Mecca of the Mostyns, the Whitleys and Pennants dwelling nearer the coast. From the outset the names of Hugh Wynne, Roger Mostyn and Robert Ellice were associated with Chester, the outworks of which were planned by Ellice. Welshmen comprised a large proportion of the garrison. The good people of Shropshire, however, had some claim and they wrote to the Denbighshire Commissioners pointing out that Salop was 'their guard from any force of the Parliament', and suggested that North Wales contributed something to the cause. Accordingly Colonel William Wynne of Melai (near Llangernyw) marched his regiment to support Lord Capell in Shropshire, while Major Robert Broughton of Marchwiel offered his services to Sir Michael Woodhouse who acted as Capell's ser-geant-major-general of foot. As the months passed the interest of Colonel Ellice and Sir Richard Lloyd centred more on Shrewsbury than Chester, doubtless because that town was nearer the seat of war. The appointment of Prince Rupert as President of Wales and commander-in-chief of the area would have been an undoubted attraction, particularly when his Highness chose Shrewsbury for his headquarters during his ephemeral command.

Charles ordered Colonel Ellice to capture Chirk Castle. This was accomplished with apparent ease, Myddelton being absent in London. His steward, Watkin Kyffin, was taken prisoner. William Maurice records:

1643. 15th of January: Chirk Castle taken and plundered by Colonell Ellis.

The loss of this important stronghold was as big a reverse to the Parliamentarians as it was a great gain to the King's party. Sir Thomas Hanmer was appointed governor for a short while but he was soon succeeded by Colonel John Watts.

In January 1643 Sir Francis Ottley

Sir Francis Ottley and his family, Pitchford Hall. He was appointed Governor of Shrewsbury in 1643 (Pilgrimages To Old Homes, Mostly On The Welsh Border, 1903. p. 317).

One of the properties built in Nantwich after the town was engulfed by fire in the late 1500s and thereby witnessed the Civil War in the town.

was appointed governor of Shrewsbury and he kept in close touch with the leading men of North Wales. Shropshire was without Parliamentary opposition until the Puritan party established a headquarters at the open market town of Wem which they proceeded to fortify. The command was conferred upon Colonel Thomas Mytton of Halston, thereby introducing a soldier who was destined to play a conspicuous part in the affairs of North Wales.

In Cheshire the Parliamentarians, led by Sir William Brereton, a baronet of ancient lineage, encircled Nantwich 'round aboute with Stronge Trenches & mudwalls of Clodds & Earthe',[26] and adopted this town as their headquarters. The principal posts along the Severn were in Royalists' hands and barge-loads of munitions and provisions freely passed along this watery highway. The crossings of the Dee were watched by garrisons at Holt, Overton, and Bangor-is-y-Coed. Denbighshire provided 400 musketeers for the purpose.[27] Well might the good people of North Wales consider themselves secure.

The loyalist baronet, Sir Thomas Aston, sallied from Chester intent on capturing Nantwich before the defence works were completed but he sustained a severe defeat by Brereton on January 28.

On February 2, Colonel Mostyn's Welsh soldiers got out of hand in Chester and sacked The Nunnery, the town house of Sir William Brereton, smashing windows, stripping off lead and carrying away furniture and goods. City officials interfered and endeavoured to restore what property they could but Brereton cherished resentment. It is probable that the tenacity of his siege was not unconnected with this incident. Sir Thomas Aston set forth again on March 11 resolved to redeem his lost reputation by an attack on Middlewich. Colonel Robert Ellice accompanied him with his Welsh regiment. In a night engagement Aston was again worsted, and Colonel Ellice was taken and marched captive to Manchester. Major Gilmore and some 600 infantrymen were among the prisoners. Ellice was exchanged in September. With him were imprisoned 'Captyn Johnes, Captyn Morrys and Captyn Eaton'.[28]

In April 1643, Prince Rupert 'entered and possessed the seditious town of Birmingham, wherein was 300 Foot and two Troops of Horse, who being gallantly charged by the Welsh-men, in less than half an hour forsook their Breast-work and retired to the Barracadoes within the Town'.[29]

That summer a party of Parliamentarians from Nantwich embarked on a nocturnal attack on the house of Sir Thomas Hanmer, in Flintshire, hoping to surprise it. They were ambushed by Welsh soldiers led by Sir Richard Willis, Capell's major-general of horse, and driven back with heavy losses.

The sale of cattle and Welsh cottons – a name applied to a coarse woollen fabric – was seriously affected by the hostilities and the inhabitants of North Wales petitioned the King for safe conduct for the clothiers and drovers to allow them to pass safely through his Majesty's army. The petition bore the signatures of Colonel Thomas Madryn, sheriff of Caernarvonshire, Rowland Vaughan, sheriff of

[26] *Hall.* p. 147. [27] Prof. A. H. Dodd. *D.H.S. Tr.* vol. III, p. 53. [28] *Hall.* p. 147. [29] *Mercurius Belcicus.*

Point of Air

English - Irish Army landed here. Nov. 18. 1643.

Mostyn
Holywell

Flint

Brereton occupied Hawarden Castle. Nov. 12. 1643.

Rhuddlan
St Asaph
Denbigh
Gwysaney
Mold
Northop

Hawarden
Chester

Conway

Ruthin

Llanrwst

Holt

Gwersyllt
Wrexham

Farndon

Brereton and Myddleton captured Holt Bridge Nov. 9th 1643.

Manley House
Erbistock
Chirk

Oswestry

Route of the Parliamentarians on their first raid, November 1643

Merionethshire, Sir William Williams, Colonel Richard Bulkeley, William Hookes, Owen Wynn of Gwydir and other leading men.[30]

The cattle trade was considerable and, in the words of Archbishop Williams, represented 'the Spanish fleet of North Wales which brings hither that little gold and silver we have'.[31]

When Rupert demanded money, the archbishop contended that it was pointless for the soldiers to clamour for wages when the country had no money with which to pay them owing to there being no free sale of cattle.

Wales was not merely called upon for men and money, there was an insatiable demand for powder and weapons. While worthy Thomas Bushell melted down family plate at the royal mint in Shrewsbury others laboured to provide more substantial support. Gunsmiths were rounded up and concentrated in the fortress town where a vigilant eye saw that the pistols, muskets and carbines they manufactured did not find their way into enemy hands.

The Calendar of Wynn Papers records that, in the summer of 1643, Robert Dolben of Denbigh was commanded to wait on the Commissioners of Array at Ruthin to arrange for his protection while he manufactured gunpowder in North Wales. He was to undertake the work at his own expense but the commissioners allowed him to dig 'all their houses for the making of salt-petre', but he was 'to leave all floors as he found them, and to offer the powder as cheap as he can afford'.[32]

This letter (written to Owen Wynn at Gwydir) imparts the information that there were many Parliamentary ships in Chester Water (the Dee estuary) intending to land at Flint.

A far-reaching move that year was the Parliament's commissioning on June 12 of Sir Thomas Myddelton of Chirk to be their sergeant-major-general for the six North Wales counties, to wage war against 'many Papists, notorious delinquents, and other ill-affected persons'. Despite his age Sir Tho-

[30] C.W.P. 1724. [31] Ibid 1748. [32] Ibid 1723.

mas proved himself a capable general and had a number of successful enterprises to his credit before the Self-Denying Ordinance relieved him of his command. On August 10, Myddelton marched north from London with forces which included seven large guns, four 'cases of drakes', and forty carriages of ammunition.

Welsh troops must have participated in many incidents of which there is no record. For instance, the *Ottley Papers*[33] show there were Welsh soldiers accompanying Lord Capell when he marched to relieve Warrington only to find that the town had surrendered, As he retired to Whitchurch an attempt was made to ambush him in 'a woody ground'. The Parliamentarians, with a party of horse attending them, were 'repulsed by our Welsh without any loss to us, or them, for all we came to knowe'.

Colonel John Owen had succeeded in getting his regiment together and led them south to where Prince Rupert was besieging Bristol. A number of Welsh, including Lieutenant-Colonel Thelwall, participated in the assault, during which Colonel Owen was severely wounded in the throat. The letter he wrote to his wife describing the mishap is extant.[34] He survived and returned to North Wales with dramatic results.

One of the leading royalists of the Wrexham district was Sir Edward Broughton, father of the Major Broughton who was wounded at Wem. He dwelt at the Old Hall which lies at no great distance from the Cheshire border. Among Sir Thomas Myddelton's soldiers who were then stationed at Nantwich were local men who were well acquainted with the district. On the morning of October 23, 1643, members of Myddelton's troop, assisted by men of Nantwich companies marched into Wales, and took the Hall by surprise, capturing Sir Edward and two of his sons, all of whom they brought prisoner to Nantwich.[35]

Meanwhile the Royalists in Shropshire were tasting the bitterness of internecine strife. Much of the money subscribed for the local cause had gone to the King at Oxford, and the trained bands were forced to raid the countryside for subsistence.

This atmosphere of Royalist discontent enheartened the Parliamentary party who renewed their efforts to fortify Wem. To give Colonel Mytton the benefit of their experience, Sir William Brereton and Sir Thomas Myddelton marched south to superintend the work. Myddelton's Welsh soldiers formed part of the garrison of Nantwich and were probably with the force.[36]

There followed a grim game of hide-and-seek played by men with sword and musket in their hands, for Lord Capell, learning that Brereton had marched towards Wem, surreptitiously assembled an army of between 4,000 and 5,000 men. Moving by night he essayed to capture Nantwich in Brereton's absence. His men reached Acton Church which lies a mile from Nantwich whereupon the town's defenders, despite their depleted numbers, sallied forth to give battle. Here a struggle raged in the churchyard and the invaders were driven to seek shelter in the church. Unable to dislodge them the townspeople returned to the security of their mud walls to await the anticipated assault. Word of their predicament was carried to Brereton who instantly halted his force and hastened back to their aid. Capell was informed of this and, after his men pillaged friend and foe alike, he hurried from Acton resolved to carry out his original plan to attack Wem. The two forces missed each other in the darkness.

When day dawned, Wem's three hundred defenders found themselves facing the advance guard of several thousand royalists. An assault was promptly delivered and a fierce battle followed on that momentous morning of October 18. Here, on the ramparts, Colonel William Wynne of Melai was slain, and his Welsh soldiers, discouraged by the loss of so popular an officer, abandoned the fight. Capell's men withdrew to Shrewsbury, ten miles away, taking with them the corpse of the colonel for interment in St. Chad's church.

Brereton's weary warriors on learning they had missed their foes again set out for Wem, finally

[33] *O.P.* p. 138. [34] *Mitre & Musket,* B. Dew Roberts p. 217. [35] *Hall.* p. 157. [36] *Ibid.* p. 155.

refusing to march further until they had rested. The fight was over when they neared Wem but they made a half-hearted attempt to harass the retiring Royalists.

Both sides were too fatigued to settle the issue. In the assault on Wem the Welsh suffered heavily. Among the wounded were Major Broughton of Marchwiel and Captain Manley of Erbistock. The exulting victors claimed that sixty Royalists were slain by one discharge from 'a case of drakes'. Six carriage-loads of dead were carted from the field and (adds the report) thirty more corpses were left on the ground. This was the worst misfortune so far experienced by the Cavaliers of North Wales. A greater shock was to follow.

Though Royalists had taken Chirk Castle the Myddelton influence was not exterminated. The Commissioners of Array at Chirk experienced difficulty in raising trained bands for the King's service and Kenrick Eyton, John Edwardes and John Trevor, three of the commissioners found it necessary to issue warrants to apprehend those who were backward in enlisting. On the very eve of the Brereton raid, Edwardes wrote to Sir Richard Lloyd: 'I have hastened the soldiers you desired, the delay has been caused by the illness of Mr. John Trevor, who could not assist me …. I have no arms with which

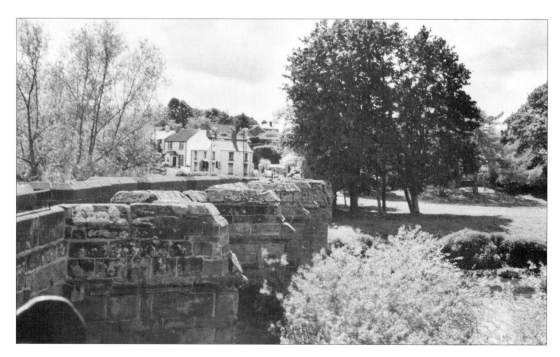

Opposite top: Holt Bridge, from an 18th Century estate map. It shows the gatehouse protecting it.
Opposite bottom: Holt Bridge today. The Parliamentarians succeeded in storming it in 1643.

to furnish the men.'[37]

In view of the menace from the Cheshire Parliamentarians the hundred of Bromfield raised 124 musketeers 'to guard the passages upon the river Dee', and provided £150 to pay them for a month. The commissioners suggested that Chirk might contribute a hundred men and £100 to support them.

Once the weather broke it was customary for troops to go into winter quarters, but Brereton, now reinforced by Myddelton decided to invade North Wales. On November 7 the combined forces marched out of Nantwich. They moved at a leisurely pace, spending the first night at Woodhey and the second at Barton-on-the-Hill.[39] As they neared Farndon they were joined by some Lancashire men under Colonel John Booth. Though the invasion was in a sense a surprise, it was not wholly unexpected. Tidings had reached the governor at Holt Castle, Lieutenant-Colonel John Robinson, who dispatched a party to cross the river and dispute the enemy's advance. The Welsh bank of the river was lined with musketeers from Colonel Ellice's new regiment, supported by Major Marcus Trevor's regiment of horse. Brereton in his dispatch claimed he had to face 'all the strength and power in Wales'. Numbers might be imposing but it will be seen from Edwardes' letter there was some raw material in the Royalists' ranks. Bells ('rung backwards') and flaring beacons spread an alarm across apprehensive Denbighshire.

At that time Holt Bridge possessed a gatehouse in the centre. This was protected by a drawbridge and strong gates. No trace remains but the structure is clearly indicated on a plan.[40] Both Royalists and Roundheads considered that it would be 'very difficult if not impossible' to force a passage. The invaders' first attempt was to send a party across the Dee in boats, but they were met by such a fierce fusillade from Ellice's musketeers that they returned to their own bank. A feint was then attempted, a large body of Roundheads marching down river as if they intended to cross elsewhere. While the defenders' attention was distracted a sudden rush for the bridge enabled Brereton's men to place ladders against the gatehouse and cut the ropes of the drawbridge. This fell down, giving access to the gates. Hand 'granadoes' were cast over amongst the Welshmen 'which struck such terror as they all run away'. The gates were forced open and the Royalists beaten from their double works. Brereton wrote that they pursued Colonel Ellice's regiment of foot, Major Trevor's regiment of horse 'and all the forces which could be arranged in the adjoining parts of Wales'.[41]

They took about forty common prisoners, one captain, four or five lieutenants, one cornet, and it was reported that there was a lieutenant-colonel also among the prisoners. 'About six o'clock Thursday evening we entered Wrexham,' wrote Brereton. 'The enimy fly apace and begin to remove all their goodes out of these partes, but Holt Castle holds out, butt is beseidged.'[42]

Thomas Malbon states that the bridge was gained about one o clock 'throughe a pollicie' without loss of a man. The King's force was supposed to be 1,000 horse and 700 foot. Prisoners sent to Nantwich included 'Captaine Preece, Captyn Johnes and Lieuftent Salusbury'.

'On Thursdaye Nighte, after they had taken Holte & left a considerable ptie theire, They marched to wrixam; where they weire well entertayned & quartered theire that Nighte.'[43]

The following morning Brereton led part of the invading force to Hawarden. Immediately the Roundheads appeared before the royal fortress the gates were opened by Col. Thomas Ravenscroft of

[37] *Mahler*. p. 166. [38] Ibid. 165. [39] *Hall*. p. 157. [40] Denb. H.S. *Tr.* vol. 4. p. 32. [41] *Chester*. vol. XXV. pp. 45-46. (quoting Portland MS 151). [42] Ibid. p. 46. [43] *Hall*. p. 157.

The reconstruction of Conwy Castle and Town walls

Col William Salesbury
This portrait is of him as
the Governor of Denbigh.
The ship probably records
Salesbury's voyage
to the East Indies when
a young man.

Pickhill, member of an old Flintshire family, who was supported by Col. John Aldersey. As Ravenscroft that day borrowed a barrel of gunpowder from Chester the cries of 'treachery' were loud. Colonel John Booth with 900 men stayed in Wrexham. There, too, was Sir Thomas Myddelton who, doubtless encouraged by the fall of Hawarden, wrote to the governor of Denbigh, Col. William Salesbury, summoning him to hand over that castle. It was a friendly missive.

'The former friendship and familiarity wch hath passed betwixt us doth not only invite but also engage me to use all possible means not only to continue but alsoe to encrease the same …. I doe hereby invite you, and desire Cod that you may for your own good embrace it, that you would please to submitt yourself to the power and obedience of the King and parliament,[44] lay down your armes, and deliver up that castle to mee ….' He signed himself: 'Your ould true friend and kinsman.'[45]

But Colonel Salesbury was of different mettle from Colonel Ravenscroft, his son-in-law. His response was courteous but firm:

'But to be playne – to betray soe great a trust as the keeping of Denbigh castle, tho' upon ever soe fayre pretences, may be acceptable to them that desire it, but in my opinion, in itself is abominable.'[46]

There the matter ended. Salesbury (who had recently received his commission from the King) and his relatives restored the castle at their own cost. In Wrexham soldiers sheltered in the parish church where they 'broke in pieces one of the best pair of organs in the King's dominions, which Sir Thomas Myddelton took for proper pillage, to make bullets out of'.[47] Another account states that Brereton went to 'Wrexham, Flint and Holywell, and did pull down the organs, defaced the windows in all the churches, and the monuments of divers, and pulled down all the arms [coat-of-arms] and hatchments'.

From Conwy Archbishop Williams complained to Ormonde.

[44] The expression invariably used by the parliament who contended they did not fight against the King, but for him to preserve him from the evil counsellors who led him astray. [45] *A.&M.* p. 214. [46] *A.&M.* p. 215. [47] *Phillips*, vol. 2, p. 114.

'For now …. the enemies are possessed of Worrall where your excellency intended to land, and entered into Denbighshire, have taken Wrexham and Ruthin (as some say), plunder up and down the whole country, without resistance; and whether with a resolution to fortify here, or to return again and besiege Chester upon the Welsh as well as the English side, I am not able to conjecture. So that if the English-Irish army shall now come over, unless it be so well provided (by sea and land) as to force their entertainment in Lancashire, Liverpool (which they now seem to neglect as I am informed), or Worrall, where it is feared they will fortify, they will be necessitated to land some-where in these parts, or at Holyhead, and so much discommodated by the poverty of the country through which they are to pass, and those two ferries at Beaumaris and Conway, which of necessity they are to waft over very incommodiously, and (as far as I can conceive) without carrying their cannon with them, but sending it by sea to meet them at Orme's Head, Abergele, Rhyddlan, or as neare Conway as the enemies' advancing will permit and give them leave. And how I shall be able to keep this town of Conway (without any power of command, but that weak one of kindred and good-will) without any assistance of souldiers or Commissions of Array, is to myself very doubtful.'[48]

Conwy Castle at this time was evidently without a garrison for Williams asked Ormonde to send by Captain Bartlett's ship one company of Yorkshiremen or Welshmen. He undertook to provide them with meat, drink, shoes and stockings, provided they came armed with some ammunition for which he would pay. The letter was written on the 12th; a more pessimistic one followed on the 18th. 'But, alas! we grow daily in more uncertainty of the landing of the forces from your parts than we were,' he wrote, little knowing that the troops from Dublin were even then being rowed ashore at Mostyn. He again appealed for his company of a hundred soldiers but this time he did not specify that they should be Welshmen or Yorkshiremen. 'I do not care of what country they are, so as they come with arms and competency of ammunition.'

An indication of the potential man-power of the area at that time is contained in this letter. If the forces from Ireland landed there, he wrote, 'they shall be waited on by two or three thousand foot at the least, and some two or three hundred horse, to the skirts of England.'[49] The old 'militia' idea had not died out – the prelate knew the men would be reluctant to serve outside North Wales! He also asks that these 'auxiliaries' should be provided with 'arms and ammunition' – the lack of which was a perennial problem to the Commissioners of Array.

From Hawarden, Brereton wrote the governor of Chester, Sir Abraham Shipman, calling upon him to surrender the city, to which Shipman sent a contemptuous reply that if Brereton desired Chester he must 'win and wear it'.

While Brereton was at Hawarden another force consisting of some 600 horse and foot marched down the road to Mold, and having possessed this town, pressed on towards Holywell and Flint. They could not have reached Flint before November 11, and as they were in retreat on the 18th, the so-called siege of the castle must have been of brief duration. A party continued along the coast to Mostyn Hall which they captured, taking four cannon, but before they could remove these pieces, a Royalist fleet of some sixteen vessels dropped anchor off the coast and the invaders turned tail.

The ships bore some 2,500 'English-Irish' (to use Archbishop Williams' term) under Sir Michael Ernley, Major-General Richard Gibson, Sir Francis Butler, Major Edward Hamond and George Wynne. With their landing the whole condition changed. Flint Castle was abandoned.

[48] Ibid pp. 93-94. [49] Ibid. p. 100.

Brereton forsook Hawarden Castle, leaving a garrison of 120 men to their fate. Colonel Roger Mostyn and Lieutenant-Colonel Thomas Davies who, according to Brereton's dispatch, 'fled', quickly reappeared and led the newcomers to Hawarden which was invested. The Welsh, some 500 strong, took over most of the duties, being augmented by a force from Chester under Lieutenant-Colonel John Robinson of Gwersyllt. The majority of the English-Irish marched into Chester where house-wives knitted stockings for the ragged warriors.

Chester was heartily glad of the respite and Lord Byron, who had recently arrived as commander under Lord Capell, was gratified to have so many trained soldiers under his charge.

Captain Thomas Sandford, commanding the firelocks from Ireland, sent a 'big letter' to the garrison at Hawarden:

'if you put me to the least trouble or loss of blood to force you, expect no quarter for man, woman or child.'

According to Orlando Bridgman, Hawarden was 'blocked up by 1,000 men, most of them of the country'. The latter would be the Welshmen under Colonel Roger Mostyn and Lieutenant-Colonel Thomas Davies. The Roundheads in reply to a verbal summons to surrender wrote: 'We fear the loss of our religion more than the loss of our dearest blood.'

After an exchange of letters the garrison finally capitulated on December 4. A condition of surrender was that the besieged should be allowed to march away with half their arms, one colour and £25 worth of goods, though, as it transpired, the Parliamentarians were badly treated by 'some of the Lord Cholmley's men'.[50] Colonel Mostyn and Colonel Davies accepted the surrender.

When visualizing incidents at Hawarden Castle it must be borne in mind that the present highway is not older than the start of the 19th century. The old road ran alongside the east face of the walls, overlooked by the barbican, the entrance, and the portion containing the living quarters. The keep or round tower was on the opposite side.

Brief though the Parliamentary raid was, it caused consternation. Henceforth the Royalists in North Wales had little sense of security. This may well have been the time when they began to deposit their valuables in the strong rooms of the castles. Sometime about Christmas, Byron assembled 4,000 foot and 1,000 horse with the idea of marching through Cheshire to link up with the Shropshire army under Lord Capell.

In the meanwhile, Archbishop Williams at Conwy had received a summons from the King to attend the 'parliament' which was to be held at Oxford. It might be well, at this juncture, to look back to see what the prelate had been doing.

Archbishop Williams, after establishing himself at Conwy, had proceeded to put the ruined castle in a state of repair, and was encouraged in this self-imposed task by his monarch who, on August 1, 1643, wrote to him from Oxford:

'And whereas you are now resident at our Town of Aber-Conway, where there is a Castle, here to fore belonging to our Crown, and now to the Lord Conway, which with some charge is easily made defensible; but the Lord Conway being imprisoned by some of our rebellious subjects, and not able to furnish it, as is requisite for our service, and the defence of those parts: you having begun at your own Charge to put the same into repair, we do heartily desire you to go on in that Work, assuring you that whatsoever Moneys you shall lay out upon the Fortification of the said Castle, shall be repayed unto you, before the Custody thereof shall be put into any other hand, than your own, or such as you shall recommend.'[51]

The archbishop had undertaken the work with characteristic zeal and thoroughness and, once the Parliamentarians had taken Flint and Hawarden castles, he evidently thought Conwy was in jeopardy

[50] *Phillips*. vol. 2. p. 113. [51] *Hacket.*

for he pleaded with Ormonde 'to spare 100 able soldiers, well commanded for officers, for the guard of this strong town and castle, where they shall have good quarters, and be ready at six days' warning to return again to Dublin'. [52]

The threat was of short duration and doubtless the prelate left Conwy with an easy mind when, towards the end of December, he rode off on the long and dangerous journey which was to carry him to Oxford where Charles had summoned his 'parliament' to meet on January 22, 1644. The archbishop lodged with the Provost of Queen's, and though he was not actually appearing as a member of the convocation, Charles asked for his advice.

He gave it fearlessly. It proved unpalatable though events were to vindicate his judgment. Bishop Hacket records the prelate's words:

'Your militia is courageous, but small, not like to increase, and then not to hold out. Your enemies multiply, and by this time your army hath taught them to fight; they are in treaty with the Scots to make a recruit; and the Princes and States beyond the seas, to their shame, give them countenance. Their treasurers at Westminster boast that it costs them large moneys every month to keep Correspondence with their intelligencers and spies about you. Your soldiers in their march and quarters are very unruly, and lose the people's affection everywhere.
'Out of these premises, I infer and engage my life to your Majesty's justice and my soul to God's tribunal that I know no better course than to struggle no further, since it is the will of God, and to refer all to the pleasure and discretion of that unkind and insolent Parliament at Westminster, but with the preservation of your Majesty's Crown and Person, to which they have all taken an oath to offer no hurt or violence …. But if your Majesty disdain to go so low, I am ready to run on in the common hazard with your Majesty, and to live and die in your service.'

Rupert and the hotheads who followed him, all of whom anticipated an easy victory, were indignant, and it might well be that from this moment Rupert was prejudiced against the prelate. The decision to appoint Sir John Owen as governor of Conwy probably had its birth at this time.

Despite the risk from Parliamentary armies the archbishop 'by easy journeys' returned safely to Conwy. Williams was at Worcester on May 6 and by the 19th he wrote from Conwy: 'I am once more come to these partes.' It was, says Ambrose Philips, 'the last journey of his life'.

While he was absent the fighting round about the Cheshire border had undergone a complete change. Lord Byron, elated at being reinforced by the veteran regiments from Ireland, took the offensive. The newcomers had seen rough service during their campaign and a cruelty, hitherto not noticeable, intruded. At the little village of Barthomley, some twenty villagers who had sought safety in the church were smoked out and cut to pieces.[53]

The officer of the English-Irish soldiers, Major Connaught, granted the suffocating villagers quarter if they came out. 'But,' wrote Malbon, 'when hee had theim in his power, hee caused theim all to be stripped starke Naked; And moste barboriouslie & contr'y to the Lawes of Armes, murthered, stabbed and cutt the Throats of xij of theim.'*

The Parliamentary cause was struck a shrewd blow by the loss of Beeston Castle on its towering crag. Malbon writes:

'On Wednesday morninge, the xiij of December 1643, a litle before Daye, and after the Moone was sett, Captyn Sandford wth viij of his fyerlocks, gott into the vpper warde of Beeston Castle, by a byeway, throughe treachery, as was supposed. For a litle after hee was entered, Thomas Steele, then

---

[52] *Phillips.* vol. 2. p. 100. [53] *Hall.* p. 159. * Lord Byron on December 26, wrote to Lord Newcastle: "The Rebels possessed themselves of a Church at Bartomley, but wee presently beat them forth of it, and put them all to the sword, which I find to be the best way to proceed with their kind of people, for mercy to them is cruelty." The letter fell into the Parliamentary party's hands and did Byron's reputation little good!

gou'nor of the said Castle, after a shorte ply [parley] betwixt theim, Receyved Sandford into his Lodginge in the Lower warde, where they Dyned together, & much Beere was sente up into the heigher warde, by the said Steele vnto Sandfords soldyers.'

As a result the sixty men of the garrison marched out with colours flying and Beeston became a King's castle. For his betrayal Captain Steele was shot behind Nantwich Church.

It was during this December of 1643 that Simon Thelwall, Member of Parliament for Denbigh borough, chose to make his journey to Pembrokeshire. He was a son of the famous house of Plas-y-Ward, near Ruthin. Though his kinsmen served the King, Simon, who was 41 when war broke out, followed the lead of Sir Thomas Myddelton. It has been suggested that the arrival of the English-Irish caused Thelwall to 'cut for his life', but the excellence of his long dispatch to the Parliament, with his detailed and lucid summary, suggests that he was officially sent South to report on the condition of affairs in that troubled region. He served as a volunteer and was given a commission as colonel of horse. His report to the Speaker begins: 'Since I departed at Wrexham from my Major-General Sir Thomas Myddelton, being foreclosed towards Wem by Lord Byron's forces, and towards Nantwich by the Irish, and having knowledge both passages to be laid for me; it pleased God, I repaired about ten days before Christmas, through some difficulties, to the good town of Pembroke, which I found environed almost on every side with adverse garrisons.' [*]

Colonel Thelwall in due course returned to Denbighshire where he played an important part, more prominent, it would seem, as an administrator than as a soldier.

Byron attacked the Cheshire Parliamentarians near Middlewich and defeated them, killing some two hundred. Colonel Robert Byron claimed 300 were slain and 274 taken prisoner. After Beeston Castle was surprised by Captain Sandford, the Royalists, encouraged by this and other successes, laid siege to Nantwich.

The King's party felt the game was now in their hands!

Beeston Castle: the lower gatehouse in 1784 (above) and the castle remains in 1850 (opposite top)

[*] Quoted in full by Phillips, vol. 2., pp. 140-148.

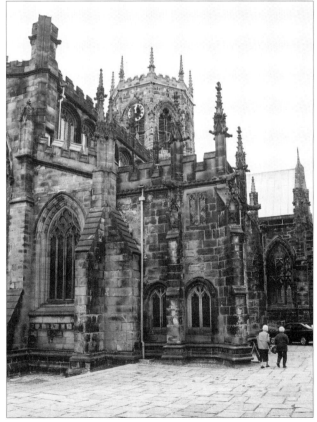

Nantwich Church, where Capt. Steele was shot for the loss of Beeston Castle to the Royalists

5

1644

With the arrival of the troops from Ireland the whole complexion of the fighting changed. More were to follow – two infantry regiments under Colonel Robert Byron (a brother to Lord Byron) and Colonel Henry Warren, with four troops of cavalry commanded by Sir William Vaughan who played a prominent part in North Wales for the remainder of the first war. Then came two more infantry regiments under Colonel Robert Broughton of Marchwiel and Colonel Tillier (or Tyllyer). In February Lord Byron ordered the deputy lieutenants of Flintshire to provide mounts for a regiment who had lost their chargers in passage.

Royalists received a reverse on January 12 when Colonel Mytton surprised a party from Chester at Ellesmere, capturing the Chester governor, Sir Nicholas Byron, uncle of Lord Byron, who quickly succeeded him.

Reinforced by the Irish regiments Byron felt confident of capturing Nantwich. It was stubbornly defended by Colonel George Booth. Lieutenant-Colonel Boughton and Captain Thomas Sandford were killed while assaulting the mud walls. Then Sir William Brereton and Sir Thomas Fairfax came to the relief of Nantwich, defeating Byron, and capturing numerous officers of distinction, not the least of whom was George Monck.

Prince Rupert having been appointed President of Wales on February 5, rode to Shrewsbury which he reached on the 18th. On March 11 he visited Chester where he was received with ceremony and ardour. Having inspected the outworks and given instructions for their improvement he returned to Shrewsbury taking the Irish veterans with him.

'He visited many of the garrisons in North Wales,' writes Roland Phillips.[54] It would be interesting to know whether the prince journeyed as far as Conwy. The archbishop mentions that Rupert 'when he was last in these parts' took men from the local regiment.[55]

Meanwhile on the Shropshire border Mytton was exercising that initiative which was to bring him fame. In June, while watching for a convoy of ammunition sent from Oswestry to Rupert, he learned that a party of musketeers were marching to Bangor-on-Dee. He surprised them at Duddleston and captured 27 out of 54. Only four bore English names. The remaining captives, headed by Quartermaster Owen Jones and Sergeant Richard Foulkes, were all Welsh.

Acting under the Earl of Denbigh, Colonel Mytton attacked Oswestry which was captured on June 24. Welsh soldiers were in the garrison. 'It is a sad sight,' runs a Parliamentary report, 'to behold the ignorance of these Welsh in these parts, and how they are enslaved to serve.'[56]

The list of officers taken includes Captain John Madryn, Lieutenant Nicholas Hookes (surely of Conwy!), Cornet Lloyd, Ensign Morgan, Ensign Wynne and Commissary Richard Edwards.[57] Mytton was appointed governor of Oswestry. The Earl of Denbigh learnt that Colonel Marrow meant to attack the town – news which caused him concern for (he wrote):

'my regiment of foot and Sir Thomas Myddelton's are grown so weake that they are not able to guarde their colours.'

[54] *Phillips.* vol 1. p. 217. [55] Ibid. vol. 2. p. 289. [56] Ibid. vol. 2. pp. 175-6. [57] Ibid. vol. 2. pp. 175.

His lordship's fears were justified. Colonel John Marrow (who, since his return from Ireland, had proved an energetic supporter of the King) led 1,500 horse and 3,500 foot against Oswestry. To frustrate this design Myddelton advanced by way of Whitchurch. He succeeded in putting the Royalists to flight but lost 'one Captain Williams'. Prisoners taken at Oswestry on July 3 included 'twenty Welsh and Shropshire gentlemen'. [58]

The victors then marched towards Shrewsbury where a skirmish occurred. Here they 'took Major Manley, major to the Lord Byron, and Governor of Bangor, within little more than pistoll shott of their workes'. [59]

This activity accounts for the absence of the Earl of Denbigh and Myddelton from Marston Moor which was fought on July 2. The Marston Moor reverse had a depressing effect on Chester and North Wales which was not lessened by the news that Rupert was riding to Chester, pursued by Brereton and Sir John Meldrum. The defeat had not improved Rupert's temper and he arrogantly demanded more men and money. While Brereton and Meldrum followed the prince, the Earl of Denbigh and Myddelton lay in wait for him, but his Highness outwitted them and reached Shrewsbury on July 20. By August he was again in Chester, quartering his forces over a wide area – some in Chester, some in Shrewsbury, others in Denbighshire and Montgomeryshire.

While in Chester Rupert made fresh demands on North Wales. On August 1 he wrote Lord Bulkeley at Baron Hill requesting him to pay by way of loan to the Archbishop of York the sum of £100 'for my use and his Majesties service'. This was followed on August 8 by a further demand, this time for the loan of 'two peeces of Brasse cannon' to be sent to Chester where the prince was devising improved defences. He obviously was acquainted with the ordnance at Beaumaris for he specifically named the guns as a culverin (18 lb.) and a saker (6 lb.). [60]

On August 5 a party of 550 of Rupert's own horse were

Above top: Sergeant-Major-General Sir Thomas Myddleton of Chirk Castle. The MP for the shire of Denbigh and Parliament's Commander-in-chief for the six North Wales counties.

Above bottom: Lady Sarah Wynne, the daughter of Sir Thomas Myddleton (spelt Middleton on this brass) who died 16th June, 1671. She was the wife of Sir Richard Wynne 4th Baronet of Gwydir. The plaque is in the Gwydir Chapel, Llanrwst.

[58] Ibid. vol. 2. p. 180. [59] Ibid. p. 183. [60] *UNV. OF N.W. Baron Hill MSS.* 5372-3.

surprised at Welshpool by Myddelton and Mytton who captured 40 troopers and 400 chargers while 'Prince Rupert's own cornet was slain'. Sir Thomas Dallison, the officer in charge, 'fled away without his breeches', in which was found a letter addressed to the prince. [61]

Myddelton augmented this useful work by driving off 200 head of cattle from the park of Powys Castle.

While Rupert was at Ruthin, Colonel Marrow led a party of horse from Chester to Tarvin. On August 21 they were badly defeated by Brereton and Myddelton, Marrow receiving his death wound. The brave officer had married a rich wife but three weeks before. Two regiments of horse rode forth to avenge his death but they, too, were routed. After this second disaster Rupert abandoned his idea of returning to Chester. Accompanied by two hundred horse, including detachments under Colonel Marcus Trevor and Sir William Vaughan, [62] he rode south from Ruthin – no one knew whither. It transpired Bristol was his destination. Vaughan and Trevor must have returned speedily for they were in the fight at Malpas on August 26.

Towards the end of August Myddelton was with Mytton in Oswestry. Orders from London directed Sir Thomas to march into Montgomeryshire, partly to disperse Royalists rallying there, partly to intercept powder which Rupert had sent from Bristol to replenish the diminishing stocks in North Wales and Chester. At this time Sir John Meldrum was endeavouring to recapture Liverpool from the Royalists.

During the night of September 3 Sir Thomas marched his men out of Oswestry and by dawn they were at Newtown where they surprised a small garrison commanded by Sir Thomas Gardiner. In addition to the governor and forty prisoners Myddelton secured thirty-six barrels of gunpowder, twelve barrels of brimstone and a large quantity of match.

His next move was to march on Montgomery Castle where dwelt Lord Herbert of Cherbury. At Myddelton's summons he instantly opened the castle gates and the Parliamentary general was able to store his precious powder inside the walls. Lord Herbert continued to reside in his castle. Myddelton. anticipating an attempt by the Royalists to recover the powder, began to replenish the castle with provisions and livestock commandeered from the countryside.

Word of the Royalist loss reached Colonel Robert Broughton, who had just been made governor of Shrewsbury, and Sir Michael Ernley. Though in ill health Ernley acted promptly. He summoned aid from all neighbouring Royalists and, advancing on Montgomery, surprised Myddelton and Mytton during one of their foraging expeditions. Mytton and the infantry took shelter in the castle; Myddelton, who had the worst of the encounter, galloped off with the cavalry to Oswestry.

Then began the siege of Montgomery Castle. The Royalists dug trenches and threw up earthworks, resolved to recapture the powder. Myddelton's determination was to break through the leaguer and rescue Mytton. At the appeal for aid Sir John Meldrum withdrew some of his forces from Liverpool, Brereton marched from Cheshire, while Sir William Fairfax, brother of the future lord-general, added a contingent from Yorkshire, bringing the Parliamentary total to 3,000 men. They converged on Montgomery which they reached on September 17. By this time Ernley's forces were reinforced by those of Sir Michael Woodhouse, now governor of Ludlow, while Lord Byron came with the men of Chester and every available soldier he could recruit in North Wales – 2,000 in all. [63]

Leaving a guard for the trenches, Byron (who assumed command) assembled the main body on rising ground behind the town, vacating the site previously occupied by the attackers. This was taken over by the newly arrived Parliamentarians. Both sides remained in these positions until the following day. While a third of the Parliamentary horse were absent in search of provisions Byron made a surprise attack. He beat back Sir John Meldrum's horse and even when the infantry fell to push of pike the Royalists appeared to be gaining the mastery. Sir William Fairfax was captured but was rescued. He then received a wound from which he died next day. Thanks to the Cheshire foot 'who

[61] *Phillips.* vol. 2. p. 194. [62] *Phillips.* vol. 1. p. 245. [63] *Parry.* p. 386.

carried themselves more like lions than men', the Roundheads rallied and completely routed the Royalists, capturing 1,500 men. The prisoners included Colonel Robert Broughton of Marchwiel, Captain Dolben, Captain Morgan, Lieutenant Morgan, Lieutenant Griffiths, and numerous others with Welsh names.

Some 500 Royalists were killed. Brereton placed his loss at 40 slain and not 60 wounded. Arthur Trevor, writing to the Marquis of Ormonde, complained:

'Our men ran shamefully when they had no cause for so great fear, so that we here are ordained to be the mocking-stock of the War.'

The writer criticizes Lord Byron:

'My Lord Byron is infinitely unfortunate, and hath now finished with your Excellency, that is to say, made an end of all your Lordship's army to a man, without any the least service; and truly, my Lord, people now begin to speak out, and say those forces were trifled away by my Lord Byron, who is here observed never to have prospered since his practice to supplant Capel, who is as prudent and valiant a person as the nation affords.'[64]

Though one might question his judgment, Archbishop Williams considered the defeat at Montgomery to be worse than Marston Moor.

Myddelton followed up this success by taking Powys Castle on October 2, and with it Lord Powys, his brother, two sons, and 80 officers and men. A parliamentary report ran:

'Sir Thomas Myddelton hath now the command of all North Wales, and can raise men there at his pleasure.'[65]

In addition to his Chirk estate Sir Thomas Myddelton had a proprietory interest in Ruthin Castle, and, pleased with his recent successes, he resolved to assault it in October 1644. Colonel Marcus Trevor had been appointed governor of Ruthin with a deputy bearing the appropriate name of Captain Sword. Myddelton, according to a letter written by Archbishop Williams, attacked Ruthin on the 19, 'admitted into the town by Trevor and his horse, who ran away, but Sword putting himself into the castle with some 80 men (the place being but in repairing), did beat him away with stones and shot, that upon two of the clock upon Monday he retired to Wem and left 100 men slain behind him.'[66] If that figure is correct there must have been fierce fighting in the streets of Ruthin. [67]

Peter Roberts in his diary records: 'That upon Sundaee ye xxth Octr. in the ye afternoone, ye

Above: An old line drawing of Ruthin Castle in the British Museum

[64] *Phillips.* vol. 2. p. 209. [65] *Phillips.* vol. 2. p. 213. [66] Ibid. p. 2125. [67] It may have been with the idea of relieving the pressure on Ruthin that Sir John Owen was ordered to rendezvous at Ruabon on October 23.

enemies, i.e. S'r Thomas Middleton Knt., & his armie, tooke Ruthyn, and imprisoned such male persons as they tooke holde of; & greate rayne and foule weather happened …. The rebells retorned and fled backe upon Mondaie, God be thanked.'

It is of interest to have Sir Thomas's own account of the incident. He wrote from Red Castle on October 29:

'Having received intelligence of the enemy's fortifying the town and castle of Ruthin, and of the raising of great forces in cos. Denbigh and Flint, being within my limits, by virtue of sending commissions granted to Col. Francis Trafford, a professed Papist, Col. Mark Trevor, Col. Washington, and others, I thereupon, with the few forces I could spare out of my several garrisons of Montgomery and Red Castle, and Col. Mitton's forces from Oswestry, marched to Ruthin, where we found the streets strongly barricaded, the town pretty well fortified, the enemy within it, and Cols. Trevor and Trafford with 120 horse and 200 foot endeavouring to defend the town & oppose us. My foot entering the town broke down the barricades and so made way for the horse, who pursued the enemy's horse through the town and almost to Denbigh, another of the enemy's garrisons, returning in safety with 24 prisoners, including a doctor, cornet and quartermaster. The enemy's foot fled into the castle which I was obliged to leave, Mitton's forces having been recalled to Oswestry upon some pretended fear of the enemy's approach thither, but before quitting the town I caused the turnpikes and fortifications to be broken down and rendered unserviceable. The castle I found to be by nature strong, of large circumference, and situated on a rock, but as yet uncovered and the walls under repair. The town adjoining was very considerable, and well suited for a garrison, it being the best situate and fairest and largest town for buildings within that county, and not above 5 miles distant from the enemy's other garrison at Denbigh. If the enemy should settle a garrison at Ruthin and fortify it, they would then be able to curb all the Parliament's friends and their proceedings in cos. Denbigh, Flint, Carnarvon and Anglesey; but on the contrary if you were pleased to enable me to locate a garrison there and fortify the town and castle, I conceive it would be a ready way for the recovery of Denbigh Castle and a speedy reduction of the aforesaid counties.'[68]

The Committee of Both Kingdoms ordered Brereton to send Sir Thomas 500 men 'about Ruthin' which, they suggested, would strengthen Chester's leaguer on that side in Wales. Brereton replied that he would give Myddelton all possible assistance but he could not see how Chester, fifteen miles distant, would benefit. [69]

The appearance of rough troopers in the aristocratic Vale of Clwyd must have come as a rude shock to many residents, particularly those who fondly hoped for better treatment from members of the same cause. Matters grew so serious that on December 12, 1644, the inhabitants and freeholders submitted a petition to Lord Byron when he was staying at Plas-y-Ward, the Thelwalls' home near Ruthin. They complained that Trevor's regiment of horse demanded contributions at will, and the petitioners asked that these men should be disciplined as they executed martial law without the consent of the local Commissioners of Array. It was feared that their depredations would ruin the Ruthin market. There had been robberies on the road and they begged that the malefactors should be executed or punished. They asked that the troopers should be distributed evenly all over the lordship, that the inhabitants should be relieved from the 'quartering' of troops and all contributions beyond the monthly assessment, and that civilians should not be interfered with without the commissioners' authority.[70] Byron admitted the demands were reasonable, coming as they did from loyalists who were willing to adventure their lives and fortunes in the King's service.[71] Colonel Trevor was ordered to make the requisite rearrangements.

Myddelton next captured the fortified abbey of Cwm Hir in Radnorshire. He was joined by Lieu-

---

[68] *Cal. S.P.D.* 1644. pp. 80-81. [69] Ibid. pp. 114 and 133. [70] *C.W.P.* 1744. [71] *Denb. H.S. Tr.* Vol. 3. p. 62.

tenant-Colonel John Carter who for the rest of his life was to be connected with North Wales. Lieutenant-Colonel Carter accompanied Colonel Beale who was dispatched by the Parliament by sea to assist Myddelton in North Wales. The original intention was for the troops to land in Anglesey but adverse winds drove them into Milford Haven. Here they were able to assist the Parliamentary cause. They marched by way of Cardigan to unite with Myddelton. [72]

Cwm Hir, lying far from the haunts of men, might have been considered immune from attack had not Sir Thomas turned his attention to it. A letter, written from Red Castle on December 9, gives an account of the assault:

'Our General, Sir Thomas Myddelton, having intelligence that the enemy had made them a garrison at Abbey Cwm-Hir, a very strong house, and built with stone of a great thickness, and the wallsand outworks all very strong, the house having been in former times an Abbey of the Papists, which i s situated upon the borders of Montgomeryshire within twelve miles of Montgomery, or thereabouts; and the country, by reason of the cruelties plunder, and unchristian usage of the cruel and merciless enemy towards them, as far as Kery, Newtown, and other places some miles distant, suffered exceedingly, and were almost utterly undone; which, notwithstanding the great strength of the enemy, our General being troubled to hear of the cruelties against the poor people by the enemy, put on a brave resolution, trusting in the Lord, and went against them and marched thither … Our general, being resolved to do his utmost for the gaining of it, summoned the Castle, but the Governor, returned a flat denial and said that he would not deliver up the said garrison to us; whereupon we immediately stormed it, and that with such violence that we soon took it by force ….
Since which our General having thrown down the enemy's works, and made the garrison unserviceable for the future, we made entrance and marched away from thence to Flintshire, where our General took great care for the securing of those parts and placed a garrison there.'

Sir Thomas Myddelton is said to have asserted he would eat his Christmas dinner in his own home at Chirk. Four days before the twenty-fifth he made an appearance:

'He would not abuse the castle with ordnance (because it was his own house) but fell on with fire-locks at a sink-hole where the governor Col. Watts, was ready to receive him; and gave a pretty number admittance (having an inner work within that hole), but when he saw his opportunity, he knocked them all down that came in, and with muskets killed of the rebels 67, wounded many more, and beat off Sir Thomas, who became so enraged that he plundered his own tenants.'

Colonel Watts gave a more balanced report to Prince Rupert, writing on Christmas Day:

'They lately besieged me for three days; their engineers attempted to work into the castle with iron crows and pickers, under great planks and tables which they had erected against the castle-side for their shelter, but my stones beat them off. They acknowledged in Oswestry they had 31 slain by the castle and 43 others hurt; their prime engineer was slain by the castle-side; they are very sad for him.'[73]

Despite this disappointing reverse Myddelton had every reason to feel satisfied with his year's work and with the condition of Parliamentary affairs in North Wales.

[72] *Phillips*. vol. 2. p. 219n. [73] *Phillips*. vol. 2. p. 224.

1645

The Royalists had lost the initiative. Jubilation followed the landing of the English-Irish army in November 1643 but when the last remnant of these veteran warriors was frittered away by Byron at the Montgomery battle, the pendulum swung. The offensive was now with the Parliamentarians and at the turn of the year Brereton established his advanced headquarters in the village of Christleton, barely a couple of miles from Chester's outworks. The destiny of Chester was linked to the two neighbouring castles (which were in Royalist hands), Beeston on its rocky crag, and Hawarden, five miles along the coastal road into North Wales–the road by which welcome provisions and coal found their way.

It is difficult to determine whether the siege of Chester should be regarded as one long investment or a series of attacks. The Parliamentary menace intensified from January 1645. On January 18, Lord Byron resolved to attack Christleton–which was protected by a mud rampart–burn the place, and, if successful, attempt to relieve Beeston Castle. But the affair was ill-managed, the pace was slow, 'a march rather for May show than a warlike expedition',[74] and Brereton, warned in advance, routed Byron's force, slaying many and taking two hundred prisoners among whom were two colonels and two lieutenant-colonels. Men from Sir Thomas Myddelton's horse and Sir William Myddelton's horse fought under Brereton. The victor wrote to the Committee of both Kingdoms:

'Beeston Castle is every day more and more distressed so, unless speedily relieved, I hope a good account may be given therof. If the force we are expecting come to our aid to make good the Welsh side, I hope to give a good account of Chester and all these parts.'[75]

About the end of January, Brereton and Myddelton 'came over the Dee to Wrexham'.[76] It was evidently their presence there that caused Sir John Owen to march on that important town which changed hands many times during the war.

William Maurice records February 5 as the date on which Prince Maurice reached Shrewsbury. After staying nine days the prince moved towards Chester:

'The first night he lay at Chirk Castle, from thence to Ruthin where Sir John Owens, with the forces of North Wales expected his coming.'

Shortly after this the Parliamentarians, taking advantage of a low tide, forded the Dee estuary and some 2,000 of them appeared before Hawarden Castle now commanded by Rupert's Scout-Master-General, Sir William Neale.

North Wales Royalists did not remain idle in the face of this new threat. On January 29, 1645, the Commissioners of Array ordered that the 'three colonels within the county' of Caernarvon should issue warrants to their several captains to have their companies ready to march with a thousand men to Conwy, 'and from thence to the confines of Denbighshire, there to attend the motions of the rebels'.[77]

[74] *Chester.* XXV. p. 71. [75] Ibid. p. 70. [76] *Parry.* p. 351. [77] *C.W.P.* 1749.

The situation was so grave that both princes–Rupert and Maurice–marched to raise the siege of Beeston and relieve the pressure on Chester. Events in England were too serious to permit the royal generals to remain long in the vicinity but their approach interfered sorely with Brereton's plans. He fought against time, and on January 26 made an attempt to storm the Chester outworks by night but the glow of matches indicated that the defenders were alert and he had been betrayed. The governor of the city, Lord Byron, meanwhile, appealed to Sir John Owen, who had recently arrived as governor of Conwy, to use his influence to secure Welsh forces to march to the relief of the city. Byron complained that he had written volumes of letters and received only promises in return[78] but no performances to help to relieve Chester. Owen soon showed that even if he could not relieve Chester he could provide something more tangible than promises. It was not long before he marched a force to Wrexham (where Brereton had been stationed), hoping to hold the bridgehead at Holt which the Royalists had secured. The news that Rupert had dispatched Maurice to redress the situation caused Brereton to send a strong party of horse and foot under Lieutenant-Colonel Chidley Coote to march through the adjoining parts of Wales to scatter enemy forces. In this they were unsuccessful but brought back 'good store of cattle out of the enemy's quarters including sixty or eighty fit for slaughter which', observes Brereton, 'will be very serviceable to our garrisons'. The writer informed the Committee that he heard Prince Maurice was at Worcester, intending to march to the relief of Chester– which much encouraged the enemy.[79]

Brereton posted a garrison at Farndon to watch the Royalist garrison at Holt Castle just across the Dee, and he endeavoured to make the best advantage of the time by marching his troops up and down the counties of Flint and Denbigh 'in order to scatter the forces collected therein and intended to join with the prince's army'.

'These are three or four thousand in number,' explains Brereton alluding to the North Wales forces, 'but the greater part being unarmed they fled on our advance first to Ruthin and then to Denbigh.'[80]

The strenuous efforts of the Roundheads proved unavailing and Maurice, on February 19, raised the siege of Chester but he did not feel himself strong enough to attempt the relief of Beeston. The prince, however, ordered a Denbighshire officer, Lieutenant-Colonel John Robinson of Gwersyllt, who at that time was governor of Holt Castle, to attempt to save Beeston. Robinson was unable to break through and lost a 'Colonel Owen' in the attempt. The prince remained at Chester reducing the perimeter of the outworks but allowing his men freedom to roam and plunder. Maurice ordered a solemn fast to be observed and also, on March 4, required all inhabitants to make a 'protestation' of allegiance to the King.

The problem of feeding the several thousand men in the trenches and villages encircling Chester must have been as serious as that of providing victuals for the besieged. From this time the counties of Flint and Denbigh were subjected to a series of raids, ostensibly for sheep and cattle wherewith to feed the hungry troops, but records show that burning, slaughter and pillage sometimes marked the trail of the raiders. This lawlessness was not confined to one party. After the forces of Rupert and Maurice had advanced to the relief of Beeston Castle, there were complaints of their ravages. An unknown Parliamentarian, in Nantwich on March 25, wrote:

'Since the King's great army lay in these parts the country hath suffered much, and they have been as barbarous in their retreat; for they have not only plundered about Flintshire, Denbighshire, and the borders of Shropshire and Cheshire, but have committed so many murders and rapines, both in these parts, as also in Herefordshire, Worcestershire, and the rest of those places they have been, that the like hath not been heard of. In Cheshire they have not only plundered about Churton, Barton, and Crew, but burnt Farndon, where we kept the pass at Holt Bridge. The Irish and Papists

---

[78] *Chester.* vol. XXV. p. 72. [79] Ibid. p. 73. [80] Ibid. p. 74.

have been at Broughton, and carried away divers Protestants of the town prisoners, and burnt down all the houses in that town. From thence they went to Christleton, and burnt down all that town, the minister's house and the church also.' [81]

Maurice, prior to this, spent one night at Chirk, followed by several at Ruthin where, writes Professor A. H. Dodd, a special brew of beer was prepared for him at the borough's expense.[82] The encouragement afforded the King's party by the presence of Prince Maurice was lessened by the disquieting news that royalist Shrewsbury had been surprised on the night of February 22 by Colonel Mytton and Lieutenant-Colonel Reinking, who captured both castle and town without difficulty.

The Shropshire Royalists had troubles enough about this time for, on February 15, Colonel John Carter, Captain 'Veiner' (Viner?) and other Parliamentarians surprised and captured Sir Francis Ottley, high sheriff of Shropshire, and with him Mr. Richard Fowler, The Grange, Littleton, with fifteen others at Hinton near Pontsbury.[83]

While Maurice was at Ruthin he issued a commission to Sir John Owen as major-general of foot and directed him to drive all Parliamentarians out of North Wales. With his headquarters at Wrexham (which had been abandoned by Brereton on the advance of the prince) Owen kept part of his force near Holt, some five miles away, to watch the passage of Holt Bridge. The situation had become tense since Colonel Michael Jones, a veteran of the Irish wars, joined the Parliamentarian army in Cheshire where he quickly made a name for himself as a brilliant cavalry commander. Early in March he captured Holt Bridge but Sir John Owen counter-attacked and regained possession. Archbishop Wil-

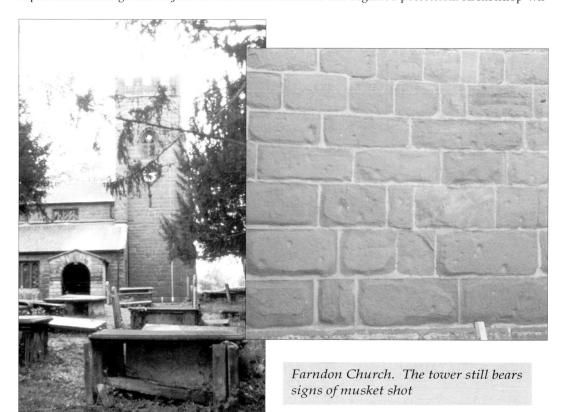

Farndon Church. The tower still bears signs of musket shot

[81] *Phillips.* vol. 2. p. 240. [82] *Denb. H.S. Tr.* vol. 3. p. 64. [83] *Parry.* p. 351.

A plan of Hawarden Castle, showing the round tower and curtain wall; the castle in   1712 (middle) and 1773 (bottom). The engravings show that the slighted castle has not changed much since the eighteenth century and perhaps since the mid-1600s.

liams was enabled to rejoice that the 'Welsh of the mountains' (evidently from his native county of Caernarvonshire) had triumphed. The Royalists' dilemma was sufficiently grave to induce Prince Rupert himself to visit the scene. On March 19 he advanced, pausing at Holt to hang twenty-four countrymen.[84] For some reason Rupert never reached Chester.

Events in England caused the royal generals to hurry away taking with them men badly needed by Byron for the defence of Chester. Their presence, though spectacular, does not appear to have achieved any practical result.

It was on March 13 that Maurice rode out of Chester; by the end of a week the tenacious Brereton had again invested the city. Hawarden, too, was to see the unwelcome sight of Roundhead headpieces for on April 3 Brereton learnt a convoy of ammunition from Anglesey was on its way to Chester:

'I marched into Flintshire to meet them,' he reported, 'but they, hearing of us, got into Hawarden Castle, whither the country people drove in many carriages, and the malignants fled thither with their wives and children.'

Engineers set about undermining Hawarden Castle hoping to secure the good store of powder and ammunition in it. Brereton, on April 3, led the remainder of his force towards Mold until he came to the Davies' ancestral home at Gwysaney: 'and fell upon the enemy there, which garrison I took from them, and therein all the Governor (a Captain) and 27 prisoners more, amongst which were some officers.'

It seems unlikely that Lieutenant-Colonel Thomas Davies was there, or Brereton would have mentioned the fact. Returning towards Chester by a speedy march, 'we gained Manly House from them, killed divers, took a captain and many other prisoners, and wounded many more besides.'[85]

Prince Rupert was expected to come to the aid of Chester again, and the Commissioners of Array for the North Wales counties were ordered to have troops ready to move at an hour's notice to assist the prince. Sir John Owen was particularly active. In addition to defending North Wales he was ordered on April 24 to march to Hereford with 1,000 men.

Meanwhile there was internal friction in Conwy. The Archbishop of York complained to Lord Digby: 'Sir John Owen is likewise governor of this place and intimateth a desire to have the Government of this Castle wch his Myte .... hadd upon high and deare considerations passed over unto me and my assignes, and wch from bare walles I have repayred, victuayled, and ammunicioned at myne owne charges.' He would, he asserted, give a better account of the castle than 'this gentleman' who without this help would never have been able to repair the town. Nor would Owen have had arms to defend it.[86]

At the moment Sir John Owen had enough military matters to occupy his entire time, but not many weeks passed before he was in a position to strike. If a feud was on the point of breaking out in Conwy, a similar situation was developing in Chester where young Colonel Roger Mostyn had disagreed with the arrogant governor.

Lord Byron, after telling Lord Digby that Prince Rupert had marched off with the remainder of the old Irish regiments, continued:

'... soe that I was left in the towne with only a garryson of citizens and my owne and Colonell Mostin's regiment, wch both together made not above 600 men, whereof one halfe being Mostin's men, I was forced soone after to send out of towne, findinge them by reason of their officers, who weare ignorant Welch gentlemen, and unwillinge to undergoe any strickt duty, far more precudiciall to us than usefull.'[87]

[84] Dodd. *Denb. H.S. Tr.* vol. 3. p. 65. [85] *Chester.* vol. XXV. p. 80. [86] *Phillips.* vol. 2. p. 243. [87] Ibid. p. 246.

The Royalists at this particular moment could ill afford to fall out among themselves. On April 15, two of Lord Byron's brothers (there were seven in all serving the King), Sir Richard Byron and Sir Robert Byron, were taken prisoners. While Brereton was intensifying his attacks on Chester and Hawarden, Colonel Michael Jones led a daring raid into the heart of Denbighshire. For this he was accused of allowing his soldiers to indulge in unrestrained pillage. This was only one of several incursions but it is indicative of what was transpiring. Colonel Jones wrote that on April 23, 'a party of 500 horse and 400 foot marched into S. Asaph twenty miles distant from Chester where they heard the enemy was. But finding it impossible by reason of their mountaines and castells to overtake them being fled thence, ye County was driven by ye assent of Sr. Th. Middleton for ye gaineing of provisions for ye Army which in a manner until that tyme was provided for by Cheshire, most of which cattel, the whole number of good Cowes not amounting to 400 nor ye sheepe to 2,000 being not fitt to be slaine.'

There follows a reference to a well-known squire's house, Plas Ucha, home of an ancestor of Thomas Pennant, the Georgian Antiquarian. 'In our return whence parte of ye Armey passing before Hugh Pennant's house divers of them were shott and one killed, a party being on their march towarde it they forsooke it. To deter others from doing ye like with ye consent of Sr. Th. Middleton ye house was ffired.' Major Hugh Pennant took a prominent part in the 1648 revolt in Anglesey.

Colonel Jones adds, 'Also at ye widdow Hanmer's howse there was a garrison of ye enemyes which killed divers of our men and hindered provisions to be brought unto Hawarden. The howse being summoned and they refuseing quarter it was stormed and all but two put to the sord and ye howse ffired.'[88]

During one of these raids Rhual, the Flintshire home of Baron Evan Edwards, was plundered. Evan Edwards was one of the Commissioners of Array for the county of Flint and had for years been Baron or Clerk of the Exchequer for the County Palatine of Chester. He had built a comfortable home on the outskirts of Mold. His younger brother, Alderman William Edwards, ironmonger, was the leader of the Parliamentary party in Chester, a friend of Sir William Brereton, and later, as a colonel, was put in charge of the captured city. This family connection was insufficient to protect Rhual.

Baron Edwards had occasion to complain that his house had been stripped and plundered by Captain Coltham and Captain Viner's men, his wife 'stript out of her cloathes by ye Yorkshire men, a box of jewels taken'. Following an investigation Colonel Michael Jones admitted the taking of the jewels but said that though Edwards valued them at £7,000 they were not worth £500. In any event they were of greater use to the public in the Treasurer's hands.[89]

A list of the missing jewels is preserved in the National Library of Wales.[90]

A Note of the Jewells My Wife Lost

Two or 3 seu'all parcells of wyer worke borders some with pearle and some Enameld only.
One Border wth Diamonds Rubies & pearle.
One Aggate Chaine thrid wh pearle.
Diverse buttons some inameld wh pearle some without pearle.
Diverse buttons wh Rubies & pearle.
24 gould buttons wh every one a diamond.
21 great wyre worke gould buttons wh pearle whereof 10 of them have Diamonds, 11 Rubies.
1 Chayne of wyer worke wh pearle, one peece of ye worke like SS.
1 gould bracelett wch goeth 6 or 7 tymes about ones Arme.
1 great Chayne of Massy gold wh 4 Rubies Inameld 22 diamonds.

[88] *Chester.* vol. XXV. p. 99. [89] *Cal. S.P.D.* [90] *N.L.W. Rhual MSS.* 115.

1 great gold neckelace wth pearle.

Divers other litle Jewells some sett wh stones some wh Aggatte.

1 Chayne wh two or three thrids of pearle & a Cornelian betwixt.

1 greate Aggate Chayne thrid wh pearle.

some wyre worke buttons wh one Ruby a peece in it.

28 pommander buttons covered wh gould inameld open worke, in evry one of the buttons in the
Midle a diamond.

1 One gould Chayne of open worke fild wh pommander 16 diamonds, diverse Rubies and pearle.

Great Company of broad flatt buttons of gould inameld wth greene white & Red, wh Rubyes.

'I will omitt to mencon what gould silver, Lynen & Apparell and household stuffe I lost for I am
hopelesse of them but of these, Christyan Charity will move restitution to the Innocent.'

Evan Edwards, who was fined £157 for his delinquency by the Commissioners for Compounding, has been regarded as 'a staunch royalist' but the degree of his loyalty is debatable. When Major-General Thomas Mytton began his invasion of North Wales he was evidently accorded so considerate a reception by the 'Baron' that he subsequently issued the following certificate:

'Right hoble.

I do hereby testifie that Mr. Evan Edwards in November 1645 did voluntarily submitt himself to mee upon my advaunce into Wales before any Garrison was reduced or the Kinge's forces in these pts subdued. And that he declared his willingness and readynes to serve the parlt whereupon I graunted him my pass and p'tection. And since, I have had good testimoney of his moderate and fair carriadge when the King's p'tie ruled in the Countrey, and that he was not active against the parliamt but p'tected the well affected (so farr as lay in his power) from the force and violence of ye King's garrisons. And since that tyme he hath constantly paid contribucon and all other taxacons there-unto. All w'ch I humbly submitt to yor honors consideracon.

yor faithfull & most humble servant,

THO: MITTON.

Halston, primo

decembr, 1646.

'This is a true Copie of Gen'all Mittons Certificate.

WILL EDWARDES.'

A similar testimonial (damaged) is in the hand of Lieut.- Colonel C. Gerrard, a veteran who partici-pated in the siege of Chester:

'To all whom these p'ntes may come–Whereas I, Gilbert Gerrard of Crewwood, in the County of Chester, Esq., being in the month of April 1645 comanded by the honourable Sr William Brereton, Baronet, as Lieften't Col'll of a Regiment of Foot then under the conduct of Col.ll James Louthian to march into the County of Flint to b'seige the Castle of Hawarden in which seidge (torn) Col.ll Louthian comanded in chief (torn) of it for the space of seaven weekes (torn) that I, the said Leift Colonell being constant at the Leagner and taking p'ticular notice of the willingness and readiness of the gent and inhabitants of the said County to contribute to the maintenance and support of the forces ingaged in the said Leaguer and inquiring of div's [divers] of the inhabitants of the said County touching the dispocon and accons of the gentry in those p'tes doe make bould to certify that Evan Edwards of Rhuall in the said County Esq., did several times voluntary and freely send unto the said Leaguer greate quantities of all sorts of provision needfull for the same, and upon inquiry made of his disposition and affeceon in & unto the late unhappy troubles of the kingdome; I was certified & informed by div'se well affected p'sons that the said Mr. Edwards neu' [never] used any violence or extremity to the Countrey in forcing contribuson to the Commissions of Array when they were in action there. And that the sd Mr. Edwards did also seu'all times advise the Countrey & places thereabout that they should readily contribute to the Parliamt fforces, by whose advice I (torn) thereabout did the more willing (torn) to the said Leaguer. All of which I (torn) witness my hand the xxth day of ffebr, 1646. G. GERRARD.' [91]

In July 1656, Evan Edwards presented a petition to the Protector for his re-admittance to the office of Clerk to the Court of Exchequer of Chester.[92] On July 17, 1660, an Order was issued by the Lords Commissioners of the Treasury to admit Evan Edwards to his office of 'Comptroller of Chester, Bewmaris and Leaverpoole', granted him by letters patent dated March 29, 1639.[93]

The 'Yorkshire horse' were evidently a source of anxiety to their officers. Sir Thomas Fairfax had to warn the commander not to let his troopers 'spoyle or plunder ye country which they are much condemned for'. The troopers should be punished for such 'wicked courses'. [94]

A more serious transgression was the plundering of the stately mansion on the Caergwrle-Wrexham road known as Plas Têg which belonged to Sir John Trevor, a loyal supporter of the parliament. A list of articles missing has been preserved: it begins with '20 Bedtickes, whereof 7 received back', and ends with '1 faire Bible, 1 Crossbow, 1 fowlinggunne. 1 great Iron Racke. Brasse of divers Andirons. Brasse Candlesticks. 3 powndes in money. The Cabinet.' This is followed by a note: 'Since then ye

Plas Têg today

[91] N.L.W. *Rhual MSS*. 136. [92] Ibid. 122-3. [93] Ibid. p. 92-53a. [94] *Chester*. vol. XXV. p. 90.

foote tooke 3 sheets and one old horse, besides such provisions as they found in ye house.'[95]

These misdemeanours added to the anxieties of Brereton who pleaded that he had not the power to hold the reins of discipline.

It would seem that the raid headed by Colonel Michael Jones was followed by another, shortly after, led by Brereton himself, for the notary public of St. Asaph, Peter Roberts, in his diary entered under the 24th, 25th and 26th of April, 1645: 'Sr. Win. Brerton and Sr. Tho. Myddleton Kt., with their army, have plyndered St. Asaph's parish, except Wickwer, and made great spoyles, &c. and defiled the Churches there &c.'[96]

Another entry reads: 'uppon Thursday the XVIth of aprill, the Towne and Castle of Denbighe were besieched by ye Parlt. armey, and ye market was uppon ye Wednesday ffollowing kept att the Elme Tree, in the bottom of the Towne, that is, in or neere the Lady Salusbury's House in the lower ende of Denbighe.'[97]

When, under the Self-Denying Ordinance, Sir Thomas Myddelton had to resign his command, the 'great force' he had vaunted in the House had, according to Colonel Michael Jones, dwindled to 160 foot and 70 horse.[98] Colonel Thomas Mytton–whose wife was a sister of the second Lady Myddelton– succeeded Sir Thomas as major-general in North Wales, assuming command in June. News that the King was marching to the relief of Chester perturbed Brereton who despaired of capturing Hawarden Castle. At a council of war on May 19 it was decided to abandon the siege and the following morning, when the tide would serve, the disappointed Roundheads waded back across the fords of the river.[99]

At this time Colonel Mostyn's force was disbanded, but the young commander had not abandoned the royal cause and before long he raised another regiment in time to return to Chester when need was great.

A strange state of affairs existed at Conwy. Sir John Owen commanded the walled town but Archbishop Williams tenaciously clung to the castle which he had restored and put into a defensible state. The prelate suffered from no delusions and he had told a kinsman many weeks before that Sir John 'looked big' on the castle and that it was evident he meant to occupy it. Conwy was not spacious enough to contain two proud men and the inevitable blow fell one evening in May.

The manner in which Sir John struck is set forth in a remonstrance which the indignant prelate sent to King Charles shortly afterwards:

'Upon the 9th of May, 1645, Sir John Owen, Governor of Conway, about seven of the clock in the evening, before the night guard was sent into the castle, the possession thereof was placed by the King in the Archbishop of York, and his assigns, upon great and valuable considerations by his gracious Letters .... did with bars of iron, and armed men, break the Locks and Doors, and enter into the said Castle, and seize upon the Place, the Victuals Powder, Armes and Ammunition, laid in by the said Archbishop at his own charge.'

The prelate demanded that the 'rabble of grooms and beggarly people' should be prevented from filching the goods stored there, but Sir John 'in a furious manner utterly refused it', and threatened to seize the plate and other valuables for his own use 'than which no rebel or enemy could deal more outrageously'. Even Owen's kinsman and namesake, the Bishop of St. Asaph, could not prevail upon him to exercise more consideration. Out the archbishop had to go, and he withdrew to his own house at Penrhyn, near Bangor.[100]

Sir John justified his conduct by writing to the King accusing Williams of treachery. To this complaint Charles replied: 'You should be very cautious how you proceed to lay Imputations upon him of so high a nature'–and required Owen to pay proper respect to the prelate. Between the seizing of

---

[95] Ibid. p. 91. [96] *Parry.* p. 368. [97] *A.&M.* p. 220. [98] *Chester.* vol. XXV. p. 99. [99] Ibid. p. 88. [100] The Remonstrance is printed in the appendix to vol. I. *The Heart of Northern Wales,* W. Bezant Lowe, and in R. Williams' *History and Antiquities of the Town of Aberconway.*

Conwy Castle and the King's reply to Owen's accusation, the battle of Naseby had been fought.

The turmoil of the proud prelate's thoughts must be imagined after he had returned to the demesne of his forebears, or as he paced the tree-lined walks of lovely Gwydir when he visited his favourite niece, Grace, who had married Owen Wynn. The time of his greatness when he was Lord Keeper of the Great Seal and the confidant of King James, the spacious days of his palace at Buckden, the throne in the minster at York, must have seemed a distant dream. He was a Caernarvonshire man again, back among his own people, and his people were faced with dire calamity.

Later he wrote: 'What they will say in the end of the day I do not know, nor do I care, if I could with mine own sacrificing keep this poor country from being ruined.' Their well-being might have then appeared of greater consequence than a tottering throne. This was the altruistic aspect. To it must be added his personal reaction–a sense of outraged dignity, and resentment at the broken pledge of the monarch he trusted. Despite this discouragement he continued to exert his influence for the royal cause, and no man laboured more assiduously than the archbishop in endeavouring to bring relief to besieged Chester.

The garden at Gwydir near Llanrwst. The cedar in the middle of the photograph is one of twelve planted to celebrate the wedding of Charles I in 1625. Four of them survive.

7

The extent of North Wales's participation in the memorable battle of Naseby is still undetermined. That some Welsh soldiers were there is apparent for in the county archives in Caernarfon are records of old soldiers who appealed for pensions as some recompense for wounds suffered on that fateful day. These simple entries tell their own tale.

> 'Robert Owen of Caerhun, maymed of the hand and wounded on the head in Nasebie fight, a very poor man.
> John Williams of Pethkelert in Nasby fight hurt in the legge and the thighe, a great wound.'

Of the regiments in which they served, of the officers who led them, no word is penned. Nor is there a list of those who fell. Imagination must fill many gaps.

When that decisive conflict left the New Model Army victors on the field the King sought shelter in the marches of Wales. Charles's aimless wanderings for the next few months are those of a bemused man, stupified by calamity yet stubbornly resolved not to yield. He rambled from place to place, seeking entertainment at Raglan, at Ludlow, at Cardiff, talking, among other matters, of making a last stand in the Snowdon mountains. There was even a wild scheme for smuggling the young Duke of York across to Dublin from Beaumaris in Captain Bartlett's *Swan* but nothing came of it. By September, Charles finally made up his mind. He would move north through loyal Lancashire and join forces with the victory-winning Marquis of Montrose in Scotland.

Protected by his faithful cavalry the King rode north. The itinerary was faithfully recorded by a gentleman trooper, one Richard Symonds, who rode in the Earl of Lichfield's troop. The officer in charge of his Majesty's life-guard was a Herefordshire soldier, Sir William Vaughan, whose presence in North Wales was soon to be felt. The King, having raised the siege of Hereford, resolved to head for Chester which was then in sore straits. Symonds noticed that their movements were watched by 'the nearest enemy' –Roundhead cavalry commanded by Poyntz and Rossiter who were specially deputed to keep an eye on the royal movements. Attention naturally centres on the New Model Army but it was not the only force under the new Parliamentary administration. There was, in addition, a Northern Army commanded by a veteran professional soldier of the Continental wars, Colonel-General Sydenham Poyntz.

On Thursday, September 18, word reached the royal party that the foe lay between them and Worcester, so Charles rode to Presteign where the night was spent. Over the mountains they went next day to Newtown, barely sighting a house after the first three miles. The next stage carried the cavalcade to Llanfyllin, passing *en route* Gregynog, the home of Sir Arthur Blayney, a devoted Montgomeryshire loyalist who later had his elbow shattered in the Beaumaris fight of 1648. Then, 'over the mountains to Chirk' where the governor, Colonel John Watts, was waiting to receive his Majesty in a home worthy of the occasion. The royal guards lay that night at Llangollen. While he was at Chirk Charles received the unwelcome news that the enemy had carried Chester's outworks. Instantly a messenger was dispatched to Lord Byron bidding him hold out another twenty-four hours as the King was coming to his rescue. Events were now shaping which were to terminate in the battle known as Rowton Moor or Rowton Heath.

On Tuesday, September 23, the King's force left Chirk. With his Majesty rode a number of noblemen, including General Lord Charles Gerard 'with his gallant troop of lifeguards'. Three brigades were commanded by Sir Marmaduke Langdale, Sir Thomas Blackstone, and Sir William Vaughan.

Holt Bridge, which changed hands so frequently, appears at this time to have been in possession of the Parliamentarians, or else destroyed, for the horsemen crossed the Dee by a bridge of boats. Hereabout the force divided. Advancing during the darkness, Langdale led three brigades down the Cheshire bank of the river. 'Their business,' Symonds explains, 'was to fall upon those horse and foot which lay before Chester.'

The King continued down the Welsh side of the Dee and crossing by the old bridge, entered the city where he was joyfully welcomed. He slept that night at the house of Sir Francis Gamull in Bridge Street with guards on duty in the road outside.

Meanwhile Poyntz, faithful to the trust imposed upon him, had doggedly followed in the wake of the unsuspecting royal army. He might have caught the Royalists utterly unprepared had not Sir Richard Lloyd, governor of Holt Castle, intercepted a letter. It was written by Poyntz and was directed to Colonel Michael Jones thanking him for standing his ground notwithstanding the King's approach. Poyntz told him of the King's 'tired over-marcht horse', which, he intimated, he meant to attack as soon as he overtook them.

Sir Francis Gamull of Beurton. Charles I stayed in his house in Chester in 1645. Based on the Farndon Church window which records events and personalities connected with the civil war.

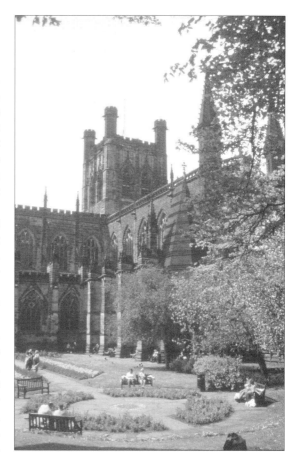

The tower of Chester Cathedral, where Charles I was nearly killed

The alarming news was speedily forwarded. It put Sir Marmaduke Langdale on his guard. On the morn of Wednesday, September 24, this veteran cavalryman faced his brigade about on the Chester side of the Dee and marched back to a spot known as Hatton Heath. Here he sighted the advancing Parliamentarians whom he charged so vigorously that he 'beat them back and took some cornets'.

Charles lost the battle of Rowton Moor not through any lack of courage of his troops but from sheer ineptitude on his part. The original plan was for Sir Marmaduke Langdale to as-sault the Roundheads who besieged Chester. During the engagement the besieged were to issue from the city and attack them in the rear. The opposite transpired. Poyntz's unexpected appearance distracted Langdale, and while he was reassembling his men on Rowton Moor, a mile nearer the city than Hatton Heath, he found himself attacked from behind by Colo-nel Michael Jones and Adjutant-General Louthian who, with 500 horse and 300 foot, rushed from the trenches to aid the northern general.

Their hasty movements created the erroneous impression that they were in flight, and a consider-able portion of Chester's garrison sallied out of Northgate to pursue them. Eastgate had been blocked up. A furious contest had taken place on Rowton Heath, and Langdale's men were routed. Poyntz pursued the fleeing Cavaliers almost to Chester walls where the victors were checked by Lord Gerard and the Earl of Lindsey who had drawn up their troops in the open.

'But those disordered horse which fled with Sir Marmaduke, had crowded all the little passes and narrow lanes between Hoole Heath and the city, a ground quite unfit for horse to fight upon; so that when a fresh body of the enemy's musqueteers charged resolutely upon them, they forced the King's horse to turn and route one another, and overbear their own officers who would have re-strained them.'[101]

A sorry sight it must have been for Charles, watching from the top of the Phoenix Tower. Earlier in the day the King had climbed to the cathedral tower but a cannon-ball carried off the head of an officer beside him and his Majesty descended to a less conspicuous vantage point.

It is estimated that over 600 men lost their lives on Rowton Moor. Among them was Bernard Stuart, the handsome young Earl of Lichfield in whose troop Richard Symonds served. Following the death of his leader, Symonds transferred to Vaughan's brigade. Among the prisoners was Lieutenant-

[101] *Hemingway*. vol. I. p. 183.

Colonel Broughton.

An unusual sidelight on the battle is contained in a memorandum written on a blank page of Clarendon's *History* by Peter Shakerley, son of Colonel Sir Jeffrey Shakerley who commanded a regiment under Sir Marmaduke:

'Poyntz coming in a marching posture along the narrow lane between Hatton Heath and Rowton Heath, Sir Marmaduke, having lined the hedges, fell upon him, and killed a great many of his men; and having so, ordered Colonel Shakerley, who was best acquainted with that country, to get the next way he could to the King (who lodged then at Sir Francis Gamull's house in Chester) and acquaint him that he had obeyed his orders in beating Pointz back, and to know his Majesty's further pleasure. The colonel executed his orders with better speed than could be expected; for he galloped directly to the river Dee, under Huntingdon house, got a wooden tub (used for slaughtering of swine) and a batting staff (used for batting coarse linen) for an oar, put a servant into the tub with him, and in this desperate manner swam over the river, his horse swimming by him (for the banks there were very steep, and the river very deep), ordered his servant to stay there with the tub for his return, and was with the King in little more than a quarter of an hour after he left Sir Marmaduke, and acquainted the King, that if his Majesty pleased to command further orders to Sir Marmaduke, he would engage to deliver them in a quarter of an hour, and told the King of the expeditious method he had taken, which saved him going nine or ten miles about, by Holt-bridge (for the boats at Eaton were then made useless); but such delays were used by some about the King, that no orders were sent, nor any sally made out of the city by the King's party till past three o' clock in the afternoon, which was full six hours after Poyntz had been beaten back; and so Poyntz having all that time for his men to recover their fright they had been put into in the morning, Poyntz rallied his forces, and with the help of the parliamentary forces who came out of the suburbs of the city to his assistance (upon whom the King's party in the city might have fallen) put all those of the King's to the route, which was the loss of the King's horse, and of his design to join Montrose in Scotland.' [102]

Richard Symonds evidently fought all through the battle and after entering in his diary an account of Langdale's victory over Poyntz at Hatton Heath, all he could wearily add was 'But they beat us agen for't'.

It was no longer safe for King Charles to remain in the city. He gave orders to Lord Byron and the commissioners 'that if, after ten days, they saw no reasonable prospect of relief, to treat for their own preservation'.

The following morning, September 25, between 9 and 10 o'clock, Charles rode across the Dee Bridge, screens having been erected to conceal the movements of the troops, and at the head of five hundred horsemen, crossed the marsh and found security in Hawarden Castle. Here the fugitive monarch stayed three hours as guest of the governor, Sir William Neale. While the King rode to Denbigh, which he reached that night, Sir Marmaduke Langdale rallied his scattered troopers by appointing a rendezvous two miles from Holt Castle.

When the trampling of five hundred chargers sounded on the night air every citizen of Denbigh must have been on tiptoe with excitement. At the foot of Lower Street lay the building of the Carmelite Friary, by that time known as The Abbey. The cavalcade toiled up the long hill, past the old Cross at the approach to High Street, and through the mighty Burgess Gate which gave admittance to the old town, and so to the great gate of the castle where the loyal governor, Colonel William Salesbury of Bachymbyd, *Hên Hosannau Gleision* (Old Blue Stockings) awaited to greet the liege lord he served so well. The governor had received his commission from the King two years before, and the castle had

[102] Quoted in full by Pennant and Hemingway.

been restored by him and his kindred at their own cost.

'Friday, 26 Sept., rested.' This succinct entry in Symonds' diary speaks volumes.

The weary monarch would have had much to meditate upon–his loyal troopers cut down in the Rowton fight and nine hundred prisoners taken to Nantwich 'whereof about twenty were of the King's own troop'.

Charles lodged in the tower called the Great Kitchen, subsequently to be known as the King's Chamber. Colonel Salesbury spoke so plainly to his Majesty for two hours in private, that the good

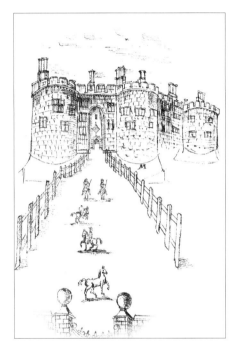

King said, 'Never did a prince hear so much truth at once!'[103] Having done so, Old Blue Stockings made a vow he would never deliver up the castle save on the instructions of the King himself.

Lord Digby was with the party and wrote to Sir John Owen at Conwy bidding him attend. Archbishop Williams also arrived at Denbigh. 'Here is now with his Majesty, the Archbishop of York, Sir John Owen and divers others,' wrote Digby to Lord Byron from Denbigh on September 26.[104]

Whether a reconciliation was achieved is not known but two significant facts emerge: one, that Sir John remained governor of Conwy; the second is that the prelate continued to labour with undiminished ardour in the royal cause, and even wrote to Owen:

'Sir John, I pray you be confident that I loue you and Honnour you, and, if you please to believe it, with the best understanding that God hath given me, well be readye to runne the same fortunes with you in this dangerous tyme and business.' [105]

[103] *A.&M.* p. 232. [104] *Cal. S.P.D.* pp. 160-1. [105] *Arch. Camb.* 1875.

Symonds writes: 'Satturday, 27, was a general rendezvous 3 miles from Denbigh.'

A hamlet known as Cyffylliog was chosen as the place of meeting, presumably favoured for its remoteness and because it lay approximately an equal distance from the castles of Ruthin and Denbigh. Green hills slope down to a vale where runs a sizeable stream in which cavalrymen could water their mounts. Walls of water-rounded stones line the narrow roads which converge from several directions, and the little church is guarded by age-old yews. It is hard to conceive Charles, King of England and Scotland, in such a setting. In the church register was a page–subsequently extracted which contained the following entry:

'Saturday, 27th. September, 1645. Be it remembered, that King Charles was the day and year above written, making his rendezvous in the parish of Cyffylliog, in a place there called Cenfesydd.'

A service was held in Denbigh church on Sunday morning, probably the garrison church at St. Hilary of which only the tower remains. Symonds records:

'About one of the clocke afternoon, the K. marched through Ruthyn, where there is a large castle and fortified, to Chirke Castle, com. Denbigh. Watts knighted. Here P. Maurice met us with his troope, and those of P. Rupert's horse that came from Bristoll, Lucas's horse, &c. toto 600 or 700.'

And so to Bridgnorth, and finally Newark and Newcastle. Wales never saw Charles again. The King ordered Sir William Vaughan to return to North Wales with his brigade to effect the relief of Chester.

With Symonds' meticulously kept diary for reference it is difficult to account for the peculiar story that the King fled to Llanrwst where the bridge was broken down to prevent pursuit!

Naseby is generally accepted as marking Charles's downfall, but after Naseby there was still some slight possibility of a rally in the west. After Rowton Moor no such hope remained. The King's fortune was past recovery.

Standing amid the ruins of Denbigh's mighty walls today, one may imagine the sombre thoughts which passed through the royal mind as the Stuart gazed down on the verdant vale so soon to be scarred by the earthworks of his rebellious subjects.

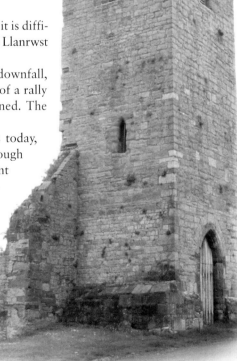

Opposite top: Chirk Castle, where the King stayed in 1645. It is shown here in 1684 and (opposite below) as drawn by Buck in 1742.

Right: St Hilary's Church tower, within the town wall at Denbigh. The nave and chancel were demolished in 1923.

Top left: Col. Thomas Madryn; top right: Maj-Gen. Sir John Owen
Bottom left: Maj. David Pennant; bottom right: Col. Hugh Wynne

The effect of the Self-Denying Ordinance was soon felt by the Parliamentary forces in Cheshire for on June 13, 1645, Sir William Brereton had been recalled to London, not only to answer the charges made against his troops for plundering, but also to serve as Knight of the Shire. The military command he held from the outset was vested in a committee, the only concession being that he was chosen as one of the five members. It was not until the middle of October that Sir William was able to return to his duties in the field and in his absence Rowton Moor was fought. Colonel Mostyn evidently made his peace with Lord Byron for, during the disturbance occasioned by the battle, he and Colonel Hugh Wynne of Bodysgallen with all the forces they could muster slipped through the cordon and rejoined the defenders in the beleaguered city.

Both sides were particularly alert, the Royalists to avert further disaster, the Parliamentary party to make the most of their triumph. The King was depressed by the news that Montrose had been defeated (at last) at Philiphaugh.

The tidings had not found their way into the streets of Chester but Byron was filled with foreboding and, three days after Rowton Moor, he wrote to Lord Digby at Denbigh:

'I do not like this return of Poyntz's horse. I fear something is amiss with my Lord of Montrose. All that can be done for the present is that the King raise the whole force of Wales and command the horse immediately to advance this way.' [106]

Top: Bodysgallen today. The part shown was built in 1620. It was the home of Col. Hugh Wynne. Below: Chester Castle today

[106] *Chester.* vol. XXV. p. 124.

The Parliamentary batteries opened a fierce fire on Chester. Though the King with his hundreds of horsemen headed for the English border, he had turned his back on Chester merely in a literal sense. The loyal city was much in his mind and heart. The course he adopted is indicated in another letter sent by Lord Digby to Lord Byron in Chester.

'His Majesty is advanced as far as Newark and we hope it will have the wished result of drawing the rebels great body of horse from the Welsh side of Chester. As for any parties they may leave, his Majesty will instantly send back Sir W. Vaughan with strength enough to master them.' [107]

The letter is dated October 5.

Sir William Vaughan concentrated on collecting forces from the various garrisons along the marches of Wales until by the middle of October he felt himself strong enough to attempt to relieve Chester. In his efforts he was loyally supported by the Royalists of North Wales. Archbishop Williams was at Beaumaris endeavouring to load a vessel with provisions in the hope that it could get through the blockade and reach Chester by water. Sir John Owen was to raise a force of cavalry though on this occasion he does not appear to have exhibited his customary zeal. Colonel Roger Mostyn escaped from Chester, crossed to Dublin, and managed to recruit some more soldiers for the King though the numbers fell below his expectation. The Lord St Pol – Byron's general-of-horse – also managed to get through the Parliamentary lines and reached Rhuddlan where he conferred with Colonel Gilbert Byron, Lord Byron's brother. The archbishop had arranged for the footmen of Caernarvonshire to rendezvous at Groes-yn-Eirias (Colwyn Bay)[108] there to be joined by a party of horse before they marched to Denbigh. The delay experienced here proved, as it transpired, their salvation.

There was to be a general rendezvous on Denbigh Green which (until enclosed by Act of Parliament in 1807) extended from the Friary fields as far as Trefnant on one side and the forest of Lleweny on the other.[109] Vaughan advanced from Montgomeryshire to unite with the North Wales infantry. His movements were not unknown to Brereton who had recently returned from London and the Cheshire baronet made arrangements accordingly.

Symonds now served under Vaughan and, thanks to his invaluable diary, it is possible to trace the royal army's progress.

Vaughan's advance guard reached Chirk Castle at 9 a.m. on October 23, the general following more leisurely. Symonds records:

'Monday, October 26. Sir William Vaughan came to Chirke. We marched to Llanannis [Llanynys], Mr. Thelwall's howse, com. Denbigh.'

This unusual diarist had a fondness for heraldry and missed no opportunity of slipping into a parish church to note heraldic adornments on tomb or painted glass. Even on the eve of battle he found time to jot down comments on the churches at Ruthin and Llanrhaeadr. On the last day of October Vaughan was at Denbigh.

Across the border Brereton was active. He dispatched Colonel Michael Jones with 1,500 horse and Adjutant-General Louthian with 1,000 foot to scatter the Royalist muster. On October 30 the Roundheads reached Mold. The next day they marched to Ruthin where Vaughan had paused so short a time before. Here they were joined by 'that active officer' Thomas Mytton who, as the new major-general, assumed command. The Roundheads appear to have taken Vaughan by surprise when, the following morning, they marched down the road from Ruthin. This is the more unaccountable because of an entry in Symonds' diary:

[107] *Cal. S.P. Dom.* (1645). p. 174. [108] Prof A. H. Dodd. *Denb. H.S. Tr.* vol. 3. p. 70. [109] *A.&M.* p. 270.

'Friday, October 31. came intelligence to Denbigh to Sir William Vaughan that the enemy under the command of Mitton was advanced to Ruthyn, both horse and foot.'

Denbigh's square-towered parish church of St. Marcella, known as Whitchurch, stands isolated on the common. At the foot of Denbigh's long northern approach was the ruined friary consisting of several buildings with a few trees nearby. Otherwise little broke the wide expanse of Denbigh Green though quicksets bordered the narrow roadways. It was here that the entire Royalist force assembled on the morning of November 1. Their total is given as 1,700 horse and 400 infantry. Their muske-teers and dragoons lined the hedges which flanked the road from Ruthin – and waited. Those who felt chill on that damp, drab morning would shortly be warmed by exercise:

'Satturday at noone wee had the alarm, for they were at Whitchurch below the towne. Their ap-proach was handsomely disputed by our horse and foot about an howre in the hedges and lane.'

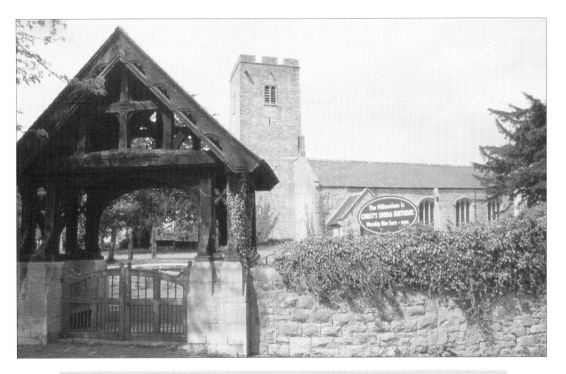

St Marcella's Church, Whitchurch near Denbigh, as it is today: not quite as isolated as it was described in the 17th century

So wrote Symonds. This was the first stage of the battle as seen through a Royalist's eyes. The Parliamentary report ran as follows:

'The Forlorn Hope, forty out of every regiment, was commanded by Capt. Otter, Captain of the Reformadoes,[110] a gallant soldier, and Captain William Edwards,[111] a Cheshire Captain and well-deserving gentleman, who, coming to Whitchurch, a mile from Denbigh, were in a lane flanked by

[110] Reformadoes were officers waiting for regiments to be re-formed. [111] This might be Alderman William Edwards, Brereton's friend, and a younger brother of "Baron" Evan Edwards of Rhual. He was later a colonel.

the enemy's horse and dragoons, so that they were forced to make good that pass with the Forlorn Hope and Cheshire dragoons, under the command of Capt. Finch and Capt. Holt, stout and resolute men. These, with the Forlorn Hope, behaved themselves gallantly, and maintained the pass till the foot came up, the most part of which, with the Warwick and Derbyshire horse, Commanded by Major Sanders and Major Hokesworth, seconding the Forlorn Hope, bare the burden of the day, whilst the Reformadoes, Cheshire horse, and 400 Lancashire foot, were intended for a greater service; for the Commanders finding that straight lane too difficult a pass to fall through upon the enemy, were marshalled in open field.' [112]

Symonds takes up the story:

'There number of foot, being 1,500 at least, made ours retreat to the towne, which was not long disputed by reason of their forward advancing. Our horse were putt to a disorderly retreat, notwithstanding Sir William Vaughan drew many of them up upon a greene neare two myles off but could not be made to stand; a party of Arcall horse charged the persuers, and were seconded by part of Prince Maurice's life-guard. The foot were let into the castle by the governor. The horse gott to Llanrwst that night, com. Denbigh, twelve miles distant. Next morning dispersed to quarters. The governour of Denbigh wrote that the enemy was in his sight above double our number.'

It was on the advice of 'some who knew the country', that Mytton moved his troops into the open:

'These last mentioned were drawn thence by Denbigh Green, a way near four miles in compass, to fall upon the enemy upon even ground, which, whilst drawn off, the foot (exceeding forward to engage themselves on the whole) beat the enemy out of the lane, and routed both horse and foot, driving them under the command of the castle, where they rallied themselves; but the Forlorn Hope, Derby and Warwick horse, with the foot, encountered them again, and utterly routed them, whom the horse chased eight miles in the way to Conwy, making great execution on the way, taking many prisoners, and 500 or 600 horse, and so long pursued that not above seven score were left together … It is conjectured by those who are best able to give account herein, that above 100 of the enemy were slain, about 400 taken prisoners, with divers men of quality. It is not known that any of ours are slain, and few wounded.'

The dispatch was dated from the town of Denbigh which the victorious troops had occupied. An interesting echo of the flight to Llanrwst is preserved in the *Calendar of Wynn Papers*:

'On Allhallowtide twelvemonth, 1645, Sir William Vaughan, having been defeated near Denbigh by Gen. Mytton, fled with the remainder of his horse, in number 900, towards the mountains, and fell that night upon the house of Sir Richard Wynn, where they stayed five days, and, on going, rifled the house.' [113]

A tumultuous time for tranquil Gwydir!

Williams asserts that the pursuit continued as far as Llangernyw. Cannon-balls supposed to have been fired in a skirmish there have been dug up in the village.[114] It is said that several soldiers killed at the time are buried in the churchyard under the east window. Though there were several conflicts in North Wales, Denbigh Green is probably the only one meriting the description of battle. William Maurice in his diary records:

[112] *Phillips*. vol. 2. pp. 282-3. [113] *C.W.P.* 1810. [114] *A.&M.* p. 218.

'Sir William Vaughan came with two or three thousand men out of Ludlow, and other garrisons in the marches of Wales, marched through Montgomeryshire towards Denbigh Castle, intending with the addition of the forces of North Wales, to relieve Chester agayne; but Colonel Mytton, hearing of his approach, drew up his forces towards him, and neare Denbigh Castle, gave him battel, wherein Sir William Vaughan was overthrown with all his army, whereof many were slayne in the pursuit, which continued six miles, even to Llangernyw.'

From his vantage on the castle ramparts Colonel Salesbury looked down upon the turmoil on the fair plain below. That night, when the tumult was over, he penned a line to the discomfited commander:

'For Sir William Vaughan.
'Sir,–I wish you to be as free from danger as I hope we are secure and in good condition here. On your foot being perceived under the castle wall I received them in tho I conceived I had no need of them for the defence of this place, yet having, I doubt not, provision enough, their valour and good service withall meriting my compassion, I freely entertained them. I judge the enemy had a force that came the other way over the Green, equal in number or thereabouts, to what you fought with. Mitton and the foot I am informed quarter in the town and most of the horse in the country about: God bless us all!

Gwydir; rifled by General Mytton's men in 1645

Your friend and servant,
William Salesbury.
Denbigh Castle, 1st Nov. 1646 *(sic)*–7 at night.
What you may resolve to take I leave to your own discretion.'[115]

Colonel Salesbury's surprise betokens his amazement at the Royalists' defeat. The victorious troops do not appear to have remained long in the vicinity of Denbigh. They had achieved their object and their presence was required at the leaguer before Chester. Symonds records that by November 4 the Royalist foot were able to march from the castle to Llanrwst. A list of regiments comprising Vaughan's army includes 200 horse under Colonel Whitley of Aston. It speaks well for the tenacity of the Royalists of North Wales that, undiscouraged by the reverse, they immediately devised fresh plans for the relief of Chester.

On November 18 Brereton was able to inform the Speaker that Beeston Castle had surrendered after a siege of twelve months. The gallant governor, Captain Valet, with fifty soldiers was permitted to march to Flint, and from thence to Denbigh and Beaumaris. The dauntless garrison in Chester made a gallant though unsuccessful attempt to blow up a bridge of boats by which the Roundheads spanned the Dee.

On Christmas Day Colonel John Carter (who was active on the Welsh side) frustrated an attempt by Welsh Royalists to drive a hundred head of cattle to the city. The relief train had almost reached Holywell when the watching Roundheads were detected and the cattle were scattered for safety among the hills. [116]

A few days later Carter's patrol was outwitted. A hundred Cavaliers galloped through the cordon and reached the city. Each horseman was burdened with seven stone of meat in addition to some oatmeal and powder. The Parliamentarians only succeeded in snapping up a cornet and a trooper as the daring adventurers broke through. From these prisoners information was extracted. They learned that in the city the poor had revolted and were cursing Lord St Pol as 'a French rogue'. [117]

General Mytton established himself at Wrexham with his force, the town becoming also the head-quarters of the Parliamentary county committee for Flintshire.

At low tide on December 30, Brereton's horse crossed from Blacon Point and thrust towards Mold, Northop and Denbigh. The foot were carried across in boats to strengthen the lines on the Welsh bank. The following day Brereton advanced to Whitchurch with 1,500 horse and as many foot[118] – too imposing a body for the valiant Blue Stockings to attack. 'The duty is extremely hard and much provision wanting,' wrote Brereton.

The Parliamentary soldiers' hardships were slight compared with the suffering endured in Chester. Welsh warriors died of starvation. Great stones, hurled over the walls into the devoted city, spread death and destruction. In order to frustrate any attempt to land provisions from Conwy, Rhuddlan and Beaumaris, where a woman spy reported preparations were being made, Brereton armed two small vessels. These were under the command of Captain Stephen Rich, the same who, some time before, sailed up the Dee and bombarded Chester with the two small guns with which his ship was equipped.

During the terrible siege of Chester the defenders included such North Wales officers as Colonel Roger Mostyn, Colonel Hugh Wynne, Lieutenant-Colonel John Robinson, Lieutenant-Colonel Peter Griffith and Captain Richard Griffith of Llanfair Isgaer.

A vivid picture of the sufferings of the besieged is contained in a journal kept by one of the garrison. The original is in the British Museum (Harleian MS. 2155) and is printed in detail in The Chester and North Wales Archaeological and Historic Society's *Journal XXV* from which these extracts are taken:

[115] Newcome (Denb.). pp. 65-66. [116] Chester. vol. XXV. p. 144. [117] Ibid. p. 165. [118] Ibid. p. 157.

'By this time they have unmusled death and sweare theyle let him loose amongst us, a wide mouth'd morterpiece in which like the mouth of Etna spitts litte mountames in our faces and grinds our dwellings into dust and ashes.

They sent us two Welsh granadoes and beat downe the end of a house in Eastgate Street without doing further harm.

Eleven huge granadoes like so many tumbling demyphaetons threaten to set the city, if not the world on fire. This was a terrible night endeed, our houses like so many splitt vessels crash their supporters and burst themselves in sunder through the very violence of these descending firebrands.

But for all this they are not satisfied, women and children have not blood enough to quench their fury, and therefore about midnight they shoot seven more in the hope of greater execution.

Either there granadoes are all spent, or elles they are too costly, and therefore to kill us with less charge, they toss us three huge stones.

Dec. 25. Because it is a festivall, instead of stones they send us in a token four granadoes, one of which burst among themselves.'

Amid cold and hunger the old year[119] passed to the thunder of mortar and culverin.

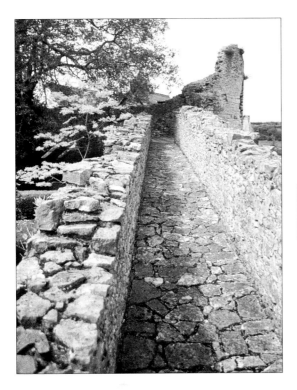

Part of the Denbigh castle wall looking to the North East Tower from the Countess Tower

---

[119] Throughout this book the year is taken to start on January 1.

9

1646

This, the last year of the first Civil War, might well be remembered as 'the year of sieges'. Though it represented twelve months of continuous strife there was little fighting in the open field. The utmost endeavours of both factions centred on Chester.

On January 2 Archbishop Williams, seated in his own house in Conwy, penned a letter to the Marquis of Ormonde, replying to a missive which the marquis had sent from Ireland on December 12 and which had, the previous day, come to hand. For a communication to take nearly three weeks to travel from Dublin to Conwy suggests adverse winds or a particularly vigilant Parliamentary cruiser. The feud with Sir John Owen had abated sufficiently to permit the prelate to sojourn in Conwy. The house, sometimes termed Parlwr Mawr or the Bishop's Palace, stood near Telford's 'Bangor Gate' where sorry fragments of its demolished walls may still be seen. Williams reported that sufficient relief from the Welsh side had reached Chester to enable the garrison to hold out another three weeks. The provisions would have lasted longer had it not been for the demands of homeless people from the suburbs whose houses had gone up in flames:

> 'The Mayor's wife [Charles Walley was mayor in 1644, and in 1645 there was no civil election] always suspected, is gone over to the enemy. Our forces from Wales, of some 100 horse (for foot we have none), under the conduct of Major Evet, put in this last supply of meal and powder, whilst the enemy were withdrawn in part to meet Sir William Vaughan, lingering at High Ercall [in Shropshire] with 1,500 horse and foot in expectation of the main supply from Oxford and Worcester under the Lord Astley and Sir Charles Lucas, who should add unto his number in horse and foot, 2,200 more. We of the Welsh being quite frightened (and three of our five counties being for a great part of them under contribution to the enemy), are not able to make above 300 horse, and scarce so many foot, being by a piece of illconduct in Prince Rupert when he was last in these parts, quite disarmed and discouraged.'[120]

Relief from Ireland was expected but the archbishop wrote that he dare not advise the marquis to send more troops until it was seen what Vaughan intended to do. While he was writing there was in his house 'a French Lord, who serves the King, Mons. de Saint Pol' who expected Vaughan to advance from Much Wenlock into Wales during the week. It might be possible for the forces from Ireland to land and wait in Anglesey or Caernarvonshire until the cavalry from the border could co-operate. But by the twenty-fifth no transports had dropped anchor in Beaumaris roads and the prelate confided in Lord Digby that there was 'no relying upon these Irish forces'.

By that time a body of North Wales loyalists had mustered for the relief of Chester. They were led by Colonel Gilbert Byron, governor of Rhuddlan Castle, and Lord St Pol (St Paul) who had 500 horse and foot, to which were added 'a piece of a regiment' (160 men) raised by Colonel Roger Mostyn in Ireland who brought both English soldiers and mercenaries from Lorraine. [121]

But all this came to naught for Mytton pounced before a junction with the English forces could be

---

[120] *Phillips*. vol. 2. pp. 288-291. [121] Ibid. vol. 2. p. 291.

affected. He chased the fleeing Royalists through Denbigh and Ruthin. Chester abandoned the struggle.

During the negotiations of surrender, Colonel Hugh Wynne of Bodysgallen was held as hostage by the Cheshire forces. Two North Wales officers were among those in the city who signed the articles of surrender. These were Colonel John Robinson and Lieutenant-Colonel Peter Griffiths of Caerwys.

The elaborate articles – they numbered eighteen – included one which gave the garrison under Lord Byron freedom to march to Conwy. 'The Welsh officers and soldiers shall have liberty to go to their own homes, all of them to have free quarters on the march, and twelve carriages, if they shall have occasion to use so many.' [122]

On February 3 the gallant defenders marched forth with the honours of war, the officers with horses and swords, the men bearing their arms.

The fall of Chester had a far-reaching effect on the Welsh counties. Hitherto the 'Parliamenteers'[123] had paid little attention to any of the strongholds except Hawarden and Holt but once the loyal city could no longer perform its tutelary task the northern shires lay open and unprotected. Triumphant Roundheads surged across the border and Major-General Mytton launched a campaign which was to place him among the war's successful generals.

The magnificent castle of Chirk was the first to be grasped. Here was no gallant resistance. John Watts, whom Charles had knighted a few months before, and John Watts, who characterised Archbishop Williams a traitor, slunk away, leaving the castle, well provisioned, to the care of Sir Thomas Myddelton's daughter. And Mytton held a receipt for a £200 bribe!

Thomas Malbon places the date as February 23, William Maurice considered it the 28th. Was it in the hope of preventing this that Sir John Owen was ordered to rendezvous at Wrexham on February 23?[124] The Lord St Paul – his name is spelt variously – is a colourful and mysterious character. He fought valiantly in defence of Chester. On January 8 an agent brought the intelligence that Lord St Paul had reached Flint Castle 'privately, without any force'.

'Upon his going away a fire was made on ye top of Hawarden Castle to give them notice at Chester'[125] – that he was safely through the Parliamentary cordon. Lord St Paul was, as it transpired, on his way to Conwy to organise a fresh attempt to relieve the city.

He escaped from Wales and was with Lord Astley when, on March 14, that veteran surrendered the last royal army in the field with the prophetic observation: 'You have now done your work and may go play, unless you fall out among yourselves.' [126] When Chester submitted, Hawarden's fate was inevitable, and its governor, Sir William Neale, having received royal permission, hauled down his flag on March 16.

The Parliamentarians were in the town of Ruthin as early as January 24 – 'most seasonable', Brereton informed the Speaker, 'for Ruthin Castle was so unprovided, as that we have now great hopes of reducing that strong castle'. The siege began about the beginning of March and occupied a matter of six weeks. The articles of surrender were signed on the 8th and the castle handed over on the 12th April. Writing to the Parliament, Mytton admitted: 'The reducing of this Castle of Ruthin hath cost me more time and ammunition than I expected when I first laid siege to it.' [127]

The articles were signed by John Raignolds, deputy governor. Of Captain Sword there is no mention; he may have lost his life in the siege.

There were good men and true in Denbigh Castle some eight miles away and they meant to make a last bid to aid their comrades in Ruthin. The day before the surrender, a party of horsemen rode out from Denbigh at dawn – sixty cavalrymen and thirty mounted firelocks – resolved to surprise Captain Richard Price's quarters, which were situated two miles from Ruthin – probably at Rhewi. Captain Price was vigilant; his scouts reported the Cavaliers' advance and the alarm was carried to Ruthin. Here Colonel John Carter was in charge of a horse guard, always on duty 'to secure the out-quarters' and frustrate any such attempt. With him was Captain Symkys of Mytton's own troop of horse.

[122] *Phillips.* vol. 2. pp. 294-297. [123] A contemporary term. [124] D.N.B. [125] *Chester.* vol. XXV. p. 171. [126] *Rushworth.* vol. 6. p. 140. [127] *Phillips.* vol. 2. p. 301.

Opposite top: Ruthin Castle today from the air. Opposite bottom: Llanrwst bridge over the River Conwy. Built in 1636, was the lowest crossing of the river during the Civil War.

Circling the raiders the Parliamentary horse surprised the King's party within half a mile of their garrison, charged them, and claimed to have killed seven. In the pursuit forty horses were taken and a number of riders among whom were Captain Morgan of Golden Grove (after whom Morgan's Mount at Chester is named), Captain Hugh Morris, Captain Wynne and Captain Pickering.[128] Colonel Salesbury disputed the figures asserting on his honour that one man only was slain.[129]

No sooner had Ruthin capitulated than Mytton pressed impatiently towards Denbigh. He apparently considered Holt Castle to be of nuisance value only and, having invested it, concentrated on his main objective which was Caernarfon Castle where Lord Byron (calling himself Field-Marshal-General of North Wales), had established his headquarters. Mytton dare not ignore powerful Denbigh but he so encompassed it that its defenders, even though they made numerous sorties, could not cut his line of communications. As the vanguard of Mytton's army advanced a party of Cavaliers disputed the way and slew a captain:

'They met with a rather warm reception from the garrison and were at first repulsed, with some loss and one commanding officer slain,' writes Williams. 'This compelled them to march on, or retreat towards Llandyrnog. But having again rallied, they returned to Whitchurch, where they lay encamped for several months, occupied in throwing up siege-works, and in constant skirmishes and sorties from the garrison who made descents upon their entrenchments and foraging parties.'[130]

As soon as the road surface permitted, the heavy guns and mortars, which had battered Chester into submission, were dragged towards Denbigh. One battery was placed on the south-western slope near the Myddelton ancestral home, Galch-hill, with the intention of breaching the castle on its most exposed side.[131] Another spot on which fire was concentrated was the Goblin Tower, part of the town wall which rises from the plain. A crescent-shaped mound close to the tower base is to be seen in the grounds of Howells School. The concave side is towards the wall and it was doubtless thrown up by the Cavaliers to protect the foundation of the tower from the bombardment which scarred its upper masonry. A contemporary account of the attack on Denbigh Castle reads:

'There are mounts raised round about it, and approaches for battering a tower called the Goblin's Tower: hoping thereby to deprive them of the benefit of a well in that tower; which, can we attain, we may then soon expect the castle through want of water–they having but one well more, which is usually (as it is reported) dry in June or July every summer.'[132]

Mytton, having satisfied himself that Salesbury's five hundred defenders were safely encased in Denbigh's walls, ventured on a reconnaissance as far as Llanrwst, a bridgehead which the King's party had failed to seize despite talk of establishing a garrison there under Colonel John Thelwall. Their oversight proved costly. It is true that Lord Byron sent an eleventh hour order to Sir John Owen at Conwy to destroy the bridge but by April 24, Mytton was already in possession. The general was entertained at Gwydir by the Wynns, and on leaving the following day he issued a warrant to Owen Wynn granting him protection 'upon pain of death'.[133]

Wynn's association with the enemy provoked Sir John Owen shortly after to drive away 200 of the Gwydir cattle – which proved acceptable to the castle larder at Conwy.[134]

A contemporary pamphlet states that Mytton drew out of his leaguer at Denbigh 'a party of about

---

[128] *Phillips.* vol. 2. pp. 301-303. [129] *Newcome (Den.).* p. 73. [130] *A.&M.* pp. 223-4. [131] Ibid. p.162. [132] *Phillips.* vol. 2. p. 307. [133] *C.W.P.* 1770. [134] Ibid. 2096-2099.

The reconstruction of Caernarfon Castle and Town walls

Penrhyn Castle on the site of John Williams' house

300 Horse and Foote, and led them in his own person, advancing neere Conway, a strong hold of the Enemies, neere which place they tooke 11 prisoners marching.'[135]

It is difficult to establish the exact moment when the erstwhile ardent servant of the King, Dr. John Williams, Archbishop of York, turned his episcopal coat, but it must have occurred about this time. Williams had retired to his house at Penrhyn (once the home of the sea-dog, Piers Griffith) which stood on a site now occupied by Penrhyn Castle. He told Maurice Wynne at Gwydir in a letter written on April 29 that he had not been used unkindly hitherto, having stated that he kept his house 'neither against the King nor the Parliament but to prevent surprizalls'.[136]

One story is that the prelate was annoyed by Byron's predatory troopers and sent to Mytton for aid – help which was willingly given. The pamphlet already quoted states: 'Yes, my Lord of Yorke was very zealous to promote this worke, keeping his house Penryne a Garison against the Lord Byron for which he suffered many bitter invectives from the said Lord.' The account also states that the former Commissioner of Array, Sir William Williams, 'also was very forward to afford the Generall all accommodations fortifying also his house against the Lord Byron'.

The writer explains that the eleven prisoners were marching from Aberystwyth with a pass for Caernarfon which they had falsified and were heading for Conwy:

'Two whereof were Irish which the General caused to be hanged immediately according to the Ordinance in that kinde. From thence they advanced to Penrin, where the General and Officers were kindley entertained and feasted (being Wednesday the 29, of Aprill.).'

Mytton's advance was by way of the old Roman road through Bwlch-y-ddeufaen (the Pass of the Two Stones). By this time he must have been joined by a considerable force for he continued his advance towards Caernarfon: .... 'where the enemy was ready to entertaine them, having lined their hedges, ditches, to obstruct their passage, and furnished the Subburbs with a great strength both of Horse and Foote'.

---

[135] *A bloody Fight at Blackwater*, London, June, 1646. [136] *C.W.P.* 2865.

Evidently the small knoll known as the Twthill figured in the operations for the account continues:

'The General having viewed their condition, divided his Body into 2 parts leading one of them himselfe towards the high Rocke, and the Subburbs on the North-side of the Towne, where the chief strength of the Enemy lay, but the dispute contrived not long; for though the enemy came out furiously yet the gallant behaviour of that small party which the General (? commanded) speedily forced them from the hedges to the houses.'[137]

Another account states that the General laid the siege with exceeding difficulty. 'The enemy have made since the siege, which hath been now very nigh one month, two desperate sallies.'[138] During the first, the garrison lost seven or eight; the second cost them 17 prisoners, including a lieutenant and four more officers. Before the forces of the Parliament arrived, Lord Byron 'burnt the suburbs, and sent Mr. Spicer, with a company of soldiers, for provision, who robbed and took all the cattle they found, and returned, but Spicer was taken'. [139]

William Maurice has his slight contribution to make to the situation:

'Towards the latter end of Aprill, Jo. Williams, Archbyshope of Yorke, yealded Penrhyn house to Generall Mytton, and assisted the Parlm in beseiging of Carnarvon, where ye Lo Byron had retreated for safety, after the rendition of West Chester.'

Whatever the cause Williams had now thrown in his lot with the victorious Parliamentarians; indeed, Mytton in a letter to London on April 30 reported that the prelate had abandoned the King's party.

It will be remembered that on the eve of war Sir Thomas Salusbury told Bulkeley of Baron Hill that in Caernarvonshire the Puritans 'bragged of a great party'. Royalist superiority had hitherto kept this beneath the surface but now that Mytton was hammering at the gates of Caernarfon and the archbishop had openly made his decision, many others followed suit. Squires who had served, perhaps with reluctance, on the Commission of Array, now turned against Byron, who, in any event, could hardly have been a welcome guest, for his troopers ranged the countryside threatening all who refused contributions. In addition to Sir William Williams of Vaenol there was William Lloyd, later to be sheriff and sacrifice his life, Colonel Thomas Madryn, and Colonel Thomas Glynne of Glynllifon, elder brother of the famous parliamentary legal light, Serjeant John Glynne. It was Thomas Glynne 'who having great power in those parts did by his invitation prevaile much for the Generalls advance', and was, in the words of the pamphleteer 'God's principall Instrument'.

Caernarfon formerly obtained relief from the sea, but the invaders now had so many ships and boats off the coast that the besieged despaired of succour. They suffered from a great want of water.[140] About May 22 Mytton sent a second summons to surrender.

While the siege was in progress Mytton dispatched three commissioners, Colonel Roger Pope, Colonel John Jones of Maes-y-garnedd near Llanbeds, and Thomas Edwardes, to Anglesey to negotiate for the surrender of the island. The Parliament attached so much importance to Anglesey that they instructed Mytton to offer a bribe of £2,000 for the island's submission.[141] On June 1 Captain Stephen Rich with the armed Parliamentary vessels the *Rupert* and *Rebecca* anchored in Beaumaris roads awaited a pass to proceed to Caernarfon.[142] The Parliamentary party were evidently active in Anglesey as Byron had to send to Viscount Bulkeley a warrant for the apprehension of Sir Robert Eyton, kt. of Beaumaris, whom he designated a spy, employed by the enemy to draw the inhabitants from their allegiance and to give intelligence to the Parliamentary forces. A Royalist officer, Major David Lloyd, former mayor of Beaumaris, was also suspect.

---

[137] *A Bloody Fight at Blackwater.* [138] *Phillips.* vol. 2. p.307. [139] *Parry.* p 362. [140] *Phillips.* vol. 2. p. 307. [141] *S.P.D.* p. 383. [142] *C.W.P.* 1776.

Supporting Colonel Richard Bulkeley, Lord Bulkeley's heir, was the more experienced soldier, Lieut.-Colonel John Robinson, former governor of Holt Castle. With his home, Gwersyllt near Wrexham, in Parliamentary hands Robinson transferred his service to Anglesey where he possessed a second house, Monachdy, on the rugged northern shore. Bulkeley complained to Captain Rich of the *Rebecca* in Friars Road that his seamen had landed in the dead of night conveying arms and ammunition to the outpost at Aberleiniog, known as Lady Cheadle's fort. [143]

While the commissioners were deliberately but successfully negotiating in Anglesey, Mytton was pressing home his attack on Caernarfon and on June 4 the mighty fortress capitulated. Byron's negotiating commissioners were Colonel Edward Vere, Colonel John Vane and Lieut.-Colonel Disney. Mytton was represented by Colonel Thomas Glynne (soon to be made governor of captured Caernarfon), Colonel John Carter and Sergeant-Major Hierome Zanchy, who commanded Brereton's troop of horse and was a fighting-preacher. Under the articles, Byron, the officers, and the gentlemen with their servants were granted leave to go to their homes or friends and they were allowed to make peace with the Parliament or else go beyond the seas. Benefit of the articles was conferred upon Sir William Byron (another of the governor's brothers), Lieut.-Colonel John Robinson, Colonel Jeffrey Shakerley of Rowton Moor fame, Archdeacon Price and several others.

The surrender of Beaumaris Castle and Anglesey almost automatically followed on June 14, Colonel Bulkeley's negotiating commissioners being Lieut.-Colonel John Robinson, Dr. Robert Price and Major David Lloyd. All in the castle were to have General Mytton's best assistance to dispense with their past delinquency and the officers and gentlemen were to have four months in which to make their peace with the Parliament. The gentlemen might remove their own property from the castle but this did not include 'victuals, ammunition, artillery, or the muskets of the veteran trained bands'.[144] Only five castles now remained – Denbigh, Flint, Rhuddlan, Conwy and Holt, to which might be added isolated Harlech.

The remains of Rhuddlan in 1742

[143] *C.W.P.* 1784. [144] *Phillips.* vol. 2. pp. 312-313.

✿   ✿   ✿

Flint was apparently closely besieged by May 22 which makes it difficult to account for the presence of Colonel Roger Mostyn at Gloddaeth on May 28. The governor of Flint was undoubtedly there for on that date he wrote to his uncle, Maurice Wynn at Gwydir, warning him to be on his guard against raids by Sir John Owen's troopers, adding that in Gloddaeth they were in continual danger from attacks by the Conwy men.[145] Roger's familiarity with the district may have enabled him to break through the Parliamentary cordon when he learnt of the menace to his property. He was in Flint Castle during the protracted siege that hot summer for his uncle, Bulstrode Whitelock asserts that he 'held it out till all provisions, even to Horses, failing him, and then rendered it up upon honourable terms'. [146] Two days after the siege began, forty-six of his cavalrymen broke away and either surrendered or went to their homes.[147] With Roger in the castle was his father's brother, John Mostyn of Maesmynan and Tregarnedd, who was a Member of Parliament for Flint county until February 5, 1643, when he was 'disabled' (disqualified) for deserting the House and being in the King's quarters.

The articles of surrender were signed on August 20. The castle surrendered on the twenty-fourth, the governor, officers and gentlemen being allowed to go to their homes and to have six months in which to make their peace with the Parliament. Soldiers were permitted to march out with the honours of war and go to their homes, 'Colonel Mytton to use his best endeavours with the Parliament on behalf of Colonel Mostyn, the Governor, and Mr. John Mostyn'. [148] When the castle surrendered Colonel Mostyn was only twenty-two years old. Impoverished, he was forced to dwell for a time in a farmhouse on his estate but his loyalty remained unimpaired and he continued to work for the House of Stuart.

There must have been fierce fighting in Flint town. The description penned by John Taylor, the Water Poet, six years later depicts a place devoid of industry or accommodation, scarred and stunned by the misfortune which had befallen it. How different from the day four years before when young Roger with high aspirations raised fifteen hundred men for his King in twelve hours!

Now Roundhead riders roamed the familiar roads. The stillness of a green countryside was disturbed by the dusty trampling of marching musketeers as 'rebels' forced their unwelcome way across the broad acres of royalist estates, and labouring gun-teams hauled culverins along leafy lanes to turn their ominous mouths against Flintshire ramparts.

The operations before Rhuddlan remain obscure. The governor, Colonel Gilbert Byron, was summed up by Archbishop Williams in a single caustic comment – 'lately married and very indulgent to his lady'.

Rhuddlan was obviously more vulnerable than mighty Denbigh. The probability is that Mytton refrained from sacrificing lives in a spectacular assault when starvation would accomplish the task. The seige began in May; by the end of July Gilbert Byron surrendered. The attackers, thus released, swelled the ranks of their comrades before Denbigh's defiant walls.

[145] *C.W.P.* 1775 & 2866. [146] *Memorials.* [147] *Phillips.* vol. 2. p. 308. [148] **Flints. H.S.** *Journal.* 1916-17. pp. 85-6.

10

By August Mytton was free to turn his attention to Conwy. Thanks to the earlier exertions of Archbishop Williams, the castle was in good repair and equipped with cannon. The normal garrison had been strengthened by men who arrived from surrendered fortresses. Sir Thomas Eyton of Eyton, Salop, was in the castle for his name appears as compounding on the Conwy articles for his delinquency. Colonel John Whitley, a younger brother of Colonel Roger Whitley, was killed while defending Conwy town.

One can only assume the composition of the force in Conwy but a memorandum prepared after the surrender of Chester in February might furnish clues. In this, Archbishop Williams inquired whether entertainment should be accorded 200 foot and some gentlemen on horseback, 50 horsemen from Holt Castle who arrived under Lord St Paul, and 80 of Lord Byron's men. In addition, there were 100 men from Ireland and 90 from Beeston Castle and Latham House, 'generally commended for their carriage' (as might be expected). There were also 70 of Lord Byron's troopers who had taken foot-arms under Captain Robert Pugh of the Penrhyn Creuddyn family.[149] Though several months had passed since these words were penned it is probable that a number of these warriors remained in Conwy. Bishop Hacket might contemptuously observe that 'the Conweiians would as soon fight for a May-poll as Sir John Owen', but the garrison gave proof of their resolution.

Archbishop Williams must have chafed under the indignity of being turned out of the castle[150] for when the attack was planned he readily participated despite his sixty odd years, and for so doing sustained a wound in the neck. Mytton's men had apparently been observing Conwy since June though nothing in the nature of an assault was attempted. The attack is vividly portrayed in a pamphlet printed on August 19, 1646: [151]

'On Saturday, the 8th of this instant, General Mytton returning to his military employment at Conwy Castle (called) a Council of War, to which was joined the grand advice of Doctor Williams, sometime Archbishop of York, where he represents unto them his intentions, concerning the surprisal of the town of Conwy, together with the former order for the managing of that service. It was concluded by all to be feasible, though full of doubt and hazard, and not to be effected without much loss, yet they resolved to use their best skill; and endeavour to commend the success and blessing to God. Resolute and approved men of his own horse and foot were employed preparations of grenadoes and ladders made ready, and provisions. The service thus prosecuted and effected.

Capt. Simkis was appointed to give and continue an alarm to the town on the North side; that while the enemy that were upon guard advanced themselves to defend and secure that part of the town, Major Elliot on the South side, and Capt. Camburs and Capt. Gethin in two other places, with three select companies of resolute men, might as they were ordered make their advantage of that opportunity... Such was the resolution and gallantry of the soldiers, that though some were knocked down and crushed with horses, others cast off the ladders (which were ten yards high, and yet proved a yard and a half too short), that they renewed the action and drawing up over the other by the arm,[152] till a considerable company were got over; which being done they fell into the town,

---

[149] C.W.P. 1763. [150] "Dr. Williams is no little vexed that Owen hath put such a trick upon him." (*Phillips*, vol. 2. p. 328). [151] Phillips. vol. 2. pp. 325-327.[152] An ambiguity in the printing.

surprised the main-guard, killed a corporal and a gentleman there, wounded many, took a major, one Capt. Wynne, an old cow-driver, four lieutenants, four ensigns, twenty-two soldiers of fortune, and fifty townsmen in arms. Many [Irish] were commanded to be tied back to back, and to be cast overboard, and sent by water to their own country. There was one great gun taken, 200 arms, ammunition answerable, wine, corn, and victuals good store, and considerable booty for the soldiers. The guards being sent for, the town secured, and all things quiet, the General sent this summons for the surrender of the castle namely:

'Sir,

I cannot but be sensible of the misery you have brought upon your country by holding this town and castle from the obedience of the King and Parliament. Now it hath pleased God to give this town into our hands I can do no less than put you in mind, that your holding of the castle can produce no other probable effect than the effusion of Christian blood, and the ruin of your country. And by what authority you do it I am ignorant: the King being come into our quarters, and made known unto you that he is not able to relieve you. I cannot omit to tell you what a desperate condition you will bring yourself and [your] estate into, if you persist in your way but a few days. I do, therefore, summon you to deliver the castle into my hands for the service of the Parliament, and expect your answer within two hours.

Your servant,

Conway, August 9th, 1646.   Tho: Mytton.'

To this Sir John Owen from the castle replied:

'Sir,

I received yours yesterday, and this day I send you mine. I wonder you should tax me with bringing misery upon this country, which my conscience tells me I am free of, especially in doing my endeavour to hold it in obedience to his Majesty.

Now you have gotten the town, I expect no other title from you than of the castle, which title I will maintain with my life. For the effusion of Christian blood, far be it from my heart, only I must seek to defend myself and those that are with me. As for the ruin of the country let the blood of those that lost it fall upon them that were the contrivers of it. I free you and yours. And if you would know by what authority I hold this place, I have formerly given you an answer. You writ that the King was in the Parliament's quarter. I believe he was never further from them; and withal you believe he hath made it known unto me he is not able to relieve me: this point I doubt very much. You tell me a desperate condition I will bring myself and estate, in persisting in not yielding to your desires. I can be nothing bettered unless you have an absolute power from the Parliament. As for your summons, I shall hold this castle as long as it pleaseth God, for his Majesty. Yet, if you shall accept of such conditions as I shall propound, which shall be honourable for us both, I will be content to treat with you only,

And rest, Sir, your servant,

J. Owen.'

Mytton replied that he was prepared to consider these proposals whereupon Sir John asked for three days in which to prepare them. They were not received by August 12 and the attack on the castle was resumed.

A strange situation must have existed within the ancient walls of the Edwardian borough. Roundheads lodged in the houses and patrolled the streets. Cavaliers looked down from the towering ramparts and doubtless took shots at any incautious Parliamentarian who strayed within range. The archbishop could not have been severely wounded. He celebrated the capture of his native town by preaching in the parish church in which he was christened. He chose a right fighting text from the first verse of Psalm 144: *'Blessed be the Lord my Strength, which teacheth my hands to war and my fingers to fight.'*

The House of Commons was informed that 'Conway holds out. Their flesh is spent, corne and Beere they have in store.' By September 14 Mytton reported 'the rendering of Conway goes on well'. Then he passed over the conduct of the siege to Colonel Jones. By October 13 it was reported that 'General Mytton had planted two pieces of cannon (very near) for batteries'.[153]

Doubtless these were on the slope above the Woodlands on the south side of the Gyffin Stream. Edmund Hyde Hall thought so when he examined the terrain in 1809:

'Some testimonies to this attack are still to be seen in the balls (three-pound shots) occasionally found, and in the battered appearance of the south wall where the town connects itself with the castle. Upon the opposite bank the line of the battery may be traced, though it has been smoothed down in a great degree by the labour of the plough.'[154]

When the castle was taken it was found to possess seven pieces of ordnance and six barrels of gunpowder, so it may be assumed that the bombardment met with a spirited response. The recent researches of Mr. A. J. Taylor have thrown fresh light on the siege. After Colonel John Carter was made governor of the captured fortress his expenses included money for repairing platforms for the great guns in the castle, and also for mounting and fitting those guns. Additional costs were for repairing the three drawbridges 'that were shattered and spoyled in the time of the siege'.[155]

There are still unanswered questions. Did the archbishop dwell in his own house? Was Plas Mawr used by the victors as their headquarters and were the coloured plaster escutcheons and crests white-washed at this period? Who were the 'other Welch' who assisted the archbishop in the assault? 'Cap-

---

[153] *Prelate-at-Arms* by Norman Tucker. [154] *Hyde Hall*. p. 65. [155] *Conwy Castle and Town Walls*. Ministry of Works' Official Guide. p. 9.

tain Wynne' was the only prisoner mentioned by name which suggests he was well known. Might he have been a Wynne of Plas Mawr? Robert Wynne, the deputy mayor whose tomb is in the chancel of Conwy church, was alive at the time. Conwy must be pictured with battle-smoke curling grey amid the yellowing leaves, and the air trembling to the roar of cannon as red-coated soldiers of the New Model Army made a garish splash of colour in the sombre streets. It was November 18 before Sir John Owen and his men marched out with the honours of war.

The three months' siege which Conwy endured cannot be compared in its intensity with that of Denbigh. It was, nonetheless, a considerable achievement on the part of Sir John Owen to withstand so long, particularly when the town itself was in his enemy's keeping. The so-called 'hanging tower' on the south side of the castle is traditionally said to have collapsed in the 18th century, because residents took too many of its stones for building their walls. This may well be so, but it is highly probable that in the first instance the foundations were weakened by Mytton's bombardment. It is the tower on the south side which has clearly been rebuilt where the bottom section fell away.

A quaint sidelight on the siege has survived. The Parliamentary commander, evidently as an inducement to the garrison to come to terms in November, wrote:

Conwaie, 10 of 9ber, 1646.
'I promise that everie musquetiere in the castle of
Conwaie shall have Ten shillings a peece when they
laie down theire armes upon Fridaie.
Thos. Mytton.'

Sir John retired to his home at Clenennau, impoverished but honoured – and inwardly resolved to draw the sword again on the first opportunity. As might be expected he was heavily fined.

It will be recollected that one of Archbishop William's conditions for supporting Mytton in his attack on Conwy was that the valuables stored in the castle should be returned to their owners. Hacket asserts: 'Mytton kept the Castle and kept his word too, to let the owners divide the goods among themselves to which they had title and could prove it.'

Opposite: Although later than the Civil War, this print of Conwy Castle and the Town wall shows the Castle and the river as it would have appeared at that time (prior to Telford's suspension bridge, of course).

Above: Plas Mawr, High Street, Conwy, photographed during the September Honey Fair. It is probably the finest surviving Elizabethan townhouse in Britain. It consists of 4 separate buildings.

11

There is a tendency to regard the Civil War in terms of land warfare overlooking the effect of maritime operations, yet the entire issue was influenced by the Navy's early espousal of the Parliamentary cause. When 1642 dawned, the King had three vessels in the Irish Sea. These, based on Dublin, were the twenty-gun ship *Swan* and the armed merchantmen *Phoenix* and *Confidence*. Early in the year the Phoenix was cast away mysteriously on the Great Orme leaving only the *Swan* and *Confidence* to fly his Majesty's war flag in these waters. If the entire story of the exploits of these gallant little craft could be written it would provide a saga of the sea. The King's ship was commanded by Captain John Bartlett, formerly a Dublin merchant, while Captain Tom Bartlett was skipper of the appropriately-named *Confidence*. John was the senior but whether these two loyal sea-dogs were father and son, or two brothers has not yet been established. Before hostilities commenced, Tom Bartlett was entrusted with the unenviable task of carrying Parliamentary commissioners from Dublin to London river in the *Confidence*. To his chagrin he was detained but managed to gain his freedom and bring the *Confidence* back to Dublin in time to plough the waves of the St. George's Channel on many risky passages. Again and again the daring *Confidence* ran the Parliamentary blockade bearing dispatches or carrying men and munitions to Beaumaris or Conwy.

In January 1643 'Captaine Baldwyn Wake, a captaine of the late King's, coming to harbour in Bewmares in co. Anglesey with a Fleete of 14 Sayle of Shippes threatened to spoyle and ruinate the sayd Towne of Bewmares and Countie of Anglisey unless hee should be supplyed with victualles and other necessaries.'[156] The reason for Wake's presence and the nature of his activities are alike wrapped in mystery but he seems to have made little use of his opportunities. He was in the vicinity on December 7, 1648, as a letter written to Mr. Michael Lewis at Beaumaris on that date indicates:

'Mr. Michael Lewes. There being a present necessity of vittualing Captain Wake, and the other shippes now with him in Chester watter, and understandinge that you have 80-100 Barrells of Beefe ready salted and fitt for Shipping at Bewmarys wee have thought to make lese of 16,000 weight of the Beefe ffor him and wee doe undertake to satisfie you fforthwth. Accordinge to such rates, as shalbe reasonably Agreed on by Capt. Chedle & your Selfe, no Corne or other provisions of vittuals, and this beinge ffor the present use of the ffleet wee make noe doubt that you will readily Comply with our order and desire, soe wee bidd you hartily ffarewell herein,
your very loveinge ffriends,
ARTHUR CAPELL,
JOHN BYRON,
NICH: BYRON,
AB: SHIPMAN,
OR: BRIDGMAN.
Chester Decber 7th. 1643.'[157]

The date suggests that Wake and his vessels may have participated in the expedition which resulted in the landing of the English-Irish army a couple of weeks before. There is no account of any naval

[156] Anglesey Field Club & Ant. Soc., *Tr.*,1948, p. 65. [157] UNV. OF N.W. Baron Hill MSS. 5367.

action off the coast as would almost inevitably have occurred had Wake been in the vicinity that summer when a small Parliamentary squadron under Captain Danske put in an appearance. The sight of the first 'enemy' warships off Anglesey caused consternation among the Royalist inhabitants. Their anxiety is reflected in a letter[158] written by Dr. William Griffith of Carreglwyd, to Thomas Bulkeley of Baron Hill, the Lord Lieutenant:

'Truely wee are shrewdly affrighted in these naked parts by three men of Warre whereof two anchor'd neare land all day yesterday and last night at a place called Yr Wylfa three miles from mee, the third at Holyhead where, it still remaineth, but that being farther from mee, and come in since the other two, I cannot give you any certaine account of it, but that it is a tall vessell bearing diverse Peeces of Ordnance …. ffor the other two as soon as I heard of their anchoring and continuance in a place unusual for shipps of that burden, I went thither in the evening yesterday to enforme my self the best I could of them, and to persuade my neighbours to keep a good watch in respect of them last night, and truly I believe all the musketts of these parts attended there last night; but surely this morning they weighed Anchors and I believe you heare of them about Beaumares before this time.

All wee could learne of them here by some that were sent aboard the greater of them was that they were men of warre full of men and Ammunition; in the greater were seene 6 pieces of ordinance ready mounted, and 8 unmounted, and the people that went aboard it, saw 40 or 50 men in one roome at two tables at dinner, what further company there was in the ship they could not see. There was one Welshman of their company with whom our men conferred, and who told them that they were sent into these parts by the Earl of Warwick to secure theis Coaste from some Dunkirkes[159] that lye in these Irish Seas. I fear that you will soon apprehend their errand concearnes us more nearly; and had they not departed from us very timely today, I was resolved to have sent a dispatch to you to advertise what unwellcome neighbours wee had …. I may add that they were inquisitive to learn of our men, how matters stood between King and Parliament, which I conceave was but to fish their disposition towards them. The Welshman of their company would not tell what county of Wales hee was, neither would hee tell us theire Capt's name. They were seene yesterday before they came to the aforesaid place of Anchorage to sound our shores as they went for 6 or 7 miles … The 2 shipps I wrote of wee guess to bee, the one of about 120 Tunns, and the lesser of about 100 Tunns, the lesser seemed to be as full of men as the other.'[160]

Before the Parliamentary ships arrived the Bartletts had been stealing across the Irish Sea with supplies for the King's forces. Sir William Brereton early in 1643 wrote:

'Captain Barkely (sic) who commands the Kings pinnace, the *Swan*, is very officious to the Commissioners of Array, and hath promised them two pieces of ordnance to guard Chester. It is said the Com'ers have given him £500 or £1,000. If some speedy care be not taken to prevent him, he may do very much mischief.'[161]

The Bartletts were joined by the Griffon and also by Captain Lloyd in the '*Swan* frigott', a small vessel, carrying only a few guns, which Mr. Aled Eames considers served as a tender to the great ship whose name she bore. In January 1644 the Parliament dispatched a squadron of five ships and a frigate to watch the coast of Ireland. The admiral was Captain Richard Swanley who flew his flag in the *Leopard Regis*, with Captain William Smith as vice-admiral in the *Swallow*. The remaining vessels were: *Prosperous*, Captain Nicholas Gottenby; *Providence*, Captain William Swanley; *Leopard* merchant, Captain John Guilson; and *Crescent* frigate, Captain Peter Whittey (or Whitley). There were also 'two Liverpool vessels'.

[158] Now in the library of the University of North Wales. [159] Pirates from Dunkirk. [160] *Baron Hill MSS. 5368.*
[161] *Chester.* vol. XXV. p. 38

Castles, principle manor houses and sites of fire engagements.
The site maps were drawn by Mr C Howarth R.C.A.

The magnificent harbour of Milford Haven became their base. Here, in addition to capturing two Royalist ships, they reduced a fort and assisted in land operations for which the admiral and vice-admiral were voted gold chains by an appreciative Parliament. They cruised north on a number of occasions. Lord Ormonde had occasion to complain that he could not send Colonel Francis Trafford and 800 men to Anglesey because of two Parliamentary ships and a frigate anchored off the coast of Dublin. Again he wrote: 'The ships imployed by the Parliament as it were blocked up these coasts, some riding upon the point of Ayre near Mosson (Mostyn) betwixt Beaumarice and Chester. The same lately took away seven barques with much scandall and insolency out of the very port of Holyhead, they being bound hither with provisions.'

This was in May 1644. One record tells of Caernarfon being captured by Swanley's fleet but confirmatory evidence is lacking. Towards the end of the war Swanley was so confident that he offered to take Dublin if he could have his force strengthened. He was hated by the Royalists as 'a bloody mariner' who flung soldiers from Ireland overboard bidding them swim back to their native land. From 1643 onwards Archbishop Williams established a service between Conwy and Dublin which was as regular as weather and watch-ships permitted:

'Let Captain Bartlett bring hither cannon and ammunition and to trust them at Conway,' he wrote to Ormonde. 'The cannon shall be safe and the ammunition paid for. I have likewise presumed to be a humble suitor unto your excellency for the greater of some four or five skiffs or frigates which lie unused, and two pieces of ordnance to be used in her.'

He suggested that Captain Bartlett towed the vessel to Beaumaris 'ready to serve your Excellency from time to time'. Some time before this the archbishop complained that there were but three or four 'fisher-boats' along the North Wales coast.

The manner in which Ormonde secured, with great difficulty, sufficient ships to transport Irish regiments across to aid the King is part of the history of the Civil War. Less known are the passages of the individual ships but casual references to Captain Bartlett or Captain Lloyd indicate that their vessels frequently arrived at Beaumaris and Conwy with powder and stores. A record in April 1645 tells of one of Bartlett's ships coming into Dublin harbour with prizes taken off the Scottish coast, but so battered was his vessel that it would take a considerable time to re-rig her.

It is difficult today to imagine Chester as the chief port for Ireland. This extract proves that vessels could sail right up to the city in Civil War days: 'My bote (the *Rebecca*) was yesterday at Chester and gave the Towne and Alarum and shott in to ye Towne with one of our Gunnes.'[162] So wrote Captain Stephen Rich on May 18, 1645. The enterprising captain proposed to Sir William Brereton that he might that night capture a King's ship which was moored off Flint Castle. He asked for more boats 'to attempt designs worth note'.

As the siege of Chester intensified Brereton ordered that a vessel should guard the approach to the river day and night 'lest provisions should be brought in by water to the besieged'. A woman spy at Conwy had reported that a vessel carrying 300 measures of wheat, thirty flitches of bacon and '4 fatt Beeves' had left Conwy and reached Mostyn but had to turn back on account of adverse winds. The vessel had on board in addition to her crew, thirty soldiers, as it was planned to capture the *Robbin* – evidently one of Brereton's watch-ships. Rich's vessel was furnished with two cannon and twelve musketeers. He assured Sir William that his own pinnace in addition to another vessel would coast up and down night and day. Later he reported: 'I have three nimble vessels fitted inne with four peeces of ordnance, one with two pieces, besides my shallops.'[163] When a last attempt to relieve Chester was being made in January 1646 the King's party had several vessels at Conwy and Rhuddlan laden with corn, bacon and other provisions.

The strength of the little Parliamentary fleet did not however suit Colonel Chidley Coote who complained to Brereton that if Chester was to be protected they must have something better than 'a stinkeinge boate or two yt are not able to doe any good'.[164]

When Chester was captured and the Parliament forces advanced into the interior of Wales, Captain Rich with the *Rebecca* and *Rupert* followed along the coast ready to cooperate. In June they were in Beaumaris roads where General Mytton issued a pass for them to proceed up the Menai Strait to Caernarfon. While at Beaumaris the crews apparently landed and Captain Rich was charged with a breach of the peace negotiations – which he stoutly denied.

All hope of Caernarfon being relieved from the sea was abandoned because the Parliament had 'so many boats and ships'.[165]

From the Royalist point of view the sea struggle ended in tragedy. The gallant *Swan* at the very close of the first war was captured by Parliamentary seamen while most of her crew were ashore in Dublin.

---

[162] *Chester*. vol. XXV. p. 104. [163] Ibid. p. 166. [164] Ibid. p. 82n. [165]*Phillips*. vol. 2. p. 307. For further details see Sir Frederick Rees' *Studies in Welsh History*, and Mr. Med Eames' article in the *Caerns. H.S. Tr.*, 1955, on *Sea Power and Caernarvonshire*.

12

During the close siege of Denbigh which lasted from April to October 1646, letters were periodically exchanged between the two commanders. All were couched in courteous terms, Mytton endeavouring to convince Salesbury of the futility of prolonging the struggle; the doughty governor steadfastly maintaining that until the King gave him leave he would not surrender his trust.

The first of these letters was dispatched by Mytton on the eve of the capture of Ruthin:

'Sir,–I can noe less than put you in mind of the losse of christian blood, the undoing of this country, and the retarding of the work of reformation in these parts (soe happily by God's blessing) not only began, but in great measure perfected in most parts of this kingdome, that you soe much cause, and will be deeply guilty of, if you persiste in your way, of your forcibly keeping this castle of Denbigh from being reduced to the obedience of the King and parliament, having no hopes of reliefe. I do therefore hereby summon you to deliver into my hands the castle of Denbigh for the use of the King and parliament, upon Monday next, by nine of the clock in the morninge; assuring you that you may have better conditions both for yourselfe and the rest of the castle with you, if you refuse not this my first summons, than eyther you or they can expect hereafter if you doe refuse it, and thereby cause mee to desire the parliament that the whoall charge of this seige may for the saving of this poor exhausted countrey from ruyne bee maintayned out of your and there estates, which will certenly be prosecuted by him who rather desires to bee unto you, as heretofore,

Your ould friend and servant,
Tho. Mytton.
Denbigh town, 17 April, 1646.

I expect your answer by 9 of the clocke too-morrow morning.'

Colonel Salesbury replied:

In nomine Jests
18th Aprilis, 1646.
'I am sorry to see the ruine of my in'ocent native countrey, for there loyalty to there King, and sensible of the effusion of christian blood, but upon whose account that which is, or shall be spilt in your attempt to force this castle from mee, being our king's own house–entrusted to mee, unsought, both by his Majestie's commission and verbal com'and, I will leave it to the Highest Judge;–and, in answere to your summons, I will say no more then that, with God's assistance, I doe resolve to make good this place till I receive our King' com'and and warrant of my discharge –to whome, under God, wee all are tyed by common allegiance; and, when I shall have need of relief, I shall undoubtedly expect it from my merciful God, who knows the justness of my cause, and soe rest Your ould friend and servant,
William Salesbury.' [166]

[166] *Newcome (Denbigh)*. pp. 77-80.

General Mytton was not the only person to appeal to the governor to abandon resistence. On May 8 a petition signed by forty-seven residents was sent to the castle, begging the governor to avoid spilling Christian blood and ruining many poor and rich by the continuance of the siege. It was evidently sponsored by the Member for Denbigh, Simon Thelwall, who had returned from South Wales where he had served as a colonel of horse. His name headed the list of what was known as 'The Bumpkin's Petition'.

A print of Denbigh Castle dated 1742 by Buck

Salesbury's reply was addressed to 'Cosin Thelwall– and the rest of the subscribers'. He wrote:–

'How I became interested in this place and command is very well knowne to the best of you; and with what moderation I have since managed it doth clerely appeare by the exhausting of my own estate for the supply of this castle (but what hath bin plundered from mee by the parliament forces) to avoyde any pressure upon the country; who cannot in justice complayne, if the practice of other garrisons be impartially looked upon; and if by the advance of this force, your condition be rendered so deplorable as you mention, I am confident I shall stand acquitted before God and every good man; seeing all I do is in mayntenance of my allegiance and in persuance of the trust imposed in mee by MY KING (whom you doe not vouchsafe to take notice of).'

He told them he could not see how matters would be improved by his surrender seeing that there were other castles of no less strength still under the King's command. He signed himself 'the King's loyall subject'. [167]

Once Caernarfon and Beaumaris were in the Parliament's hands Mytton again summoned Salesbury to surrender, this time on June 24 but with no better result. Salesbury retorted that what Caernarfon and Beaumaris did was no affair of his, he intended to continue to hold Denbigh for the King:

'As for the ruine of this innocent countrey, I am hartily sorry, that soe noble a gentleman, soe generally bee-loved as yourself, of soe antient, and soe worthey a stocke, should bee made the prime actor therein.' [168]

[167] *Newcome (Denbigh)*. pp. 84-86. [168] Ibid. p. 90.

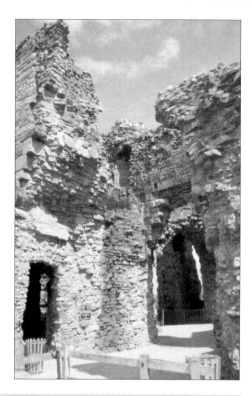

Top left: *The Countess Tower, looking towards the Goblin Tower on the town wall;* top right: *The Great Gatehouse block from the interior;* bottom left: *Remains of the Great Gatehouse, the main entrance to the castle; bottom right: The Green Chambers*

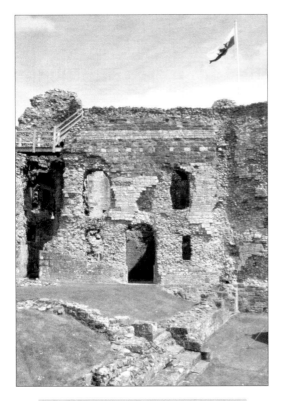

*The Great Kitchen Tower, where
Charles I stayed in 1645*

*Remains of the Postern Tower
and Upper Gate*

The south Curtain wall from the Mantlet looking towards the Treasure House Tower

Salesbury asked permission to send two gentlemen to the King to learn his pleasure. This Mytton was compelled to refuse as Parliament had directed that no such concession should be granted.

Conwy town having been taken, Mytton tried another summons, this time on August 30. 'I hope you will not make your countrey so miserable, in persisting any longer in houlding out this castle,' he wrote.

Again heading his reply *'In nomine Jesu',* Salesbury answered:

'Sir, I shall ever acknowledge your curtesies, tho' unable to requite.–For the condition of our King and his kingdomes, if God have soe disposed, blessed be his name and welcome bee his will. In my answere to your second summons I desired your consent to send a gentleman or two to our King, to knowe his pleasure; but I received noe answere from you therein as yeat; the same desire I doe now second, being confident I shall speed, as others, who had the like granted from you; expecting your answere,

I rest, your servant,

William Salesbury.

'Sir,–I doe returne, per this Drume, Sir John Trevour's letter and the Diurnall.' [169]

Mytton in reply assured Salesbury that he had received a command from the Parliament not to suffer anyone to go to the King 'upon any pretence whatever'. By this time it was evident that the troops which besieged such strongholds as Flint and Rhuddlan had now swelled the ranks of the besiegers for Salesbury in his reply, sent the same night (August 31), began:

'The coming of more forces to beseige this place will noe way move my resolution; who preferre noe ende to the acquitting myself like an honest man in that trust which my King hath committed to mee, which I am fully satisfied can never be done before my King receave an accompt of my pro-ceedings (and without that, to deale freely with you) I have such an engagement upon mee, that I will not entertayne any overture of this nature;–and since I must beeleeve that your hands are tyed up, yeat I am so much concerned in this business, that I must apply myself to other means in that perticular for my satisfaction; which will take up some time; and if I must quit the place, I professe, I had rather you had the honour of it, than any other person in England, of your party; tho' give me leave to tell you, that the addition of a new force, bee the consequence what it will, will but add to my honour which is all I have now left to care for.

'I remayne your servant,

'Ult. Augti, 1646.   William Salesbury.' [170]

A message was entrusted by the governor to one of the loyal Thelwalls who managed to get through the enemy's lines and ride to the King in Newcastle with the following message:

'In nomine Jesu.

'May it please your Majesty, I have presumed to make my humble address to you by this gentleman, Mr. Eubull Thelwall, to let your Majesty understand that this castle hath now for severall months byne closely besieged; what matter of action hath in that time happen'd, I humbly refere your Majesty to his relation, wherein I do beseech your Majesty to give him creddit; praying for your Majesty's health and happiness, I remayne,

Your Majestie's loyall subject,

William Salesbury.'

---

[169] Ibid. pp. 93-94. [170] Ibid. pp. 96-97.

The King replied from Newcastle on September 13.

'Coronell Salesbury, I hartely thank you for your loyall constancie, and assure you, that whensoever it shall please God to enable me to show my thankfullness to my friends, I will particularly remember you. As for your answer, I refer you to thease messengers, to whom I have clearly declared my minde; commend me to all my friends, So I rest,
'Your most assured friend,
Charles R.'

The messengers bore the following warrant:

'TO OUR TRUSTY AND WELL-BELOVED COLONEL WILLIAM SALESBURY, GOVERNOR OF THE CASTLE OF DENBIGH, IN WALES. CHARLES R.

'Whereas, Wee have resolved to comply with the desires of our parliament in every thing which may bee for the good of our subjects, and leave noe means unassayed for removing all difference betwixt us–therefore wee have thought fitt, the more to evidence the reality of our intentions of sittling a happy and firm peace, to authorize you upon honourable conditions, to quit, and surrender the castle of Denbigh, entrusted to you by us, and to disband all the forces under your commands; for which your soe doeing this shall bee your warrant.
'Given at Newcastle, the 14th of Sept. 1646.'[171]

More than a month passed before the garrison marched out and it is difficult to account for this lapse of time. Archdeacon Richard Newcome, from whose *History of the Town of Denbigh* the above correspondence is extracted, quotes the *Memoranda* of Wm. Morris for Sept. 28, 1646:

'Mr. William Salusbury of Rug, after he hadd sente to the King to shew in what case the countrey stood and what misery they suffered by reason of the leaguer, and also how his souldiers in the castle were infected with divers diseases, was commanded by the King, and delivered up the castle to them upon the 26th Oct.'[172]

Williams states that the troops under Salesbury engaged the Parliamentarians in constant skirmishes and, in frequent sorties, descended upon their entrenchments and attacked their foraging parties. Details of one such happening have been preserved. Newcome quotes from 'MSS Memoranda in the possession of the heir of Llwyn'. This reads:

'Edward Wynn, 4th son of Edward Wynn, the only son of Maurice Wynn of Gwydir and Catherine of Beren, by Blanch his wife, daughter of John Vychan of Blaen y Cwm, was captain of a company of foot in Denbigh castle in the service of Charles the First, was wounded in a sally made by the said garrison against the beseigers under Sir *(sic)* John Carter, and in three days after died of his wounds, and was interred with military honours at Llanrhaiadr, being conducted as far as Ystrad Bridge, where he had three vollies, thence taken by a party of the Oliverians, who likewise conducted him to his grave after the same manner'.[173]

---

[171] Ibid. pp. 100-103. [172] Ibid. p. 103. [173] Ibid. p. 106.

Captain Wynn's tomb, a raised slab, is conspicuous in the churchyard in front of the east window. The inscription may still be read:

'Here lyeth ye Body of Capt Edward Wynne 4th son of Edwd Wynne. He dy'd in the defence of Denbigh Castle when besieged by Oliver Cromwell's army.'

The tomb of Capt. Edward Wynne, Llanrhaiadr. The medieval glass in the east window was stored in a nearby wood for safe keeping during the Civil War and Commonwealth.

Mention of Cromwell's name is misleading; he never fought in North Wales. Carter was not knighted until March, 1658,[174] and was again knighted by Charles II at the Restoration.

Williams writes: 'On the way to Whitchurch is a place still called *Captain Bridge,* where tradition tells us a great battle was fought, and where a captain belonging to the garrison fell.'[175] No bridge is to be seen at the spot now. The stream has diminished to a rivulet and is carried by a culvert under the Ruthin road.

In their report prepared about May 22, Lieutenant-Colonel George Twisleton, Lieutenant-Colonel Thomas Mason and Captain Richard Price described the governor as 'a verie wilful man'. Events confirmed their opinion. It had been a tedious siege. Williams, writing in 1856, states that 'Cannon-balls have frequently been dug up about the Castle, but they are mostly eight-pounders, and none, we believe, exceed 32 lb.'[176]

The articles of capitulation were signed upon October 14.[177] Mytton's commissioners were Colonel Simon Thelwall, M.P., Lieutenant-Colonel George Twisleton, Lieutenant-Colonel Thomas Mason, Roger Hanmer, Esq., Thomas Edwardes, Esq. (who also served as a commissioner with Colonel Mason at the Beaumaris surrender), Captain Robert Farrar and Nathaniell Barnett, clerk to the commissioners. Colonel Salesbury's commissioners were Lieutenant-Colonel (Peter) Griffiths (of Caerwys), Colonel Wynne (probably of Bodysgallen), Major Francis Manley of Erbistock, Major Reynalds (probably the governor of Ruthin), John Eaton, Esq., John Thelwall, Esq., and Kenrick Eyton, Esq.

The articles, 16 in number, are too detailed to be reproduced in full[178] but some extracts may serve,

[174] *C.W.P.* 2151. [175] *A.&M.* p. 228. [176] *A.&M.* p. 229. [177] *S.P.D.* pp. 234-237. [178] *A.&M.* pp. 234-237 and *Cal. S.P.D.*

'No. 2. That Coll. William Salusbury, gouernr of ye towne and castle of Denbigh, wth his servants, and all that to him belongs, and all officers and souldiers of horse and foote, as well reformed officers and volunteere souldiers as others, and all other officers with theire seuants, and all yt appaynes to them, shall march out of ye towne and castle of Denbigh, wth theire horses, and armes proportionable to theire prsnt or past com'ands, flying colours, drums, beatinge, matches light at both ends, bullet in the mouth; eury souldier to have 12 chardges of powder, match and bullet p'portionable, wth bag and bagage p'perly to them belonginge; and all p'sons of quality clergymen, and gentlemen, wth theire seuants, horses and armes, in like manner wth bag and bagage, and all goodes to them p'perly belonginge to any place withn X miles, such as the gournor shall make choyce of; where, in regard ye King hath noe armie in the fielde, or garrison vnbeseidged, to march to; the com'on souldiers shall laye downe theire armes (theire swordes excepted): wch armes, soe layed downe, shall be deliuered vp to such as Generall Mitton shall appoynt to receiue them.'

Sufficient carts and teams were provided. No one was to be reproached, or have any disgraceful speeches or affront offered them. Major-General Mytton allowed Colonel Salesbury for his present subsistence so much of his own property, corn, grain and provision now in the castle as he should consider expedient 'by reason all his estate at prsent is seized vpon, and employed to the vse of ye State'. All persons comprised within the articles should have a certificate to that effect.

Only one piece of ordnancc is listed as being captured in the castle. Arms to the number of 200 were handed in after the formal march from the castle – a significant number seeing that the original total of defenders was placed at 'very nigh 500 able-fighting men'. [179]

There were also in the castle many gentry and some riches, 'many barrels of meal, a great quantity of wheat, with other corn and victuals very plentiful. Some hundred weights of lead and bullets, no great quantity of powder and match, which they most wanted.' [180]

Sir William Myddelton, cousin of Sir Thomas, acted as the officer in charge of the siege under Mytton, and was nominally appointed governor of the captured castle. This was probably a gesture of courtesy as his grandfather had been governor in Elizabeth's reign. It was not long before Lieutenant-Colonel George Twisleton became military governor of Denbigh Castle, and alderman of the borough – an office he occupied for about twelve years.

More attention could now be paid to Conwy which, under Sir John Owen, still defied the encircling Parliamentarians. Sir John, and his brother William who commanded Harlech, had apparently come to a mutual arrangement whereby each would hold out as long as the other. John gave way first, and on November 18, the Conwy garrison marched out into the town which their adversaries had occupied for a matter of three months.

As the year drew to a close only two castles in the land flew the royal colours – little Holt beside the Dee, and far-off Harlech on its cliff top overlooking Cardigan Bay.

Before December was ended the Parliament passed an order for the 'slighting' of the castles of Flint, Rhuddlan, Ruthin, Hawarden and Holt – the latter even before it was in their hands, so sure were they of its capitulation. Stout walls which had resisted cannon fire were blown up by engineers.

❊ ❊ ❊

Holt, which stood on the river bank a short distance from the arched bridge which spans the Dee below Farndon, was in the hands of a Denbighshire worthy, Sir Richard Lloyd, one of the irreconcilables who meant to fight to the bitter end.

[179] *A.&M.* p. 225. [180] *Phillips*. vol. 2. p. 329.

'Holt hath been besieged ever since the taking of Chester,' was the comment in a Parliamentary report in May. 'It is a very strong place. Starving is the only way that we can use against the place.'[181] It had caused Mytton trouble even as early as April when he reported:

'The siege of Hoult hath of late been of great difficulty and hazard to those few men I have there, for the drawing off of the Cheshire fire-locks from that service without my privity gave the enemy an advantage to burn the guard the fire-locks kept (which cost the country much to fortify), and about forty dwelling-houses more in the town, and exposed my men (who lay in open quarters, and fewer in number than the enemy within were) to their power, which necessitated my men to be upon continual duty.'

But, despite resistence and destruction, the siege had to end and in January, 1647, Colonel John Carter, concluded the articles of surrender with Sir Richard Lloyd. On January 13, Colonel Roger Pope accepted the surrender in the absence of General Mytton.

Only Harlech remained, the last castle to hold out for the King in England and Wales. On March 15, 1647, the articles of agreement were concluded. The governor, Colonel William Owen, appointed as his commissioners Sir Arthur Blayney and Captain William Edwards. General Mytton was represented by Thomas Edwardes, described as 'Adjutant-General', and Major Edward Moore. Officers and soldiers were allowed to march out with full military honours to a place within four miles and there lay down their arms. There were in the castle, Mr. John Edwards of Chirk 'who being somewhat aged died in February', in addition to his son, Captain William Edwards, Lieutenant Roger Arthur and other officers. John Edwards and his son William had previously been in Denbigh during the siege. Besides these there were twenty-eight common soldiers. Comment is made that on March 14, 'Mr. Robert Foulkes, being in the castle, died, and was buried at Llanfair.'

Holt Castle in 1620 from Lloyds "History of Powys Fadog", Vol 1 p 360

[181] *Phillips.* vol. 2. p. 308.

The keys were delivered to General Mytton on March 16. [182]

The following tabulated list of the dates on which the castles surrendered must be regarded as an approximate guide. In some instances the date refers to the signing of the articles of surrender; in others to the actual vacation.

1646	Date	Governor
CHIRK	February 23[183]	Sir John Watts
HAWARDEN	March 16	Sir William Neale
RUTHIN	April 12	Col. Mark Trevor
ABERYSTWYTH	April 14	Col. Roger Whitley
CAERNARFON	June 4	Lord Byron
BEAUMARIS	June 14	Col. Rd. Bulkeley
RHUDDLAN	July (end)	Col. Gilbert Byron
CONWY (town)	August 9	—
1647		
FLINT	August 24	Col. Roger Mostyn
DENBIGH	October 26	Col. Wm. Salesbury
CONWY	November 18	Sir John Owen
1647		
HOLT	January 13	Sir Rd. Lloyd
HARLECH	March 15	Col. Wm. Owen

---

[182] *Phillips*. vol. 2. pp. 332-4. [183] William Maurice gives the date as the last day of February. Malbon states the garrison 'stoole all pryvately awaye'.

✿   ✿   ✿

Once hostilities ceased the victorious Parliamentarians were confronted with problems of a new order. They had to set in motion the administrative machine. Economy demanded that they should disband the armed forces as rapidly as possible yet they must retain sufficient garrisons to prevent disgruntled Cavaliers from revolting. They had to attend to the sequestration of Royalist estates. Adventurers felt the urge to feather their nests with as little delay as possible. Conscientious officers were concerned with the injurious effects of relaxed discipline.

In the summer of 1646 troopers stationed in the Vale of Conwy became 'very troublesome'. Grace Wynn at Gwydir found that the country was so full of soldiers that there was no going out without danger. From Trefriw to Penmachno the country people were troubled by the lawlessness of three troops of Cheshire and Lancashire horse. Mention was made of a rifled trunk or two, and the soldiers' threats to extend their depredations as far as Dolwyddelan if their pay was not forthcoming. Some soldiers who called at Gwydir were civil, others were very rude. More soldiers departed to cross the mountains to Harlech to assist in the siege operations there. [184]

The problem of finding accommodation for mounted men was continually under discussion. Archbishop Williams considered horse 'a cruel burden' and advised Parliament to 'disband or dispose of the troops in Wales as fast as you can because of their unruliness, and to suppress all useless garrisons which will but suck out the maintenance of the army'. Mytton, having fallen ill, returned to his home at Haiston whence he wrote Cromwell emphasising that Caernarvonshire was 'not a fit county to accommodate horse'. [185]

Correspondence of the period abounds in such expressions as 'the insupportable burden of the free quartering of troops', or 'the insufferable burden it groans under'. In January, 1648, Fairfax issued instructions for disbanding the forces in North Wales. Garrisons, however, were to be retained at Conwy, Caernarfon, Beaumaris, Denbigh and Red Castle (Welshpool). Caernarfon, Denbigh and Red Castle were to retain each one gunner, two matrosses (assistant gunners) and one marshal. Gunners received 1s. 4d. per day, a marshal 10d. and a matross 4d.[186] Archbishop Williams strove to have the number of men in the garrisons reduced and succeeded in getting the quota at Conwy placed at forty with fifty at Caernarfon.

In March that year came a welcome announcement. 'The inhabitants of Caernarvon have paid in their proportion of the disbanding money and are, therefore, not to have any free quarter put upon them.' [187] The prelate doubtless thought only of sparing the purses of his countrymen; Colonel John Carter, governor of Conwy, viewed the diminution of the forces with apprehension.

Following an insurrection of the inhabitants of the upper parts of Caernarvonshire, he unburdened himself to Fairfax. His troopers, he wrote, which were to quarter there had been beaten out of the counties 'in opposition and contempt of authority of your Excellency and Parliament'. When they had beaten and disarmed officers and soldiers the insurgents called them 'rebels that fought against the King'.[188]

No sooner had the Royalists driven the troops of horse out of the hinterland than they rose in the lower parts of the county 'and fell upon some of the garrison soldiers of Conway, who were sent out to assist the Constables in gathering in the contributions laid, by their own warrants, for the maintenance of the garrison'. Having wounded the officers and some of the soldiers, they took their arms away and held them prisoners. 'And all this they have done unto men quiet and civil in their quarters, that never did the country one pennyworth of harm or wrong.' [189]

In such an atmosphere resentment at the treatment accorded the King in captivity proved inflammable material. In the spring of 1648 the smouldering embers of Royalist indignation burst into flame.

---

[184] *C.W.P.* 1802. [185] Ibid. 1837. [186] Ibid. 1845.[187] Ibid. 1850. [188] Ibid. 1811.[189] Ibid. 1811.

13

1648 The Second Civil War

It was not until the closing stages of the first Civil War that the tranquillity of Caernarvonshire was disturbed. In examining the Quarter Sessions records for 1642-1645 in the County Archives little reference to hostilities will be encountered. [190] The justices were normally occupied in dealing with assaults, abuse, trespass and thefts. Occasionally when a war-note is encountered it derives from resistance to constables when they endeavoured to 'press' men for the armed forces. A case occurred in October, 1643. A justice of the

peace, Humffrey Jones of Penrhyn, heard a charge of assaulting two petty constables preferred against Thomas Lewis, a Llandegai miller, and his two sons, David Thomas Lewis of Pentir, and William Thomas Lewis of Vaynol. The men had refused to accept press money and slighted the officers' authority. When the constables were escorting them to Penrhyn, the senior defendant threw one of the constables to the ground, beating him and drawing blood. He called upon his sons to beat and kill the other constable, exclaiming that it was 'as good for them to venture their lives there as elsewhere'. The accused were committed to prison and, after appearing at the Quarter Sessions, were 'sent to the King's service'. The sheriff at the time was Colonel Thomas Madryn who, a few years later, became an outstanding Parliamentarian.

Disturbances were not invariably of this nature. The secluded churchyard of Llannor, near Pwllheli, was the scene of strife one Sunday morning. Dissension arose when a recusant family (that of Griffith Wynne of Brynhynog, gentleman, and his wife Dorothy) were reproached for not attending the parish church. Upon this Dorothy expressed a wish to wash her hands in Protestants' heart's blood, and hoped that all who would not be converted to the Popish religion should have their heads 'cut off like crows' heads', They were accompanied by several soldiers among whom were Lieutenant-Colonel Pugh and Captain William Edwards. Weapons were drawn and in the affray Captain Edwards was struck on the brow with a stone.

On another occasion when a constable was trying to impress Thomas Griffith of Llanaelhaiarn, a bystander, Harry Edwards, who went to the aid of the constable, nearly lost an eye.

Once Lord Byron established himself at Caernarfon in the spring of 1646 the county felt the rough grasp of his avaricious hand. His lordship dispatched parties of war-hardened veterans to collect money for his depleted war-chest. Robert William and David ap Robert of Llannor, demurring at

Above: Llannor Church, the scene of an affray (see text above)

---

[190] The writer is indebted to the former County Archivist, Mr. W. Ogwen Williams, M.A., for his ready assistance.

having to pay in excess of their contribution, were informed that, unless they did so they could 'expect noe lesse than to be plundered by a company of horsemen sent about for that purpose'.

Dame Elizabeth Bodvel, mother of the Royalist, Colonel John Bodvel, had cause to complain of a party of horse calling to collect contributions levied by Lord Byron. She had, at the time, fourteen soldiers quartered in her home, and because she could not accommodate the troopers they brought straw and threatened to burn the house and to carry her off. It is reassuring to find an instance of a 'maimed soldiers' mize', proof that locally at all events some compassion was felt for those who suffered in the war.

❂   ❂   ❂

The Second Civil War, as far as North Wales was concerned, resolved itself into Sir John Owen's revolt in May, 1648, and Colonel Richard Bulkeley's uprising in Anglesey in September that year. To these might be added sundry plottings which intensified with the advent of the Restoration.

Not far from the London-to-Holyhead road near Pentrevoelas is a humble cottage with a massive porch. Inside this is a wall sundial on which is carved MOVNT-V-RANDEV[O] and the date 1648. [191] The thick walls of the house are pierced in several places by small square loopholes as if for musketry. Local tradition claims that this is the spot where Sir John's Cavaliers rallied in the momentous spring of 1648. The position of the sundial indicates it is not in situ.

Horse and foot to the number of a couple of hundred made their way surreptitiously to the meeting place. Most of the volunteers were officers. Messengers arrived with the enheartening news that small parties of indignant Royalists were wending their way from mid-Wales to swell the ranks. Disquieting rumours of the unrest filtered through to the parliamentary strongholds, causing apprehension, for the garrisons were all below strength. On May 9, sheriffs, justices of the peace, and other leading Parliamentarians held a meeting at Wrexham where it was decided to put the country 'in a posture of defence' against all who were in arms to resist the Parliament. The declaration was published in all six North Wales counties, and with it an appeal for volunteers and funds.

The sum of £6,000 was to be collected each month and the six counties pledged themselves to help each other. Persons ready to volunteer for service in Denbigh county were to send their names to Lieutenant-Colonel George Twisleton, governor of Denbigh; the High Sheriff, Sir Thomas Myddelton; or Simon Thelwall, the elder, of Plas-y-Ward, Member of Parliament and colonel of horse. The leaders in Flint were the High Sheriff, Colonel Thomas Ravenscroft, Colonel John Aldersey (these two, it will be recalled, were in charge of Hawarden Castle when it surrendered to Brereton in 1643), John Salisbury of Bachygraig, and Captain Luke Lloyd. The arms of the inhabitants in the counties of Denbigh and Flint were to be stored in Denbigh Castle. Ruthin and Rhuddlan castles were to be made 'more untenable'. [192]

Major-General Mytton was in Caernarfon Castle and with him the new High Sheriff, William Lloyd of Plashen (whose signature is to be seen on documents in the Archivist's office). The seriousness of the situation was impressed on the commander-in-chief when, on riding to Beaumaris, he found the gates closed in his face. Captain Thomas Symkys, who once commanded the general's own troop of horse, had gone over to the rebels!

In this time of crisis the most active officer and the one exhibiting the most initiative was undoubtedly Colonel George Twisleton, the governor of Denbigh. Assembling sixty or seventy mounted men he rode into the Snowdon fastnesses hoping to prevent the arrival of Royalists from the south and, if possible, to catch the ringleader himself.

Those who rode out with Sir John Owen included Colonel Richard Lloyd of Llwyn-y-Maen, Shropshire, Lieut.-Colonel Scriven, Colonel Lee, Morgan Herbert and Captain Edward Herbert, his son,

---

[191] Illustration in *The Heart of Northern Wales*. vol. 2. p. 488. [192] *Phillips*. vol. 2. p. 372.

Captain Blodwst, Captain Kynaston, Captain Phillips, Sir Arthur Blayney, Mr. Herbert Vaughan, Lieutenant-Colonel Hughes, Captain Morgan and Captain Brynkir. They were with Owen when, at the head of a hundred volunteers 'almost all of them being commanders', he rode into Dolgellau. Here they stayed two nights and, on their departure, 'paid for their quarters', explains the scribe virtuously, 'and did no man harm'. [193]

They rode to Dyffryn Ardudwy, thence into Caernarvonshire, and back to Ardudwy. This was about mid-May. Meanwhile Colonel Twisleton and Captain Roger Sontley, having ridden from Denbigh, arrived at Dolgellau after Sir John had departed. Here they learnt that 'some foot came over Dyfy from Sir Richard Price to Sir John Owen', so they took horse for Penal and thence to Towyn. At Llwyngwril they overtook some of the footmen for whom they searched 'who, thinking they had been some of their own men, made no resistence nor shift for themselves, and therefore about forty-eight were taken prisoners, among whom were Captain Vaughan, Henry Vaughan's son of Golden Grove.'[194]

The successful Parliamentarians returned to Dolgellau by six in the evening. About midnight they took their prisoners and marched by way of Bala back to Denbigh. Meanwhile word reached Sir John Owen that his enemies were at Dolgellau so he turned back from Ardudwy but learning he had missed his quarry, he headed for Caernarvonshire. So it was that early in June Sir John came bravely down from the hills and turned his face towards Caernarfon.

General Mytton was anxious to crush the uprising before it attained dangerous proportions and he sent to Twisleton at Denbigh instructions to raise as large a force as possible to strengthen Caernarfon. The original orders were to advance by way of Llanrwst bridge. Meanwhile the parliamentary commander, learning of Owen's proximity, decided with the meagre forces at his disposal to make contact with the Royalists. To discourage any latent loyalist sentiment among people in the neighbourhood he made several sallies, the High Sheriff, William Lloyd, taking command of the horse. Colonel Thomas Madryn also assisted.

On Saturday, June 3, a small force of horse and foot were making their way along an old road which is now practically obliterated by the woods in Glynllifon Park. The advance guard of Owen's party appeared and there was a sharp clash. Sheriff Lloyd at the head of twenty horse bore the brunt of it, Mytton, who commanded sixty foot, being farther behind. The sheriff, wounded in some seven places, was unhorsed and taken prisoner. Mytton by a skilful movement was able to retire to Caernarfon where he found temporary security behind the stout walls. Nevertheless he dispatched a messenger post haste to Twisleton, urging him to hasten to his aid. In the meantime Twisleton had collected some seventy soldiers from Chester and, uniting these with the Denbigh garrison, he hurried to join Colonel John Carter at Conwy. According to Edmund Hyde Hall the force travelled by way of Bwlch-y-ddeufaen, dragging two small field-pieces with them. [195] Their intention was to reinforce Mytton in Caernarfon but it was not to be. For Owen, hearing of their approach, abandoned his vigil at Caernarfon and leaving a small party to prevent Mytton emerging, he led the remainder to intercept the advancing relief column. As his men splashed through the shallows of the Ogwen River they sighted their enemy advancing along the flat lands which border the mouth of the Menai Strait.

The entire story may be told in the words contained in 'The Narrative' which was submitted to the Parliament after the clash at Y Dalar Hir on June 5, 1648:

'Sir John Owen, Commander in chiefe of the enemies Forces (and whom they called) and formerly Major Generall against the Parliament, with a hundred and forty horse, and one hundred and twenty foot or thereabouts, was growne so strong by some addition from the Countrey, that Major Generall Mitton together with William Lloyd Esquire, High Sheriffe of Carnarven, were forced for their security to repaire to Carnarvan Garrison, upon Saturday the third instant. Major Generall Mitton with the Sheriffe and what horse were in the Garrison, being about twenty, and some Foot

[193] *Parry.* p. 390. [194] Ibid. p. 390. [195] *Hyde Hall.* p. 238.

to the number of sixty or thereabouts, marched forth (sic) the enemy: met them within three miles of the Garrison; the Sheriffe who led the horse was so farre ingaged, that being overpowred, he could not come off, but after long strugling, having received seven or eight wounds, became their prisoner, whose barbarous usage towards him can hardly be related; they carried him, whilst he was able to sit, from place to place on horseback, his wounds never searched nor dressed, which had they been, its conceived they had not proved mortall, as by a Chirurgeons attestation appears, given by him under his hand, as followeth.

The Chirurgeons Attestation.
"William Griffith, Chirurgeon, being sent for to dresse some men belonging to Sir John Owen, found the High Sheriffe of Carnarvanshire, wounded in seven severall places, besides burnings and skars, but no considerable helpe afforded for the healing of them, being unsearched, untended, unrolled, from Saturday in the forenoon, untill Sunday night only some shallow pledgets of Lint on the superficies of the Orificies, which wounds (I believe) were all curable, if he might have rested in a settled place butt; being marching in wind and raine, and cold getting into the wounds must needs cause death, and this I testify under my hand.
William Griffith."

'But when his strength began to faile, they carried him upon a Beare; and all this not sufficing to take away his life they threw him off the said beare with such violence that he presently died, having continued in the languishing condition aforesaid, from Saturday till Monday following, after his wounding; fresh cloaths being brought to him, Sir John would not suffer him to be shifted and Major General Mitton, sending to desire that he might come to Carnarvan to have his wounds dressed, with engagement that after his recovery he should render himself prisoner, it was wholly refused, and no answer returned thereunto.'

From this it will be seen that the inhumane treatment of the High Sheriff and his untimely end made a profound impression on General Mytton and his colleagues. Normally the first thought of an officer who has crushed a revolt and captured the instigator would be to report the success of his operations, but in this instance the conflict is relegated to second place. Having unburdened his mind the writer then turns to what has become known as the battle of Y Dalar Hir. So far as numbers were concerned it did not merit so imposing a designation yet the engagement resulting as it did in the capture of Sir John Owen was undoubtedly important. Both sides were without distinctive uniforms and as neither side wore scarves or brassards (which is apparently what is meant by their being 'without bands') and having war-cries of a similar sound, confusion resulted. The pamphlet continues :

'Colonel Carter Governour of Conway, and Lieutenant Colonel Twisselton, Governour of Denby used their best endeavours to suppresse the Forces raised by Sir Owen (sic) as aforesaid, and havin mounted thirty foot from Denby Castle with Colonel Jones his Troop, and about thirty Volunteers mounted, being some late disbanded officers and others well-affected in Denbyshire, as also seventy Foot and thirty Horse, procured from Colonel Duckingfield, Governour of Chester, together with thirty of Colonel Carters souldiers marched towards Carnarvan, intending before ingagement with the enemy, to adde some of the Forces in Carnarvan; but the enemy prevented this, and met them upon Munday, the fifth of this instant moneth, upon a plaine near the sea-side betwixt Bangor and Aben (Aber); the Forlorns of both Parties being drawne forth, charged each other with great resolution; but ours at last were forced to a disorderly retreat; the enemy pursued with much courage, and were entertained by our reserve, after some long encounter, to their totall routing; and in their retreat Captaine Taylor singled out Sir John Owen, and after some short encounter wounded him,

The map contains the following labels:

Lady Cheadle's Fort
Almshouse
Red Hill
Cadnant landing place
MENAI STRAITS
To Caernarfon
Bangor
R. CEGIN
R. OGWEN
Penrhyn
Beaumaris
Gallows Point
Y Dalar Hir
Aber
Boats led by Major Cheadle
Conwy
Col. Twisleton's advance.
ROMAN ROAD.
R. CONWY
Tal y Cafn Ferry
From Denbigh
Llanrwst Bridge
Gwydir

Sir John Owen captured June 5. 1648.

Site of the two engagements of 1648, Y Dalar Hir and Beaumaris

and unhorsing him, took him prisoner; there were of the enemy slaine about thirty, whereof three Captains, one Captaine Madrin; Captaine Morgan, and another, and fifty eight taken prisoners, most horse, whereof many of quality, as by the list appeareth; they threw away their Armes, and most of them possessed by us; few of them had escaped, but that our words were somewhat alike in sound, and the signall on both sides the same; their word was Resolution, ours Religion; the signall was without bands, so in the disorderly pursuit, we knew not each other; about fifty of their horse got away in a body, and carried three of our men with them, which we hear since they have put to death, it being according to their resolution, as some of the prisoners confest, not to give any quarter to any they took. Sir John Owen, after he was disarmed, upon discourse uttered these words; though you have defeated me, yet foure score thousand men, now in Armes in Essex and Kent will not be baffled therewith; and seemed therewith much to comfort himselfe.'

This pamphlet must be accepted as an official document as it was 'ordered by the Commons in Parliament assembled, that this Narrative, together with the Letters be forthwith Printed and Published'. Having presented his brief summary of the fight the writer reverts to the death of the High Sheriff:

'By the Barbarous, and unchristian-like usage aforementioned by the said Sir John Owen and his rebellious crew, towards the aforesaid Gallant Gentleman, the late High Sheriffe of Carnarvan (who with his life, gave testimony of his good affection to Parliament, Maugre[196] the late aspersions endeavoured to be fastened upon him by some persons really disaffected both to him and Parliament) as also towards others taken by them prisoners, all unbyased men and of any ingenuity and conscience, may discover their bloudy resolution, and others of their stampe towards the Parliament and their adherents. Did not God in mercy prevent the execution of their bloudy designes, as

[196] NOTE. *Maugre*= in spite of. The treatment of Lloyd might have been prompted by personal animosity. Professor Dodd points out Lloyd had been put under arrest when war broke out as one of the trio of 'disaffected' spirits in Caernarvonshire (*vide Caerns. H.S. Tr.* vol. 14, p. 26).

he hath been pleased most eminently of late (especially in this expedition, and that successe in Kent, and other parts of the Kingdome so manifest) which is hoped and desired, may prove as an eye-salve to open the eyes of such, as have been, or are apt to be deceived by the plausable Pretences of Malignants and Cavaliers, and serve as a motive to all honest and religious men, to lay aside divisions, and to unite against the common adversary, for the preservation of Religion, and publick peace of the Kingdome.'

Mytton's letter to the Speaker in which he signs himself 'Tho: Mitton', is virtually a repetition of the facts though he mentions that when the sheriff was taken, the Royalists also captured two private soldiers. The parliamentary party secured a Royalist lieutenant and an ensign, and 'killed one of theirs'.

Mytton asserts that he personally sent three letters to Sir John Owen asking him to release Lloyd until his wounds were healed, adding, 'I did engage my selfe that he should become a prisoner againe.'

The dispatch sent jointly to the Speaker by Colonel John Carter and Lieutenant-Colonel George Twisleton (included in the brochure) reveals the writer as something more cultured than a rough soldier. It is unlike Carter's crude style and was probably Twisleton's work:

'Honourable Sir,
The sad distempers of these times had reached these countreyes in a great Measure, and threatened sad things to these Parts, had not God been pleased to give the Enemy a blow, and such an one, as we hope will crush and destroy all their hopes in these Parts; and it is exceeding seasonable, all circumstances considered, the relation whereof we leave to this bearer, whose favour and courage, much conduced to the service; Sir John Owen hearing of our march, and suspecting our intention, which was to joyn with Generall Mytton, he as he since confessed, resolved to engage us to hinder it, and accordingly marched with all the strength he could make, which was of Reformados and Fightingmen about 250, all well appointed, and of Countreymen a numerous many, and met us between Bangor and Aber in a very faire plain upon the Sea-side; where he found us ready to entertain him, having had intelligence of his advance, we were horse and foot 200 and upwards, the dispute was desperate and hazardous, but at last (although at first our forlorn was routed) through the resolutions of the Officers and Reserves, the Routed Partie rallied, we utterly routed the Enemy, killed and tooke many; and with no few knocks to our selves; this indorsed list showes you the names and qualities of the Prisoners and their number; we dispersed also all the Clubmen that were gotten together, there is some horses of the Enemies gotten away which we could not immediately pursue, our horse being wearied in the fight and march, but intend to give them little rest in these Parts. We thought it our duty to present you with this accompt, wherein we would ascribe all to that good hand of God that fought with us and for us.
We are, Honourable Sir,
Your most humble and faithfull Servants,
JOHN MARTER[197]
          GEORGE TWISLETON.'

---

[197] An obvious printer's error.

A LIST OF THE NAMES OF THE PRISONERS BOTH OFFICERS AND SOULDIERS

Sir John Owens Maj. Gener.,
Mr. Richard Lloyd Colonell,
Mr. William Owens, [198]
Mr. Hugh Budurdah,
Mr. Joshua Cole,
Mr. Robert Wynn,
Mr. James Kinaston, Capt.,
Mr. Matthias Lloyd,
Mr. John Wanteon,
Mr. Thomas Lloyd, Lieu.,

Mr. Robert Wynn, Lieu.,
Mr. John Mathews,
Mr. Samuel Conway,
Mr. Will. Sanders, Capt.,
Mr. Gilbert Fox, Capt.,
Mr. Arthur Stapleton Cornet,
Maurice Griffith, servant to Sir John
    Owens,
William Hide of Cheshire,
John Harrison of London.

Richard Thomas, John Thomas, William Pym, Robert Jones, William Pirhard, William Jones, Hugh Roberts, Robert Davies, William Richard, Richard George, Owen-ap-William of Caernarvanshire.
Ralph Davenport of Lancashire.
Evan Roberts, Thomas Jones, John Davies, Hugh Greene of Denbighshire.
Robert Johns, John Hughes, William Danis (No County specified), William Calladay of Hartfortshire.
Walter Morgan of Glocestershire.
Robert Creswell, William Creswell, Walter Roe, Thomas Stockwell of Shropshire.
Christopher Elmor of Lincolnshire.
David Williams, Henry Pughe of Merionethshire,
Robert Williams of Flintshire.
David Ellis of Montgomeryshire.
Benjamin Par of Carmarthenshire.
John Morris of Cardiganshire.
John Crosse, Thomas Crosse, Jeffrey Burch, John Clark of Worcestershire.
Rich. Baxter of Staffordshire.
Isaac Edwards of Anglesey.
John Cadwaladr of Carmarthenshire. [199]

The diversity of districts illustrates how life was dislocated by the disturbance of war.
Another pamphlet prints 'A Letter from Chester, of the great Victory against Major Generall Sir John Owen'. It reads:

'Noble Sir,
There began a new insurrection in North Wales, Sir John Owen, the Kings old Major Generall, with Colonell Floyd and others were joyned, to the number of 200 besides 200 Country-men which they had raised in those parts, and were daily increasing in Merionethshire.
Major Generall Mitton, with Mr. Lloyd High-Sheriffe of that County joyned and sent to the Committee of North-Wales to assist them with what Forces they could.
We had informations here that they were resolved to give no quarter to any that served the Parliament. And by letters from Liverpool it was said that they had discovered, that had the Cavaliers had

---

[198] Sir John's son. [199] A Narrative, Together with Letters Presented by Captaine Taylor, To the Honourable House of Commons, Concerning the late successe obtained by the Parliament forces in Caernarvanshire in North Wales. against Sir John Owen, and his forces, consisting of Malignant Papists and Cavaliers. As also, Of his barbarous and unparallel'd inhumane usage towards the High Sheriffe of the said County, and others of the Parliaments party taken prisoners by him. LONDON, Printed for Humphrey Harward and are to be sold at his Shop at the *George* upon Ludgate-hill over against the *Bel-Salvage*. 1648.

power in their Design against that Town, they had not only killed all that have joyned with the Parliament, but to put their wives and children to the Sword.

There need not much to persuade a readinesse to joyn in the suppressing of Sir John Owen; And a messenger was dispatched to Major-Generall Mitton and the Sheriffe, to assure them of speedy supplyes, and the time and place appointed.

But before they could come up, Major General Mitton and Mr. Lloyd the Sheriffe, a ingaged with them, and had a very hot fight, routed the forlorne, and did good execution.

But Reserves comming up and overpowering us, Major Generall Mitton was worsted, And the Sheriffe with some others taken.

Mr. Lloyd the Sheriffe had seven wounds, And Owen promised him upon his Honour that he should have care taken of him, for curing his wounds, yet nevertheless a guard was set upon him, and hee was carried up and down from place to place, his wounds, bleeding about the streets, and no Chirugion admitted to dresse him, and at last stript and throwne upon the ground, where he lay till he bled to death.

Collonell Carter and Collonell Twisleton with a party of Horse and Foot coming up had notice of that unhappy ingagement with the enemy before they came, and were sorry for the losse of that gallant man, yet they (after debate amongst the Officers) resolved to ingage Sir John Owen if they could.

And accordingly (marched up to them) faced each other, And their Forlornes met, and fought furiously, But Col. Carters men had the worst then.

Relief being come up from both (after another dispute) both sides were at a stand, But after some charges the Parliaments Souldiers worsted them, and brak in upon them, doing execution, which they followed so close that they put them to a totall rout, so that there is now no visible fight in the field.

I have sent you (here inclosed) a List of the particulars, and doubt not but the Parliament will proceed to execute Justice against them for murthering the High Sheriffe of that County, doing his Office.

Chester 8 June, 1648.'

A List of those particulars that were killed and taken by Colonell Carter, and Col. Twisleton in North Wales.
Taken Prisoners.

Major Generall Sir John Owen taken prisoner, and wounded with three cuts on his head by Captaine Taylor, who hath his Buffe-coate, and pulled him off his Horse.

Collonnell Floyd a notorious Cavalier, that formerly served the King.

> 10 other considerable officers.
> 60 Prisoners taken.
> Most of the Horse.
> 200 Armes.
> 30 Slaine of the Cavaliers.
> 4 slaine of Col. Carters men.
> Many wounded on both sides.
> Good Pillage taken which they plundered from the Country.
> June 10, 1648. Imprimatur Gilb. Mabbot. [200]

---

[200] *From N.L.W.*

❂ ❂ ❂

With these prosaic returns ends the strange story of the encounter known as the 'battle' of Y Dalar Hir. The account would be even more interesting if all the officers mentioned could be identified. It savours of the incongruous to think of this modest meadow-land attracting the attention of the House of Parliament and setting tongues talking in far-off London. 'Hir' signifies 'long', and 'dalar' is the name applied to the turning place at the end of a furrow. An English ploughman would term it a 'headland' but to translate it thus would be misleading. Interpret the word how one may, the scene today retains its homely rustic atmosphere which holds no hint of war or politics.

The whole episode, trivial to the military mind, is not without fascination. There is something incredibly daring about Sir John's lonely rendezvous, and the manner in which his horsemen rode boldly down to pen the parliamentary commander in his great castle at Caernarfon. In contrast is the hectic mustering of the parliamentary horse and foot. In both forces were veterans and volunteers, men of quality and humble musketeers, shoulder to shoulder in their eagerness to settle the issue. When men like Captain Roger Sontley or Captain Edward Taylor rode the lanes of Caernarvonshire they were far indeed from their Bromfield homes.

The alleged murder of the High Sheriff (who was akin to the Royalist Lloyds of Bodidris), and the cold-blooded shooting of the three Roundhead captives, suggest a callousness which is ill-pleasing. At the same time these incidents serve to impress on the mind something of the fierceness of the passions stirred by the plight of the imprisoned King. Charles's followers foresaw the end of their royal master unless they, by their exertions, could save him from the headsman's axe.

The valorous Captain Taylor was sent to the capital as bearer of the good tidings and was duly rewarded by a grateful Parliament with a present of £200. After strutting for this brief moment on the nation's stage, Taylor resumed a less conspicuous existence in his native haunts near Wrexham where he became a respected member of the County Committee. The family of the sheriff who had sacrificed his life for the cause he espoused received compensation extracted from the estate of the captive Sir John Owen.

Insignificant though the clash at Y Dalar Hir appears it was not without importance. Had the scales tipped the other way the whole aspect of the uprising in North Wales might have undergone considerable change. The Anglesey Royalists would doubtless have united with Owen; Cromwell, hastening from captured Pembroke, might have been forced to turn aside, and his surprise attack on the Duke of Hamilton's invading force at Preston would have been delayed.

Today the placid pastures beside the Menai Strait are undisturbed save by grazing sheep or flocks of sea-birds. It is hard to catch an echo of discordant war-cries and the clash of arms.

14

The reverse at Y Dalar Hir in no wise disheartened the Royalists in North Wales. While the energetic Captain Roger Sontley of Bron Deg was hunting fugitives in the vicinity of Dolgellau, and General Mytton and Colonel John Jones were at Pwllheli, several dashing blades in the Vale of Clwyd began plotting to rescue Sir John Owen from Denbigh Castle where he had been incarcerated. And notwithstanding a company of Roundheads being stationed in Bangor, a party of Royalists from Anglesey crossed the Menai Strait one July evening and carried off nearly forty of the enemy whom they found near Aber. Shortly after, the Anglesey men crossed to Caernarfon and took some men and horses about Chyrmog (Clynnog?). [201]

The plotters at Denbigh were headed by several local men, among them Major John Dolben of Segrwyd, Captain Charles Chambers of Plas Chambres, a Captain Cutler, and Captain Richard Parry of Plas Llanrhaiadr, a descendant of Bishop Parry of St Asaph. They paved the way for their exploit by bribing several of the garrison. William Maurice in his diary makes brief reference to the incident:

'1648.–About the end of June, Mr. Dolben and Mr. Chambers of Denbigh hadd a design to take the castle of Denbighe, they scaled it in the night, and aboute sixty men got into the ulter-ward, but they were discovered, and some of them taken; they both plundered, but escaped, as is said.'

A printed account–Denbigh Castle surprised for the King, by 60 Cavaliers &c. supplies more detail:

'Noble Sir.–We finde the King's party still very active in these parts; those in Anglisey that revolted will not accept of the indempnity, but resolve to keep the island for the King. Sir John Owen is acting in Denbigh castle, where with his confederates, the castle was very neare being surprized. On Monday night last, the captaine of the guard being gone to bed, they began to act their design. And there was engaged in this business for surprize of Denbigh castle (where Sir John Owen is prisoner) a corporall and a sentinell belonging to the castle, of the parliament souldiers, who had (it seems) been wrought upon by those who carried on the design, to whom large promises were made. These men we have discovered, besides some others whom we cannot yet find out, to have been corrupted by Serjeant-major Dolton,(sic) [202] Captain Cutler, Captain Parry, Captain Charles Chambers, and some others, who were the chief actors in this plot. There was a party of the cavilliers that came that night with scaling ladders, who came privily to the walls without giving any alarm at all, the corporall and the two sentinells of guard being privy to their design and confederacy. And about some 60 of the cavilliers had scaled the walls, and had got over without any opposition at all, and were within the walls at least an hour before any alarm was given, and it was a hundred to one that we had not been all surprized and ruined, but we were miraculously delivered. The aforesaid three score cavalliers that were got over, were so near entrance into the inner ward of the castle that they had but only one horselock to break, which the corporall was ready to have assisted them in, to open one of the sally ports. It so pleased God that the captain of the guard could not sleep in his bed, but was much troubled, tho' he knew not for what, and at last he resolved to rise and to walk the rounds with his

---

[201] *Parry.* p. 391. [202] This must mean Major Dolben.

souldiers, for which purpose he did get up accordingly. When he had drawn out some souldiers to walk with him about the rounds, he went with them, untill at last he espied a party got over the walls, and scaling ladders upon the walls, whereupon the alarum was given to the castle, and the towne also by these means took the alarm. But they all yeilded themselves prisoners at mercy, only some few that had got back again over the wall. And upon remark of the business, the corporal was discovered to be going with them to help them to open the gate. I hope this will be a sufficient warning to them all to look well about them both in that castle and also in other parts about us. Chester City, the 8th of July, 1648.' [203]

It is not surprising to learn that before the month was out 'Sir John Owen was sent to Windsor Castle, upon a charge of high treason and murder against him, for the business in North Wales.' [204]

The conspirators were in no wise daunted by their narrow escape for William Maurice shortly after had occasion to make another entry in his diary:

'July.–In this monthe, aboute the 16th., Dolbein and Chambers with their companye came before Denbighe Castle, and, in a bravado, discharged their pistols and went away.'

According to Sir Frederick Rees, the Parliamentarians who betrayed the castle were Corporal Sutton and the two sentinels Privates Williams and Ashmount. The captain of the guard was Sergeant Owen.[205]

It must have been a period of anxiety for the Parliamentarians not merely in North Wales but throughout the entire country. The uprising in South Wales, headed by the former Parliamentarian leaders, Laugharne, Rice Powell and Poyer, was sufficiently serious to warrant Cromwell's appearance in person. Fairfax was wrestling with troubles in Kent and at Colchester. From Scotland the Duke of Hamilton threatened an invasion which brought Cromwell hastening from Pembroke the moment the fortress capitulated. In all parts disgruntled Royalist officers were restless and rebellious. Anglesey was no exception. Lord Byron had been secretly plotting in Lancashire and Cheshire, but seeing greater possibilities of success in isolated Anglesey he made his way thither fondly hoping he would be hailed as the Field-Marshal-General he designated himself. Anglesey, prompted by his suggestion, had, that July, published a manifesto, declaring for the King. It was signed by Viscount Bulkeley who, besides being the island's outstanding personality, was also colonel of a trained band.[206] The thirty-six other signatories included his young son, Colonel Richard Bulkeley, Captain Thomas Symkys, former parliamentary governor of Beaumaris Castle, Colonel John Robinson now living at his Anglesey home, Monachdy, Dr. William Griffith, Carreglwyd, Colonel John Bodvel, Richard Wynne (? of Gwydir) and other leading royalists.[207]

A council of war having been held at Llangefni it was resolved that all the islanders between the ages of 16 and 60 should subscribe to a declaration proclaiming their loyal principles. The task of drawing up this document was conferred upon two clergymen, the Rev. Michael Evans, chaplain to Lord Bulkeley, and the Rev. Robert Morgan, rector of Llanddyfan, 'who had skill enough to draw it in high swelling words and bitter language', commented the Beaumaris schoolmaster, William Williams, who wrote an account of the momentous happenings, 'and subtletie sufficient to impose it upon a well-meaning gentry and soldiery, yet wanted discretion to pen it in that wary way, and prudent style, as the state of affairs at that time did require'. [208] The manifesto was dated July 14, 1648.

When word was received of the invasion from Scotland led by the Duke of Hamilton, the Anglesey Royalists thought their opportunity had come. A party crossed to Llanrwst to seize the bridgehead there. Here they were joined by Colonel Roger Whitley, the Flintshire soldier who had already lost

[203] *Newcome (Denbigh)* pp. 110-113; *A.&M.* p. 241; *Parry.* pp. 380-381. [204] *Parry.* p. 384. (quoting Whitelock's *Memorials*). [205] *The Second Civil War in Wales.* Cymmrodorion Soc. *Trans.* vol. 1930-1931, p. 28. [206] Baron Hill MSS. 5370. [207] Parry. p. 387. [208] Ibid. p. 387. where the Manifesto is printed in full.

The reconstruction of Denbigh Castle and Town walls

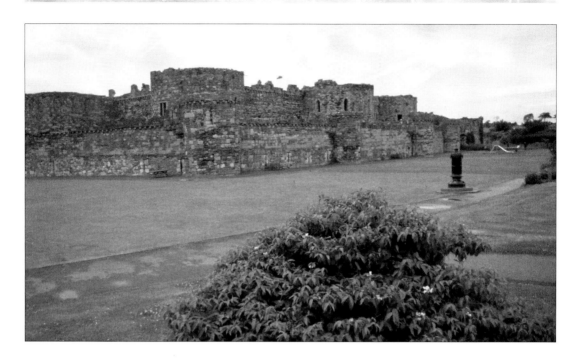

Above: Beaumaris Castle and Beaumaris Green
Below: Cadnant Landing, where the Parliamentarians came ashore on Anglesey

two brothers in the service of the King. Their hopes were shattered by the devastating victory Cromwell gained at Preston, and the adventurers withdrew to Anglesey. Here they were joined by Sir Arthur Blayney, the Montgomeryshire knight. Other volunteers included Major John Dolben, Captain Charles Chambres, Captain Robert Hughes, Captain William Eyton, Mr. Richard Parry and others from Denbighshire; Major Hugh Pennant, of Plas Ucha, Whitford, an ancestor of the antiquarian, Mr. Thomas Griffith and Mr. Thomas Davenport from Flintshire, Captain John Morgan and others from Merionethshire. Lieut.-Colonel Hugh Hookes,[209] doubtless of the Conwy family, headed the Caernarvonshire contingent. Other newcomers were Sir Faithful Fortescue (whose defection affected the issue at Edgehill) and Samuel Singleton.[210]

Parliament, well aware of what was happening, appointed a commission of five to cope with the situation: Sir Thomas Myddelton, former major-general, his eldest son and heir, Thomas Myddelton, Major-General Thomas Mytton, Colonel Simon Theiwall, the Member of Parliament, and Colonel John Jones, Maes-y-garnedd.

About a thousand men, horse and foot, mustered at Ruthin and marched by way of Llanrwst bridge to the Conwy Valley gathering volunteers on their way. At Conwy the party divided, some 1,500 marching to Bangor, and the remainder going by water to the Cegin Creek. The crossing of the Menai Strait was made possible by the fleet of boats collected by Major Richard Cheadle, an enemy of the Bulkeley family.

It was stated that as soon as the 1,500 horse and foot appeared at Penmaenmawr – if it was low tide they probably marched along the shore – Royalists on Beaumaris showed their defiance by firing cannon and muskets, beating drums and blowing trumpets 'which the enemies took little or no notice of'.[210]

After delaying four or five days at Bangor to complete preparations, the Parliamentarians were 'wafted over to Cadnant in Anglesey, about Sept. 15,[211]1648, near the fall of night; John Wiggins, of the town of Bangor being their guide'.[210]

The scene as the soldiers scrambled over the seaweed-covered rocks and struggled into the dingle must have presented a nocturnal picture which was ill pleasing to Royalist eyes. Despite the brave noise and clamour on Beaumaris, the Royalists with one exception did nothing to prevent the landing. Major Hugh Pennant rode up with his troop on hearing of the attempt, but by that time the musketeers were ashore. From positions behind rocks and hedges they poured in a storm of shot which caused him quickly to retire. At Porthaethwy (Menai Bridge) about a quarter of a mile distant 'a strong guard of foot under the command of two officers' had been stationed but they quitted their posts not without strong suspicion of treachery, for it was afterwards currently famed that one of them had received *50l* from General Mytton, before hand, for betraying the island, and that *50l* more were promised him after he should betray it, but never paid, as all traitors are commonly cheated by those that employ them; it being a maxim among enemies themselves, to love the treason, but hate the traitors.'[212]

The following day Mytton moved his army into position preparatory to an attack on Beaumaris. In Anglesey the command of the island forces had been given to young Colonel Richard Bulkeley, heir of Viscount Bulkeley, it being 'to the Welsh nation's honour' to be led by one of their own people and not by a stranger. When this decision was made Lord Byron in disgust withdrew to Monachdy where he was guest of Colonel Robinson until a favourable wind could carry him to the Isle of Man where the great Earl of Derby was all but 'King'.

Mytton's men marched by way of Llandegfan until they could form up with their left flank not far from the almshouses which, bearing the date 1613, still stand beside the upper road. The islanders commanded by Colonel Bulkeley with Colonel Roger Whitley as second-in-command, formed in

---

[209] In Conwy church is a memorial to the wife of a Lieutenant Hugh Hookes. She died in 1632.
[210] *Parry.* p. 388. [211] Sir Frederick Rees places the date as the end of September. [212] *Parry.* p. 388.

what were known as St Mary's Fields, in the land below Red Hill park. Their left rested on the road not far from Gallows Point. Colonel Bulkeley's regiment of foot was in the Harp Field. The Beaumaris Company, commanded by Captain Sanders, and other infantrymen were on Red Hill fields. 'The horse were scatteringly drawn; some in the way to the almshouses, some at Mr. R. Vaughan's house (Tros yr Afon), some in the lands of the towne and elsewhere.'

Thus the two forces waited the signal to engage. It was not until three o'clock in the afternoon of October 1 that General Mytton gave the word to advance. The account written by Schoolmaster

Williams is so detailed as to imply he was present during the action which lasted for a couple of hours or more. His account reads:

'The enemy made the onset, and were stoutly repulsed by Captain Sanders and the towne's company, from the hedges in the Harp Field, but the foot in the other fields did all betake themselves to flight in disorder. Major Pennant and his troop charged the enemy, in the lane coming down from the park towards Mr. Richard Vaughan's house, and was like to take Colo-nel Louthian prisoner; Sir Arthur Blaney and his troop charged in the back lands, and was danger-ously wounded in the arm, his elbow being shattered to pieces. Colonel Bulkeley his own troop, consisting of gentlemen, made a valiant charge upon Brickes Fields, encountering with Captain Benbow, but being overpowered by far greater numbers, were forced to retreat to the barricades near Mary Ned's house, and there another charge happened, when, on the Roundhead party, Cap-tain Benbow and Vavasor Powell (a military preacher) were wounded, and on the cavalier side, not far from the same place, one Mr. Price,[213] vicar of Bettws Abergele, in the county of Denbigh, got his mortal wound; at the same time one Captain Lloyd, of Penhwnllys, being commanded to guard the church, he locked up his men in it, and ran himself away, taking the key in his pocket, whereupon he was called Captain Church to his dying day. These men, from the steeple and church leads, and some others from Court Mawr garden, played very hotly upon the enemies, and killed several especially Captain Hancock of Colonel Louthian's regiment, his Lieutenant and Ensign in the clay pits and back lanes. The islanders were so full of disorder and confusion in this fight (and indeed, it might be called an affray or scuffle rather than a fight) that they were easily routed and dispersed, Colonel Bulkeley, Colonel Whitely (sic) and most of the commanders retiring into the castle; but let it be understood, that a great party of the island forces being the men of Talybolion and Llison, the two remotest comotes of the island under the command of Colonel John Robinson, were not come to the place of battle this day, but in their march, about Traeth Coch, hearing of the defeat of their friends at Beaumaris, returned to their own houses. Of the enemy were killed this day about forty,

Opposite top: Major General Mytton. Archbishop John Williams switched sides from the King on condition that the chattels of local people held for safe keeping in Conwy Castle were respected. Mytton kept to his agreement when the Castle fell in November 1646.

Opposite bottom: The alms houses of 1613 above Beaumaris where the left flank of Mytton's force formed up for the attack

Above: The fields at Redhill near Beaumaris

[213] Apparently a young man fresh from Oxford. The Rev Richard Price took office at Betws-yn-Rhos in 1644; the next vicar in 1660.

*The Bull's Head where Gen. Mytton made his headquarters at Beaumaris.
It was remodelled in 1766.*

and of the islanders about thirty, but near four hundred taken prisoners; and now General Mytton having routed the field, and entered the towne of Beaumaris, he sent a drum to the castle, to demand the body of Colonel Bulkeley and Colonel Whitely, which, if refused to him, he would put all the prisoners taken that day to death; upon which the two colonels surrendered themselves, to save more effusion of Christian blood, and lay prisoners at the Old Place (Henblas?) until they were ransomed. The island forces then scattered.' [214]

General Mytton is said to have made his headquarters at the Old Bull Inn. The leading Royalists submitted, and articles were signed whereby the islanders agreed to pay £7,000 within fourteen days to Colonel George Twisleton, who was appointed treasurer, the money to defray the wages of the officers and soldiers employed in the expedition. When this was done the general undertook to mediate with the Parliament on their behalf.

As the articles of surrender were entered into on October 2, it was obvious that no time was lost in coming to a settlement. Colonel Bulkeley is known to have gone 'beyond the seas' and Colonel Robinson fled to Ireland.

❂   ❂   ❂

After King Charles was beheaded, Sir John Owen, in company with the Duke of Hamilton, Earl Holland, the Earl of Norwich (Goring) and Lord Capell, stood trial. The Duke, Holland and Capell lost their heads, but Sir John, somehow, was reprieved. He returned to Clenennau (which had been

[214] *Parry*. pp. 388-389.

plundered in his absence) and despite a heavy fine, he was able to spend the remainder of his days in comparative peace. The esteem in which he was held is indicated by John Taylor, the Water Poet, who recorded that he rode to 'a place called Climenie, where the noble Sir John Owen did, with liberal welcome, entertain me'.[215]

Rupert offered Owen a high post with the army in France but Sir John felt he could still serve his sovereign better at home. Professor Dodd points out that Owen was three times put under preventive restraint – in 1651, 1655 and 1658[216] – but he survived to see a Stuart on the throne again. Holding the post of vice-admiral of North Wales he lived until 1666. Sir John lies interred in the South Caernarvonshire church of Penmorfa (near Porthmadog). The sword which Lord Capell presented to him from the scaffold is now a cherished possession of his descendant, Lord Harlech.

Owen's old enemy, Archbishop John Williams, died at Gloddaeth Hall in 1650 and is buried at Llandegai Church at the entrance to his estate at Penrhyn near Bangor. His effigy with a ponderous Latin epitaph by his biographer, Bishop Hacket, is on the south wall of the chancel.

Colonel John Carter, the Buckinghamshire adventurer who came to North Wales in 1644, married, in 1647, Elizabeth Holland, heiress of the Kinmel estate near Abergele. He was ambitious, aspired to Parliament, and was knighted by Cromwell in 1658, but after the Lord Protector's death began to trim his sails and was able to assist in the Restoration and so get a second knighthood from Charles II. His colleague, Colonel George Twisleton, married the heiress of Lleuar in South Caernarvonshire and is buried in St Beuno's Church, Clynnog Fawr.

✪   ✪   ✪

The unrest which persisted long after the suppression of the 1648 revolt was probably greater than is realized. 'Several emergencies occasioned by insurrections of the malignant party' were mentioned in 1654 by Carter when he applied for the refund of money he alleged he had expended. He claimed that he had spent the sum of £504 in victualling and repairing Conwy Castle. A committee appointed to investigate reported that Carter had spent his own money. [217]

In 1655 the Parliament decreed that the castles of Conwy and Caernarfon must be slighted and their garrisons transferred to Denbigh and Red Castle.[218] For some reason these two splendid piles were spared the fate of the neighbouring fortresses but, whatever the reason, it is certain it would not be sentiment.

The extent of the unrest has not been brought to light but sundry references indicate that a number of Royalists stubbornly persisted in their intrigues against the unwelcome government.

Though Colonel John Robinson had been forced to flee from his Anglesey home, Mynachdy, he renewed his opposition immediately he was safely at Dublin, and in 1649 Major General Mytton learned that Ormonde had given Robinson a commission to seize the island of Bardsey. Mytton frustrated this by dispatching Ensign Aspinall with thirty men to the island. Three days after their arrival at Bardsey they were able to seize 'Colonel Gerrard, Mr. Conwy, and six gentlemen more who landed there to surprise the island, took their boat and sent them prisoners to Caernarvon'. The report adds that the pirate who set them ashore and was an Irishman 'fled away'.[219]

There was a widespread conspiracy in 1655 but the few Caernarvonshire names involved in it were, writes Professor Dodd, 'mainly obscure ones'.[220] This, of course, excludes Sir John Owen who was one of those arrested. Some light is thrown on this abortive uprising in Caernarvonshire by several letters exchanged between the governor of Conwy, Colonel John Carter, who was at the time visiting Cromwell in London, and his deputy, Lieutenant Thomas Kynaston whom he left in charge of

[215] *A Short Relation of a Long Journey.* p. 11. [216] *Caer. Hist. Soc. Tr.* vol. 14. p. 30. [217] *Cal. S.P.D.* 1654. p. 18. [218] Ibid, 1655. p. 232. [219] *Parry.* p. 385. [220] *Caer. H.S. Tr.* vol. 14. p. 31.

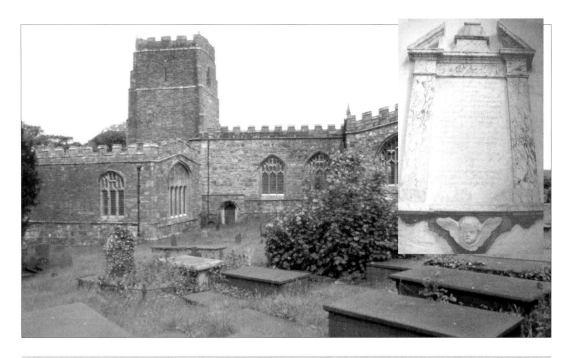

St Bueno's Church and the memorial to Col. George Twisleton (inset). He died Boxing Day, 1714, aged 92 years. The Church is one of the finest Tudor churches in Wales.

Llandegai Church, where Archbishop John Williams is buried, and his memorial

Archbishop John Williams

Conwy Castle. The originals are at the University of Wales, Aberystwyth. The first letter from Carter, written in March 1655, was in reply to a report from Kynaston to Cromwell informing him of a conspiracy detected near Conwy, the leader of which was one Bayly, possibly of the Anglesey family of that name.

When John Taylor visited Conwy in 1652 he wrote: 'I lodged at the house of one Mr. Spencer (an Englishman) he is post-master there.' [221] Spencer had been an officer in the parliamentary army of invasion and it was his astuteness which uncovered the plot.

Kynaston had been warned by General 'Lord' Lambert to be on his guard and, writing to the Lord Protector, he assured him that he had shown 'double diligence'. He informed Cromwell that Ensign Spencer, formerly an ensign to Colonel Carter, and at this time postmaster of Conwy, 'by discoursing with a neighbouring inhabitant discovered something relating to the listing of some men designed for the putting of the bloody plot against the present Government into execution'. William Stodart, a Justice of the Peace, examined suspected persons and took depositions. Kynaston wrote that the names were now enclosed but there is no sign of them. Edward Williams, one of the prisoners examined, was sent to the common gaol 'as conceived guilty of high treason'. Two others had entered into recognizances for their appearance when required.

'Mr. Bayly,' lamented Kynaston, 'the man mentioned in the examinations, is returned home amongst his neighbours.' Kynaston added that as Bayly had been so far engaged in this 'inhuman action' he could not understand how the man had been so soon cleared.[222] Colonel Carter's reply is given in full:

'For Leftennant Tho Kinnaston
at Conway Castle,
Co Carnarvon sheere.

The little church at Penmorfa, near Porthmadog, and the grave of Sir John Owen. The large tomb chest is traditionally accounted for by a story that the grave includes not only Sir John, but his horse too. He died in 1666. The church dates from the 14th century.

[221] *A Short Relation of a Long Journey.* p. 8. [222] *The Family Papers of Owen and Stanley of Penrhos, Holyhead.* University of Wales, Aberystwyth (1951). v. No. 212. I am indebted to the Librarian, Mr. Emyr Gwynne Jones, M.A., for calling attention to this correspondence.

These With trust and speede.

Lett Kinnaston,

His Hieness the Lord Protector received yre letter and the Examinations of the persons suspected to bee ingaged with Bayly in the Plott and hee comanded mee to write unto you to continue y'or care in enqui'ring out the rest of theare complacies for certainly theare are many yet undiscouered that were ingaged with them. The examinats say that Evan Jefferise tould John Evans that hee heard Wm. Wms., Ed. Wms. and diuers others in Isaph had promised to apeere in Armes under Bayly at an howers warning.

Its thought fitt that you send for that Evan Jefferise into Custodie and find owt the bottome of those mens ingadgm't (engagement) to Bayly; lett Jefferise proue how they became ingaged to Bayly as hee saith hee heard they weare. Else keepe him in ye Castle till you heare further and if hee doe prooue it against ym or any of them or others send souldiers and fetch them into ye Castle and theare keepe them safe till further Order and send mee word with speede what you doe hearein, and examine strictly what proofe can be made of Bayliss ingaging any & upon my receipt of it you shall receiue further Orders touching him also. Send also for Mr. Tho Williams of Llanbaglans man who Jefferise said was twice desired by Bayly to beare armes under him and let him be carefully examined to prooue that Bayly soe attempted him as Jefferise saith. You are desir'd to bee uerry carefull of ye Castle with ye few men you haue to preuent any surprise, and to yse all yore indeavours to find out ye truth of these things and to.. . them up with all the speede you can send.

yre uerry loving friend,

    March the 5th.   Jn Carter.

    1654.

    yre coppise I also receiued safe.'

'For Liftent Kinnaston

at Conway Castle in Carnarvon sheere.

Sir, yres I received and am comanded to tell you that yre care in this business is verry well aprooued of. I know you will continew it. If you doe heare of any that weare out in ye insurrection or knowing of it weare in redyness to joyne send for them in. It may be Mr. Madrin (to whom I have wrote) will giue you notice of some such. Thean will bee a speedy coorse taken for to safe you in the case of such as you haue in custodie and weare really in ye plott. You did not send mee ye names of all such as you haue secured. If any are secured up suspition only and yt noe proofe is against ym of theare beeing of ye plott such you may release taking good security for theare quiet liuing for ye future and for aparance on notice left at theare houses. As for ye victualling of Conway & better manning it some speedy course will bee directed what shall be don with that and all other Garisons in Wales. In ye meane while I know you will bee as careful of it as you can with ye men you haue. I hope this storme is blowne over every wheare.

in hast I rem

yre asshured frind,   Jn Carter. [223]

    the 21st March. 1654.'

  Roger Mostyn's brief incarceration in Conwy Castle in May 1658 suggests that he was involved in some plot but nothing seems to have come to light beyond Whitelocke's two references to his obtaining Roger's release on parole two days after his arrest.

---

[223] *Penrhos MSS*. v. 32a & 32d. University of Wales, Aberystwyth (Punctuation added).

Chirk Castle today. Top left: The north front; top right: the gatehouse; bottom left: the west front; bottom right: the east frontage from the garden with later building on the left following the partial slighting of the castle

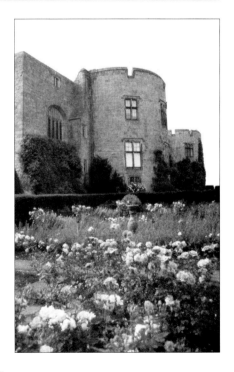

✪　　　　　　✪　　　　　　✪

Once death removed the firm hand of Oliver from the helm of the ship of state, hopes of the Royalists soared. Unrest intensified. Confusion in Westminster and disorganisation in the army lifted high the aspirations of all who prayed for the restoration of a Stuart. Action in this area centred on the former ardent Parliamentarian, Sir George Booth, the Cheshire baronet. It was the veteran warrior Sir Thomas Myddelton of Chirk Castle who sparked the political powder in North Wales. Despite his eighty years he brandished his sword in Wrexham market-place and proclaimed Charles as King. Sir George Booth and the Earl of Derby combined to swell the throng of jubilant loyalists. To Myddelton flocked Royalist neighbours, Sir Edward Broughton of Marchwiel, Captain John Edwards of Chirkland, Colonel John Dolben of Segrwyd near Denbigh, Captain Richard Dutton of Keven-y-Wern, Captain Charles Chambers of Plas Chambres and others of Sir Thomas's erstwhile opponents. Age deprived Sir Thomas of leadership but his cloak fell upon the shoulders of his heir, another Thomas.

These men marched to Chirk Castle, began to fortify the stronghold, and awaited the storm which would inevitably break.

Sir George Booth gathered four thousand enthusiasts about him, never doubting the rest of the land would follow suit. News of the outbreak stung London into activity. The Parliament's best general, 'Lord' Lambert, set off at the head of five thousand parliamentary soldiers intent on extinguishing the fire of revolt before it spread. Booth took Chester without a shot being fired. Liverpool and smaller places were quickly in the hands of the Royalists. Warrington was chosen as their headquarters. When it was learnt that Lambert was approaching by forced marches Booth endeavoured to negotiate but Lambert believed in the 'root and branch' policy of Cromwell. With a curt negative rejoinder he prepared to attack. His Roundheads swept down upon the Royalists at Winnington Bridge and an utter rout was only prevented by Captain Edward Morgan of Golden Grove sacrificing his life to enable the residue of Booth's forces to escape.

In a week Liverpool and the other towns which declared for Charles were in parliamentary hands again. Lambert marched on Chirk Castle which he proceeded to bombard. A mortar was placed on a nearby knoll. There was no water supply in the castle. Quickly Chirk capitulated and the aged Sir Thomas saw his palatial home once again in alien hands. He, himself, was declared traitor and his estates sequestrated.

Young Captain Richard Wynn of Gwydir was caught up in the uprising though the part he played is uncertain. It was sufficient to land him in Caernarfon Castle where the turncoat tyrant, Colonel Thomas Madryn, former sheriff, was governor. The rounding up of the conspirators is briefly but vividly sketched in a few letters among the Wynn Papers. Robert Price of Gilar (probably the same Robert Price of nearby 'Place Yollin', who compounded in 1649 for delinquency in arms)[224] wrote to his neighbour, Lady Grace Wynn, warning her that parliamentary troopers were searching for her son:

'Madam

John Evans, the trumpeter, and another trooper was here yesterday being sent purposely by Captaine Sontley: to sumon and require my neighbour Mr. Ellice Price; my sonne; and others to appear: and sub-mitt themselves unto Cap. Sontley; he gives them a weeke's tyme to come in; and to bring in their horses and Armes; promising to use them Civilly; and to show them all fav'r that shall lye in his power in the future if they submit [themselves?] [225] and come in to him. I understand by the troopers and by another friend that came yesterday from Wrexham that severall gentlemen as namely: a sonne of Mr. Salusbury of Boch Egraig: Mr. Puliston of Emrull, Cap: Chambers & others have submitted already, and that they are civilly treated; I hope to understand more of their p'sedings at

---

[224] *Cal. Committee for Compounding.* vol. 3. p. 1890. Price was not fined! [225] Damaged.

Bromfield ere longe. The two men that were here did onely enquire where Mr. Richard Wynne was, and I answered them the truth: that I did not know where he was but I did believe that he was not at or neer home. Sr George Booth for certain was taken at Newport Pannell: Noe other for certaine newes all being quiett in Yorkshire and all other places, as they say.

I shall trouble yr Ladyship no further; but onely subscribe that I am really, Madam,

yr humble & faithfull servant,

Robert Price

Geeler, 4th Sepem, 1659.

Lt. Col. Ed. Broughton is sent prisoner to Chester; it is feared that he shall lose his life upon account of having broken a former Paroll.' [226]

Price's next letter (on September 14) advised Lady Wynn that 'Col. Madryn must be made their friend if her son's estate is to be saved from the sequestrators.' Mr. Ellice Price was back from Wrexham having made his peace with the authorities. His excuse was that he had only called to see Myddelton on business. What Lady Wynn had to do must be done quickly. 'Colonel Madryn expects to be courted, and, if it be handsomely done, he may soon be gained.' [227]

Lady Wynn 'courted' successfully. The bribe must have been substantial, for on September 30 young Richard was back at his home, Caermelwr, Llanrwst, with a pass. The 'courting' was periodically resumed until Charles was on the throne. Sir Richard that same year (1660) became the fourth baronet on the death of his father. He was made chamberlain to Queen Catherine, and is said to have presented a large Conwy pearl for inclusion in the new regalia which replaced the one lost in the wars.

Captain Roger Sontley who was so active a member of the parliamentary County Committee, exhibited such zeal that he found himself ere long in a Royalist prison. The tables were reversed. In 1665 Sontley, still in Denbigh Castle, wrote to Sir Richard begging him to secure him his liberty.[228]

Sir Thomas Myddelton was not long denied his home. A rebuilt wall at Chirk shows how the place was 'slighted', though not entirely wrecked. The Restoration was at hand. Sir Thomas received £60,000 to recompense him for his losses. His son was made a baronet.

A number of North Wales Royalists were nominated Knights of the Royal Oak. The knighthood never materialized for it was feared such recognition might have reopened wounds the nation desired to heal. Such nominations would have been conferred only upon men who rendered exceptionally distinguished service. The fact that some recipients are now hard to identify is an indicaton of the way in which records have been lost.

Colonel Roger Mostyn was rewarded by Charles II with a knighthood, quickly followed by a baronetcy. Colonel Roger Whitley became Receiver General. He entered Parliament, turned Whig, entertained William III, and served as mayor of Chester.

Major Francis Manley, thanks to his brother John, obtained a post under the Commonwealth, turned Royalist at the Restoration, and rose in the legal profession to become a judge and gain a knighthood. Colonel Hugh Wynne continued to take an interest in the Caernarvonshire military affairs and served as a Deputy Lieutenant. Colonel Roger Mostyn and Colonel William Price continued to place their military experience at the disposal of the country by serving in command of the local militia. Mention is made of their companies in the Progress of the Duke of Beaufort through North Wales in 1685, by which time these erstwhile dashing Cavaliers had become revered veterans. 'Old Bluestockings', weakened by the memorable siege, appears to have died about the time the King returned from his wanderings. The honours which would have been bestowed upon him went to his loyal second son, Charles, who served with the colonel during the siege of Denbigh.

Exiles flocked back from the Continent. Colonel Robinson of Gwersyllt, near Wrexham, found his home restored 'by some alien hand' – presumably that of the above mentioned Roger Sontley. The men who had sacrificed and suffered for their King might now sheathe their swords.

---

[226] National Library of Wales. *Wynn (of Gwydir) Papers*. No. 2193. [227] *C.W.P.* 2195. [228] *Ibid.* 2446.

*The memorial to General Sir John Owen erected c 1700
on the east wall of St Beuno's Church, Penmorfa*

Knights of the Royal Oak

The following list of those nominated Knights of the Royal Oak is extracted from Parry's Royal Visits and Progresses.
ANGLESEY: *John Robinson Esq., William Bould Esq., Thomas Wood Esq., – Bodden Esq., Pierce Lloyd Esq.*
CAERNARVONSHIRE: *Sir John Owen's heire.*
DENBIGHSHIRE: *Charles Salisburie Esq., Euball Thelwall Esq., Foulke Middleton Esq., John Wynne Esq., Sir
Thomas Middleton, Knt. (of Chirk Castle, of Westminster after, spent most of his estate), Bevis Lloyd Esq.,
John Lloyd Esq.*
FLINTSHIRE: *Sir Roger Mostyn, Knt. of Mostyn, Bart., Sir Edward Mostyn, Knt., John Salisbury, of Bachegrag,
Esq., Robert Davies Esq., John Puliston Esq., John Hanmer, Knt., Bart., William Hammer, Esq.*
MERIONETH5HIRE: *William Salisbury Esq., William Price Esq., William Vaughan Esq., Howell Vaughan Esq., –
Anwyl, of Parke, Esq., Lewis Owen Esq., John Lloyd Esq.*
MONTGOMERYSHIRE: *John Pugh Esq., – Owen Esq., of Ruserton, – Blaney Esq., Roger Lloyd Esq., Richard
Owen Esq., Richard Herbert Esq., Sir Edward Lloyd, Edmund Wareinge Esq.*

A Final Word

When the fighting ended the time came for counting the cost. In Caernarfon, for instance, the inhabitants were taxed for supporting the garrison in Caernarfon castle – taxed until complaints of overcharging were made to the justices. The Parliamentarians put down Sunday fairs, suppressed alehouses, endeavoured to stop Sunday travelling, and even penalised a poor woman who carried a basket of nuts on Sunday.

The quay of Caernarfon town, the shire hall, and the church of Llanbeblig were 'said to be ruinous and in great decay' according to a presentment made to the grand jury in January, 1649.

While local hunters were far afield stalking human foes on the field of battle the wild life of the county flourished unchecked to such an extent that the justices offered bounties for the slaughtering of foxes, polecats, hedgehogs, wild cats, stoats, otters, weasels, and two creatures by the peculiar names of 'fitchewe' and 'fayrebade'. These were evidently of small size for the bounty was only 8d. as for stoats and weasels, whereas 10/- was offered for a fox, and 2/- for an otter. Ravens figured on the condemned list, and crows were listed at 6d. a dozen.[229]

The appearance of the war-wracked country is implied in words written by John Taylor, the Water Poet, who rode this way on his nag, 'Dun' in the summer of 1652. Flint Castle he noticed was almost buried in ruin. As for the town there was 'no saddler, taylor, weaver, brewer, baker, botcher or button-maker'. He laments, 'They have not so much as the signe of an alehouse, so I was doubtful of a lodging.' There was little to be seen in Rhuddlan beyond 'a wind and war-shaken castle'.

Of Conwy he wrote: 'There is a good defensive castle which I would have seen, but because there was a garrison I was loath to give occasion of offence or be much inquisitive.'

Undoubtedly he was wise – Colonel John Carter was the governor! Caernarfon impressed him as invincible. His five hours' inspection produced an unexpected sequel:

'When I thought I had taken my leave for ever of it, then was I merely deceived; for when I was a mile on my way, a trooper came galloping after me, and enforced me back to be examined by Colonel Thomas Mason (the governor there) who after a few words, when he heard my name, and knew my occasions, he used me so respectfully and bountifully, that (at his charge) I stayed all night, and by the means of him, and one Mr. Lloyd (a Justice of the Peace there) I was furnished with a guide, and something else to bear charges for one week's travel; for which courtesies, if I were not thankful, I were worth the hanging for being ungrateful.' [230]

Though the warriors of the King had laid down their arms they were by no means broken in spirit. In the Caernarvonshire archives is a presentment of a grand jury in 1648 who, despite parliamentary occupation, boldly protested against the killing at Llandegai of their 'neighbour and fellow subject', Robert ap William ap Robert of Llanllechid by Captain Oakes and his company. 'We also conceive that ye Troopes of horse commanded by Capt. Yong and Capt. Viner a charge upon the said County to be (blessed be God) uselesse amongst us and consequently an unnecessary charge.'

A warrant was issued to the sheriff and constables to demand a ten shilling fine from Thomas

[229] The Caernarvonshire County Archives. [230] *A Short Relation of a Long Journey.* p. 8.

Glynne of Plas Newydd, esquire, for using the name of Christ in vain.

The calendar of prisoners in 1651 shows that William Jones, gentleman, was in the county gaol for uttering contempt of the present government.

In the alehouses a similar spirit of resentment was exhibited. A former Royalist soldier, one Lewis Morris of Llanddinolen, was prosecuted for abusing the government. He was in an alehouse when a parliamentary soldier named Robert Vaughan, who served in the Caernarfon garrison, entered with a sword at his side. Morris taunted him, asserted that he had been a Cavalier, and added: 'a turde in the States' teeth and I care not if they and all Roundheads were hanged'. [231]

Constables were appointed to keep watch and ward on Sundays to report and charge any persons found breaking the Sabbath. Such was Caernarvonshire under the unpopular puritan regime.

Captain William Oakes, the Parliamentarian who called forth this protest from the Caernarvonshire jury following his slaying of a man at Llandegai, turned his coat before the Restoration. In September, 1660, he wrote, on behalf of Sir John Carter, to Lieutenant Thomas Kynaston who had been transferred from Conwy to Beaumaris. Addressing him as 'Honest Godson', Oakes stated that it was Sir John's command that Kynaston slept in Beaumaris Castle every night and that he be 'vigilantly careful of the same for his Majesty's service'. No person whatsoever under any pretence was to come into the castle without first having order from the governor, Sir John Carter.[232]

Disappointment must necessarily be felt at the paucity of information to be extracted from church registers of this period yet the very omissions are indicative of the upheaval of the times. Conwy Church registers – which somehow survived – throw no light on the war scene. After 1641 a large portion of a leaf has been cut away, and entries were not resumed until 1644. In that year there were 14 deaths and 15 baptisms; in 1645 6 deaths and 11 baptisms – none, apparently, directly attributable to the war. The year when Conwy was under siege, 1646, when the entry of deaths would have held particular significance, contained only one entry, that of a baptism. A few more baptisms occur until 1650 and then 'from here great irregularities and omission until 1699'. [233]

The grave stone to Rowland Pugh in the chancel of Conwy Church (see p. 123)

(see p. 123)

[231] Notes by the County Archivist, Mr. W. Ogwen Williams. [232] *Penrhos Papers*, v. p. 301. [233] *The Registers of Conwy.* 1541-1793. Alice Hadley (1900). p. 138.

Of possible interest is a monumental inscription on the north side of the chancel. It is to Rowland Pugh of Mathavarne, in the county of Montgomery, esquire, who died on St Stephen's Day, 1644. It is difficult to account for his presence in Conwy unless there was some association with the war.

Miss Hadley writes: 'The income of the vicar, Hugo Jones, appointed in 1642, was sequestrated in 1650.' [234]

The new system introduced during the Commonwealth is indicated by entries (upside down) made in 1655 and 1656 by 'Capten John Arundell, register'. One marriage entry for 1657 has been inserted after 1778.

Arundell turned Royalist. Sir John Carter addressed a letter to him in Conwy on January 29, 1661, desiring him to inform Kynaston at Beaumaris that he was to disband all Lord Bulkeley's soldiers 'without a penny of money'. [235]

❂　　　　　　❂　　　　　　❂

To trace all the North Wales Royalists who participated in the Civil War is a hopeless task. Unless persons are specifically mentioned in the articles of surrender it is difficult to learn the identity of those who fought tenaciously for the King. Though the Calendar of the Committee for Compounding assists it does not always elucidate. Names which might be expected to appear are missing. Under the Denbigh articles, Thomas Whitley of Aston compounded and was fined £125 for 'deserting his habitation and going into the garrison held against parliament' but there is no mention of his son, Colonel Roger Whitley, governor of Aberystwyth. No explanation is offered for the presence in Conwy Castle of Sir Thomas Eyton of Eyton (Salop) who compounded under the Conwy articles and was fined £818 (altered to £976). Some names signify little. It is difficult to identify John Williams of Llanywith (Llannefydd) who was under age when he fought through the siege of Denbigh but was fined £66.

Henry Taylor published a list of 13 Flintshire 'knights and gentlemen' who compounded for their estates. Somehow the names of Colonel William Salesbury of Bachymbyd and Rûg, the governor of Denbigh, and his loyal son, Charles, have intruded into the Flintshire roll. They were fined £781. Admitting they had both borne arms, Charles begged to compound for his father and himself explaining 'his father was too infirm to travel'.

The names Taylor extracted from 'the printed general catalogue of sufferers' does not invariably correspond with the Calendar of the Committee for Compounding. For example, the Calendar records Thomas Pennant's ancestor, Robert Pennant of Downing, as being fined £40.6.8 'for delinquency in taking up arms for the King'. In Taylor's list the fine is £298, and David Pennant of 'Bighton', gent. is given as paying £42.14 compared with the Calendar's £197 'on Denbigh articles for delinquency in arms'. Thomas Pennant in his History of the Parishes of Whiteford and Holywell states that the Bychton estate paid only £42.14 in the general composition but Robert Pennant of Downing was fined no less than £298 – presumably because some young man in the house at Downing fired on a parliamentary detachment and wounded a cornet.

The six months' siege of Denbigh attracted so much attention that the names of any of the heroic defenders are acceptable. Those who compounded under the Denbigh articles and were fined for delinquency in arms included: Colonel John Thelwall, Plas Coch (£117), Robert Parry, Llewenny (£28), Colonel Thomas Davies, Gwysaney (£51), Edward Goodman, Nantglyn (£46.10.8), Captain John Edwards, Chirk (£80), John Eyton (senior) of Leeswood (£172.15), and his son, John Eyton, junior (£42), Colonel Peter Griffiths, Caerwys (£113.13.6), John Jones (senior), Halkin (£156.11.4), Edward Lloyd, Hersketh, Mold (£64.10), and his son Thomas who petitioned that his estate should be sequestered to meet his father's delinquency fine as Edward Lloyd died shortly after the surrender. Gabriel Roberts, Segrwyd, was not fined. Major John Dolben was fined £107.

[234] Ibid. Intro. xv. [235] *Penrhos Papers*. v. p. 20. No. 32c.

Richard Dutton of Keven-y-Werne, co. Denbigh, was fined £185.6.8 for his delinquency which was 'going to Oxford and adhering to the forces raised against the parliament'.

Robert Price, Plas Iolyn, admitted being engaged in the late wars against the Parliament, but was not fined.

Sir William Gerard, a prominent Lancashire Catholic, was among the prisoners taken at Denbigh.

Colonel Richard Lloyd, Llwyn-y-Maen, Shropshire, captured at Y Dalar Hir, who fought in both wars, was fined £480.

Colonel John Bodvel of Bodvel, Caernarvonshire, a former Member of Parliament who turned Royalist and served in Anglesey, had his affairs in so complicated a condition that the Calendar devotes several pages to an attempted elucidation during which it states that since his articles 'Bodville has been in the company with Charles Stuart, the late pretended King of the Scots' in Holland and elsewhere.

Taylor's list includes: Robert Davies, Gwysaney (£645.11.4), William Hanmer of Fenhall (£1,370), Edward Phillips of Worthenburg (£24), and Roger Mostyn 'of Mostin, Esq.' (£825). [236]

The Calendar describes Colonel Roger Mostyn as late governor of Flint Castle. He compounded for delinquency under the Flint articles but begged further time to pay his fine as 'through the opposition of Holt Castle, where many of his writings are, he cannot perfect his particular'. The time limited by the articles had nearly expired. Five weeks 'delay' was granted.

Major Francis Manley, Erbistock, was another admitted under the Denbigh articles and was fined £75. Thomas Hanmer of Apley Castle, Salop, was admitted to composition but on January 28, 1646, was still 'a prisoner at Wem'.

Captain Valet, the heroic governor of Beeston, was present during the siege. Malbon writes: 'The said vallatt wth his Soldiers havinge a Convaye wth theim was broughte vnto Denbighe, whether hee had a desyre to goe.'[237]

❀   ❀   ❀

At the Restoration the humble warriors who had suffered for their King were not wholly forgotten. In January 1661 Caernarvonshire Justices ordered Major William Spicer (who had assisted in the defence of Caernarfon Castle), with Alderman William Thomas of Caernarfon and William Robins, gentleman, to call maimed soldiers before them to ascertain if they were worthy of relief. The thirty-seven names submitted on one list include a Captain Richard Vaughan. The detailed list speaks so eloquently that it is printed without comment:

'Roland ap Robert Edmund, an adged man of 63 yeares, hath been served in Scotland and other places under Sr John Owen, hath a slender wound on the knee.

Robert Owen of Caerhun, maymed of the hand and wounded on the head in Nasbie fight, a very poor man.

John Griffith ap Hughe of Langwnadle, wounded in several places upon several parts of his body.

Roland Hughes of Caerhun, wounded in the head, necke and shoulder.

John Williams of Pethkelert, in Nasby fight hurt in the legge and the thighe, a great wound.

Thomas ap Richard Owen of Nevyn, wounded on the shoulder.

Edward Griffith of Bryncroes, wounded on the head.

Roland Owen of Clynog, hurt and made a criple.

Hugh Owen of Aberdaron, shott and cut in two places, namely on the shoulder and arms.

David Owen of Conway, shott under the eye very dangerously and the bullet remained under the ear, and have several wounds.

William Morris of Llanarmon, quite maymed and half lost his right hand being shott with a Canon bullett.

John Owen of Llanyestyn, wounded in the thigh and hurt and have lost the use of his left hand

[236] *Cal. of Com. for Comp* p. 143. [237] *Hall.* p. 181.

being maymed of itt.

Symon Davies of Castell, wounded in divers places as in the thigh, side and his head.

Hugh James of Llanvihangel, an old soldier greatly wounded and have served under several commanders.

William Lloyd of Llanvairisgaer, hurt and wounded in divers parts of his bodie.

Edward Ellis of Carnarvon, hurt and wounded on the shoulder and have lost ye use of his arme under Capt. Brynkir.

William ap Richard of Llanbeblig, shott at Whitchurch in the right arm, and have lost the use of.

William Griffith of Llanllechid, aged 87, an old soldier to Queen Elizabeth, King James and the late King, hath several wounds and lost two sons in the King's service and is most considerable (i.e. worthy of consideration).

John Ellis of Llanbeblig was shott in the legge a slight wound.

Robert Evans of Bangor lost his left hand and hath other wounds received on the King's service.

David Thomas of Llanllechid shot and hurt in several places of the body, very sore hurt and the skull crackt.

Rytherch ap Edward of Llysfaen, aged 76 years, have served in Queen Elizabeth's time and in the King's service and have several wounds received in their service and deserveth consideration.

Symon ap William Lewis of Llanbeblig, shott under the eare and out at the chop, and also in the shoulder whereof he still languiseth.

Evan ap Ellis of Llandden has several wounds and cuts, a very poor man.

Harry ap Rees of Llanllechid, aged 72 years, has lost the use of both hands in the Kings service.

Humphrey John William of Pwlheli has lost ye use of his left Arm and is a very poor man and deeply hurt.

William Roberts of Carnarvon hath been shot in the foot and wounded in the head.

Maurice Hughes of Ynyskynhaynon, an ancient man, and shott in ye knee and thereby lost the use of one side and a very poor man.

Jane verch Hugh of Carnarvon, a poore widow of 80 years of age whose husband was a Taylor and was killed in Ireland under my lo. of Ormonde in ye late King's service by reason whereof she is deprived of her livelihood and is in great poverty and deserveth to be considered.

Edmund Wynne, late soldier to his Mat.^e Charles the first in severall parts of England and Wales, hath had severall shott in his body during the said warre to his great detriment.

David Lloyd, late of Llysfaen, was a soldier to his Majestie Charles the first in several parts of England, shott in the knee.

John ap John Lewis of Rhug, aged 74 years, an old soldier and have great and many wounds on several parts of his body.' [238]

Elsewhere there is a record of a petition to the Caernarfon magistrates[239] – 'John ap John Lewis, have done service in warre for his countrie for the space of nine yeares at Ireland and Scotland, and now beeing poore and aged and not haveing wherewithall to maintaine himself desireth that yr worships be pleased to comisserat his distressd case & to allow him some maintenance & reliefe out of the maimed-souldiers mise as formerly ye petr (petitioner) was wont to have.'

There is a natural tendency to regard the wars of the past from the viewpoint of officers. Perhaps this is inevitable as this is the source from which information usually springs. It is, therefore, not unseemly, that this record of the struggle should conclude with these references to the humble warriors whose faithful service made great issues possible but whose names remain unrecorded in the annals of the race.

[238] Caernarvonshire County Archives. I am indebted to Mr. W. Ogwen Williams, M.A., County Archivist, for his kind assistance in obtaining this information. [239] Caernarvonshire County Archives, 1655 file.

APPENDIX A

PREPARATIONS BY THE ANGLESEY COMMISSION OF ARRAY

January 27mo. Proposicons to bee considered of by the Comee of Arraye and peace for the County of Anglesey.

1, THAT in this time of imminent danger wherein wee are now threatened wth an invasion from seuall pts there be some speedy course resolved on, and seriously putt in execuccon for the defence of the Island wch is to be done by frequent musteringe and trayneinge the whole fourses of the County requiring all men w'soever by their bodies or purses or both to endeav'r the safety & preservation of themselves & their Countrey and that under such a penalty to be inflicted upon defaulters as shall be able to p' cure or enforce obedience.

2, By levyinge of moneys for the p'urement of Ammunition & fire armes.

3, By fortifying the maritime partes and landing places of the Island.

4, By supplyinge the seuall Garrisons of Beaumaris and Holyhead wth necessary provision for six months at least and by causing the monthly contribucons to be duely paid in for the support and the encouragement of the Soldiers in each Garrison and by punishinge such as are refractory therein.

5, By takeinge some p'indent and discreet course for the Disapointment of practices against the peace and welfare of this Country if uppon due examinaton any such appear to bee, or be probably suspected.

*UNV. OF N.W. **Baron Hill MSS, 5363.***

APPENDIX B

BEAUMARIS BEEF FOR CAPTAIN BALDWIN WAKE

To our Very Loveinge Ffriend Mr. Michael Lewes, These. in Bewmares.

Mr. Michael Lewes. There being a present necessity of vittualing Captaine Wake, and the other Shippes now with him in Chester watter, and, understandinge that you have 80—or 100 Barrells of Beefe ready salted and fitt ffor Shippinge at Bewmarys wee have thought to make lese of 16,000 weight of the Beefe ffor him and wee doe undertake to satisfie you fforthwth Accordinge to such rates, as shalbe reasonably Agreed on by Capt. Chedle and your Selfe, no Corne or other provisions of vittualls, and this beinge ffor the present use of the ffleett wee make noe doubt that you will readily Comply w'th our order and desire herein, Soe wee bidd you hartily ffarewell, herein,

Your very loveinge ffriends,

ARTHUR CAPELL

JOHN BYRON

NICH: BYRON

AB: SHIPMAN

OR: BRIDGMAN

Chester, Decber 7th 1643.

UNV. OF N.W. Baron Hill MSS, 5367.

APPENDIX C
ORDER FOR A GENERAL MUSTER IN ANGLESEY

Whereas it is found necessary for the Defence of this Island that the traine Band Souldiers & others able to beare Armes should be duly exercised according to the discipline of Warre, that they may be the better enabled (by the frequent use of their Armes) for the preservaton of their Country, Wee doe therefore hereby desire and authorise your Lop: to send Orders unto your chief officers & Capte of the Hundrede of Tindethway, Menny, & Dunkellin, Requiring them to issue their Warrante to the high Constables of their respective Comote, comanding them to Sumon in all the able Men both horse & foote w'hin their several Comote, to appeare on Bewmaris Greene furnished wth their best Armes, on the first day of St. John Baptist, by nyne of the Clocke in the Morning, there to be exercised as aforesayd. And in Case any should make default in their appearance, we doe hereby enable your Lop either to imprison, or impose such other punishm't upon them, as yor Lop shall think fitt in their behalfe. Hereof Wee expect yor Lop will not faile. Dated at Bewmaris.

14th Junii 1644.

        JOHN MENNES. W. BOLD.

        THO: CHEDLE. H. OWEN.

        O. WOODS. HENRIE WHYTE.

        DD: LLOYD.

To the right Hoble the Lo; Visct
Buckeley, Colonell of a Regimt
of the trayned Bandes wthin the
Comte of Tindethway, Menny &
Dunkellin.

[Lop = Lordship]

UNV. OF N.W. Baron Hill MSS, 5370.

APPENDIX D
RUPERT DEMANDS A LOAN

To the Right Honerable Thomas, Lord Buckley, Viscount Cassells, These–

In ye Assembly of ye Members of both Howses of Parliamt att Oxford It was concluded by the Kinge's Majestie, and the Members there assembled that for raysing of Moneys for mainteynance of ye Armye, Letters under his Mat[ts] signett or Prince Seale should bee directed to such Persons as are nominated by the Members of the Houses to be able to Lend and contayned in Schedules affixed to ye Commissions for Subscriptions issued unto ye respective Counties.

The Moneys to bee raised by that way of Loane in ye Sixe Counties of Northwales, and ye Countie of Salop the King's Majestie hath by his Letters to ye respective Sheriffs ordered to bee payd to Mee for the use of the Armye under my Command. Therefore that the present occasions of supplying the Armye requires a speedie advance of money, I doe hereby desire you upon receipt hereof to pay to the Lord Arch Bishop of Yorke whome I have entreated to receive the same, the summe of *One Hundred* xx pounds, being the summe Concluded by his Majestie and ye Members of the Howses to be lent by you and specified in the Schedule before mentyoned for wch you shall receive a sufficient discharge upon the Prince Seale in that behalfe. In the meanetyme a discharge of soe much received by the Lord Arch Bishop of Yorke for my use and his Majesties service shall oblige me to procure such other more formal discharge as shall bee thought necessarie. Soe not doubting of yor conformitie herein.

I rest, yor Lopps ffrend,

RUPERT.

Chester the first
of August 1644.

UNV. OF N.W. Baron Hill MSS, 5372.

APPENDIX E

COMMISSION FOR COLONEL THOMAS DAVIES

Charles R.

Right trusty and well beloved Wee greete you well. Wee having given our Comission to our trusty and well beloved Colonell Thomas Davies to raise one Regiment of ffive Hundred ffote and Dragooners for our service and the defence and security of our Counties of fflynt and Denbeigh have thought fitt to recommend unto you and to lett you know that although other persons may have received Comissions to raise forces in those parts who have therefore the precedency yet wee knowing the ability of Colonell Davies who hath served us, and our late Royall father of blessed memory in all our expeditions, cannot but esteem him fitt to have that respect as to be preferred to the Priority of Comand (especially in the County of fflynt) which our pleasure is your Lordhsipp see performed upon all occasions that may offer themselves for our service. And so we bid you heartily farewell.

ffrom our Court at Oxford this 19th of July, 1643. To our right trusty and wellbeloved– Arthur
> Lord Capell our Lieutenant Generall of our forces in the counties of Chester,
> fflynt &c.

Ld. Capell.

N.L.W.   Some Gwysaney Letters and Papers. p. 1.

APPENDIX F
MAURICE REQUIRES ORDNANCE

(To Lord Bukleley).

My Lord,

Upon advertizement received that his Ma^{ty} hath some peeces of Ordnance in the towne & Castle of Beau Morise I shall desire yor Loppp to give pres'nt Order that one of the best Sakars may bee sent hither for the use & safety of this City until such tyme as it can bee provided otherwise. And for that purpose I have appointed Colonell Moystin to convoy the same from Conwy to Chester. I shall onely pray yor Loppp to give speedy Order that the Sakar may be forthwth sent to Conwy wch is all att present but that I am

My Lord,

Your Lopps affectionate ffreind,

MAURICE.

Chester.

28 of ffebr. 1644.

UNV. OF N.W. Baron Hill MSS, 5376.

APPENDIX G
PROVISIONS FOR CHESTER

for my Lord Buckley.

My Lord,

I have sent unto the Comissioners of your County forr such a proportion of Provisions as are absolutely necessary forr the preservation of the Citty and Castle of Chester.

I shall desire you therefore not to faile to take the Care and performance of this business into your hands and to see it done with all the Speede and diligence and to be assisting to the Commissiary or his Deputy who attend you to this effort.

And I do hereby give you all power and Authority to see this my desire putt in execution and to use such means to compell all refractory and unwilling or disaffected persons to performe the same as you, in your discretion, shall think fitt and so rest

My Lord,

(29 Feb, 1645)

MAURICE.

Your Lo: ffreind

UNV. OF N.W. Baron Hill MSS, 5377.

APPENDIX H
BEAUMARIS AND HOLYHEAD NEGLECTED

Whereas I am informed that the Castle of Beaumaris and fort raised att Holyhead are very much neglected being not garnished with men provisions and armes nor such guardes kept and duty performed which is necessary for the securing of the same and that the Cannon in eyther or both of them lieth unmounted and uselesse.

These are strictly to require Tho: Lord Bulkeley in whose hands I am informed the Castle of Beaumaris now is and Owen Woods Esq., into whose care I am also informed the fort att Holyhead is committeed, to see that both the sayd Castles and forts be garnished with soldiers and provisions and the cannon mounted and all necessaries supplied according to the care required in so high a concernement.

And of this I desire the sayd Lord Bulkeley and Owen Woods Esq. not to fayle as they will answere the contrary upon theyr lives.

Given under my hand this 25° of ffebr.

1644.

MAURICE.

To the Lord Bulkeley & Owen
Woods Esq. att Beaumaris or
elsewhere.

UNV. OF N.W. Baron Hill MSS, *5378.*

APPENDIX I

Sir Thomas Salusbury was with his regiment at the capture of Brentford as the following extract from the *Memoirs of the Civil War* by John Gwyn of Trelydan testifies:

'The very first day that five comrades of us repaired from the Court of Richmond to the King's Royal Army, which we met accidentally that morning upon Hounslow Heath, we had no sooner put ourselves into rank and file under the command of our worthy old acquaintance Sir George Bunckley, then major to Sir Thomas Salisbury, but we marched up to the enemy, engaged them by Sir Richard Winn's house and the Thames side, beat them to retreat into Brainford, beat them from the one Brainford to the other, and from thence to the open field.'

(Copied from Montgomery Collections. xiv. p. 329.)

BIBLIOGRAPHY
MANUSCRIPT SOURCES

Rhual MSS and Documents (1949). National Library of Wales.

Gwysaney Manuscripts. University of North Wales.

Baron Hill Manuscripts. University of North Wales.

Kinmel Manuscripts and Documents. University of North Wales.

Quarter Sessions Records. Caernarvonshire County Archives.

Presentments. Caernarvonshire County Archives.

Unpublished thesis. *Sea Power and Welsh History.* Aled Eames, M.A.

Pedigree of the Morgans of Golden Grove, prepared by the late H. B. Hughes Esquire of Kinmel Hall.

The history of the family of Heaton of Plas Heaton. (Family MS.)

Gwysaney Deeds, Documents and Papers. National Library of Wales.

The Family Papers of Owen and Stanley of Penrhos, Holyhead. University of North Wales.

PRINTED SOURCES

Calendar of State Papers, Domestic.

Calendar of the Committee for Compounding.

Calendar of Salusbury Correspondence (edited by W. H. Smith, M.A.). Board of Celtic Studies, History & Law Series No. xiv.

Calendar of Wynn (of Gwydir) Papers, 1515-1690 (edited by Sir John Ballinger). National Library of Wales.

List of Sheriffs of Wales. Public Record Office.

Dictionary of National Biography.

Pedigrees of the Anglesey and Caernarvonshire Families. J. E. Griffith (1914).

Cromwell's Army. Sir Charles Firth.

Chester and North Wales Archaeological and Historic Society *Journal* Vol. XXV. *The Siege of Chester* by the late Canon Rupert Morris, M.A., D.D., edited and completed by P. H. Lawson, A.R.I.B.A. (1923).

An Account of the castle and town of Ruthin. B. Newcome (1829).

An Account of the castle and town of Denbigh. R. Newcome (1829).

Memoirs of the Civil War in Wales and the Marches. J. Roland Phillips (1874).

Ancient and Modern Denbigh. J. Williams (1856).

Historic Notices of the Borough and County-town of Flint. Henry Taylor (1883).

History of the City of Chester. Joseph Hemingway (1831).

Studies in Stuart Wales. A. H. Dodd, M.A., F.R. Hist. S.

Mitre and Musket. B. Dew Roberts (1938).

Royal Visits and Progresses to Wales. E. Parry (1850).

The Ottley Papers. Shropshire Archaeological Society.

A History of Wem. S. Garbett (1740).

A History of Shrewsbury. H. Owen and J. B. Blakeley (1825).

Diary of the Marches of the Royal Army during the Great Civil War. Richard Symonds (1839).
    Camden Series. Royal Historical Soc.

The Parliamentary History of Wales. W. R. Williams (1895).

A History of the Puritan Movement in Wales. Thomas Richards, M.A., D.Lit. (1920).

Memorials of English Affairs. Bulstrode Whitelock (1853).

Religious Development in Wales. Thomas Richards (1923).

History of Hawarden. Richard Willett (1822).

Montgomeryshire Worthies.

History of the 13 townships of the old parish of Wrexham. A. N. Palmer (1903).

History of the Parish Church of Wrexham. A. N. Palmer.

Old Wales.

History of the Great Civil War. S. R. Gardiner.

Oliver Cromwell. John Buchan.

A History of Nantwich. J. Hall (1883).

Progress of the Duke of Beaufort through North Wales in 1684. T. Dineley (1883).

A Record of Caernarvonshire, 1809-11. E. Hyde Hall. Caernarvonshire Historical Society. Record
    Series No. 2.

The Heart of Northern Wales. W. Bezant Lowe, M.A.

Scrinia Reserata (Life of Archbishop John Williams). John Hacket (1693).

Conway Castle and Town Walls, A. J. Taylor, M.A., F.S.A., F.R. Hist. S. (Ministry of Works).

Tours in Wales. Thomas Pennant. (1883).

The History of Chirk and Chirkland. Margaret Mahler. (1912).

Honourable Society of Cymmrodorion. *Transactions.*

1927-28. John Williams of Gloddaeth. Judge Ivor Bowen.

1930-31. The Second Civil War in Wales. Sir Frederick Rees.

Archaeologia Cambrensis.

1846. Diary of William Maurice.

1869. Unpublished Correspondence between Archbishop Williams and the Marquis of Ormonde.

1887. Correspondence during the Great Rebellion. (Welsh compounders)

A Tourist's Guide through the County of Caernarvon. P. B. Williams
(1821). Appendix gives Charles I's letters to Commissioners of Array.

Anglesey Antiquarian Society and Field Club Transactions.

1948. Colonel Richard Bulkeley's death (from N.L.W. MSS 9080E).

1952. Anglesey in the Civil War. A. H. Dodd

Denbighshire Historical Society Transactions.

1954. The Civil War in East Denbighshire. A. H. Dodd

1955. John Robinson, Civil War Colonel. Norman Tucker

1956. Denbigh's Loyal Governor. Norman Tucker

Flintshire Historical Society's Publications

1916-17. Articles for the surrender of Flint Castle. H. Taylor

1952-53. Flintshire and the Puritan movement. T. Richards

1953-54. Flintshire Politics and the 17th Century. A. H. Dodd

1957 Colonel Sir Roger Mostyn, First Baronet. Norman Tucker

Caernarvonshire Historical Society's Transactions

1948. Culverins for Charles. Norman Tucker

1949. Some Pages from the History of Pant Glas, Ysbyty Ifan. R. T. Jenkins, O.B.E., M.A., D.Litt.

1952. Civil War Colonel, Sir John Carter. Norman Tucker

1953. Caernarvonshire and the Civil War. A. H. Dodd

1955. Sea Power and Caernarvonshire. Aled Eames, M.A.

Llandudno, Colwyn Bay and District Field Club Proceedings.

1953. Captain Morgan's Lonely Grave. Norman Tucker

The Parish Registers of Conway. Alice Hadley (1900).

A Short Relation of a Long Journey. John Taylor (1652).

The Dissenters Burial Ground, Wrexham. G. Vernon Price, M.B.E., F.R.G.S.

ACKNOWLEDGEMENT

The writer wishes gratefully to acknowledge his indebtedness to the following:

The Rt. Hon. LORD BAGOT for permission to photograph the portrait of Colonel William Salesbury at Blithfield,

Mr. A. D. H. PENNANT, Nantlys, for the inclusion of the miniatures of Wm. Robinson and Colonel John Robinson, the portrait of Major David Pennant, and the plan of Holt Bridge,

Mr. W. W. HARRIS and Mr. E. EMRYS JONES for their photographs, The BRITISH MUSEUM for the print of Sir John Owen, Miss MOFFAT and Miss HULL, Gloddaeth Hall, for permission to photograph the portrait of Col. Hugh Wynne,

Mr. CLARENCE ELLIS M.A., F. R. HIST.S., for scrutinizing the page-proofs,

Mr. FRANK PRICE JONES, B.A., honorary editor of the Denbighshire Historical Society, and Miss K. M. COOKS, F.L.A., honorary secretary of the Llandudno, Colwyn Bay and District Field Club, for the loan of blocks,

Dr. S. W. PATTERSON (Ruthin Castle Limited) for use of the copyright photograph of Ruthin Castle,

The NATIONAL MUSEUM OF WALES for allowing the reproduction of the portrait of Colonel Thomas Madryn,

Mr. CHARLES W. HOWARTH, R.C.A., for the battlefield maps and line drawings, Mr. ASA DAVIES, for assisting with the indexing, and Messrs. GEE & SON, Ltd., for their efficient co-operation.

Publisher's acknowledgements for this Edition

Landmark wish to acknowledge the assistance they have received from many people during the assembly of illustrations. Several people gave much help and these included:

Cadw, including Castle Custodians, especially at Denbigh Castle; Mr Fraser (re Penmorfa church); Sir Wm. Gladstone; Sheila Jones; Matthew Johnson; Irene Moran; Derrick & Shirley Pratt; Beryl Rounds; John Tucker. The reconstruction drawings of Caernarfon, Conwy and Denbigh Castles are by Ivan Lapper and were supplied by Cadw: Welsh Historic Monuments. Crown Copyright

Conwy Castle Today

Top: The roofless Great Hall and Chapel against the Prison Tower and the South West Tower (left and middle). The Kitchen Tower is on the right.
Bottom: A similar view but this time from above the Great Chamber. To the left is the King's Tower and to the right corner is the Chapel Tower.

Top left: The north wall of the castle with its four towers and the east barbican. There was a gate here for boats to land visitors to the royal apartments.

Top right: The west barbican defending the main gate, photographed from Porth Y Sarn

Bottom: The south side of the castle. The Bakehouse tower collapsed and was rebuilt years later in 1887. The pseudo-tower on the right is railway architecture.

The Upper Gate (Porth Ucha), the principal gate into the town, was heavily defended.

Gate 10 - This was turned from a tower to a gate by Thomas Telford in 1827

The inner side of Mill Gate (Porth Y Felin) in Rose Hill Street

The northwest flank, with towers in Town Ditch Road and Mount Pleasant

Top: The Entrance Gatehouse Left: The Eagle Tower with the Queen's Tower beyond Right: The Queen's Tower from the Lower Ward

The view to the Upper Ward from the Lower Ward

From the left, the Granary Tower, the North-East Tower, the Watch Tower and the Queens Gate; taken near the junction of the Upper and Lower Wards

From the left, the Eagle, Queen's, Chamberlain and Black Tower which guarded the south front by the river

The town wall with the West Gate which gives access to High Street

Top left: the gate house; top right: the inner facade of the gatehouse. Cadw describes this building as "one of the most striking compositions of military architecture from the 13th century" – (Castle Guide); bottom: the site of the hall against the west curtain wall

Top: The castle from the south east, showing the south west tower (left); the south east tower and the Gatehouse (right). Bottom: The Gatehouse and flanking corner towers

Top: The view from the north west corner.
Bottom: the familar view of the castle from the south, showing its commanding position.
The sea came much closer when the castle was built (to the foot of the rocks)

Top: The Gatehouse, which dominates the ruins. Bottom: The remains from the north east

The castle remains adjoining a pleasant hotel just south of the town centre. The remains are therefore generally only available to guests. The most striking remains are of the towers on the north side (top right). There are some interesting remains to explore (top left), but much of the remains are incorporated in later work (below).

Top left: The North West and North East Towers, looking east.
Top right: The North West Tower and west curtain wall.
Bottom: Remains of the Great Tower

BEAUMARIS CASTLE TODAY

Top left: Looking through the Gatehouse towards the Great Hall
Top right: The Gatehouse and Moat
Below: The Gatehouse from the South East Tower

Top: The curtain wall and moat on the south side of the castle
Below: The Great Hall and Inner Ward

BEESTON CASTLE

Although, like Chester, this castle was in Cheshire, not North Wales, it was closely linked with the North Wales campaign. Here are views of the castle today.

Top left & bottom: The Lower Gatehouse. Top right: remains of the west curtain wall

Top: The commanding position of the castle is well illustrated here.
Bottom: Remains of a tower on the west curtain wall

For Denbigh Castle, see pp 86-87, for Chirk, see p. 117

Royalist Officers
Of North Wales
1642-1660

A Provisional List

compiled by

NORMAN TUCKER, F.R Hist.S.

Above: The Inner Gatehouse, Beeston Castle

Previous page top: Colonel Sir Roger Mostyn, knight and baronet
Previous page bottom left: Colonel John Robinson, Governor of Holt Castle
Previous page bottom right: William Robinson of Gwersyllt, a Commissioner of Array

Preface

BY

Brigadier PETER YOUNG, D.S.O., M.C., M.A., F.S.A., F.R.Hist.S.

The names of the great warriors of our Civil Wars are still familiar: Cromwell and Rupert; Fairfax and Goring; Hopton and Waller; but all too little is remembered of the lesser men who played their parts in that great struggle. Particularly is this so of the Royalist armies. Thanks to the work of Sir Charles Firth and Godfrey Davies a good deal is known of the Regimental History of Cromwell's Army, though even in that field much remains to be done – how little, for example, is known of the army that Waller led to disaster at Roundway Down.

Most of the papers of the Royalist commanders – muster rolls, lists of quarters, pay warrants, all that would help to build up their Order of Battle – disappeared in the days of defeat after Marston Moor and Naseby; no doubt burnt as often as not to prevent them falling into the hands of the Roundheads.

Yet something remains, and from sources of the most varied kind Norman Tucker has built up his picture of the Cavaliers of North Wales. This was a region of great importance to the Royalist cause. The majority of the inhabitants were loyal to the King, who recruited freely in the six counties. The castles of Edward I were still valuable strongholds. Only from the east was there any threat from the Parliamentarians. North Wales protected the rear of the circle of Royalist fortifications around Chester, itself vital as the port for Ireland. The cattle trade of the region was an additional asset. None of the great battles of the war took place in North Wales, and this fact has perhaps tended to obscure the importance of the region to the Royalist war effort. It cannot perhaps be rated as high as that of the Northern Counties whence the Marquis of Newcastle drew his strength, or as Cornwall and the West where Hopton formed his army, but these were more populous regions.

The men of North Wales were slow to admit defeat. Caernarfon Castle did not fall until June 4, 1646, while Harlech, with its garrison of 42 stalwarts held out until March 16, 1647. Every breath of hope for the Royalist cause fanned the smouldering flames. In 1648, 1651, 1655 and 1659, Broughtons or Bulkeleys, Owens or Lloyds were ready to draw the sword once more.

In these days we have much economic and political history thrust upon us, and rightly so: but when all's said and done the fundamental test of a man's beliefs is whether he will fight for them. If little is known of some of these old heroes who helped to hammer Britain into shape, at least it is a worthy work to record their names, and for this labour of love we owe Norman Tucker a real debt. To this work he has brought an enquiring mind, a vast knowledge of his sources, endless patience and a flair for detail, which others who labour in this field can only envy. It is difficult indeed to gauge the performance of generals and armies without knowing in some detail the resources at their disposal. For this reason any sort of Army List is meat and drink to the Military Historian, and for this reason alone a work of this kind is welcome. Its interest to the genealogist and antiquarian is perhaps even more obvious.

It is very much to be hoped that, inspired by Norman Tucker's example, others may feel tempted to undertake similiar studies of other regions. He has blazed a trail.

P.Y.
17 SEPTEMBER, 1961.

Abbreviations and Sources

A.A.S.	Anglesey Antiquarian & Field Club Soc. Transactions.
Arch.Camb	Archaeologia Cambrensis. (Vol. i, contains Win. Maurice's Civil War diary.)
Baron Hill	Baron Hill MS. (Bulkeley documents) UNV. OF N.W.
Brogyntyn	Brogyntyn MS. (Lord Harlech collection) N.L.W.
Burne & Young	The Great Civil War. (Lt.-Col. A. H. Burne & Lt.-Col. Peter Young.)
B.M.	British Museum.
C.A.M.	Calendar of the Committee for the Advance of Money. P.R.O.
C.C.C.	Calendar of the Committee for Compounding. P.R.O.
Clenennau	Clenennau Letters & Papers from Brogyntyn Collection. N.L.W.
C.M.S.	Caernarvonshire Maimed Soldiers mize. County Record Office.
Crosse	Crosse of Shaw Hill MS. N.L.W.
C.S.P.D.	Calendar of State Papers Domestic. P.R.O.
C.W.P.	Calendar of Wynn (of Gwydir) Papers. N.L.W.
Culham	A List of Arms delivered at Culham Camp, 23 May, 1643. P.R.O./ W.D./55. 1661.
Chirk Castle	Chirk Castle MSS. N.L.W.
C.H.S.	Caernarvonshire Historical Society Transactions.
D.H.S.	Denbighshire Historical Society Transactions.
D.M.S.	Denbighshire Maimed Soldiers mize. Chirk Castle MS. N.L.W.
D.N.B.	Dictionary of National Biography.
D.W.B.	Dictionary of Welsh Biography.
Dodd	Prof. A. H. Dodd, Studies in Stuart Wales.
Gwynn	Captain John Gwynn. The Military Memoirs, ed. Sr. W. Scott (1822).
Gwysaney	Gwysaney Deeds and Documents. N.L.W.
Hacket	Scrinia Reserta (Bishop Hacket's life of Archb. J. Williams).
Hall	J. Hall. A History of Nantwich (quoting Malbon's diary).
Harleian	Harleian MSS. B.M.
H.M.C.	Historic Manuscripts Commission.
I.O.	Indigent Officer. From a List of Officers 1663. P.R.O. S.P. 29/68.
Llanfair	Llanfair and Bryn Odol MS. N.L.W.
L. & W.	London and Westminster District of Indigent Officer.
Mitre & Musket	Miss B. Dew Roberts (1938).
Montg	Montgomery Collection of the Montgomery Historical Soc.
Morris	Canon Rupert Morris. Siege of Chester. Chester & North Wales Antiquarian and Hist.Soc. Vol. xxv.
Newcome	Richard Newcome. History of Denbigh (1829).
N.L.W.	National Library of Wales.
Ottley	The Ottley Papers. Shropshire Antiquarian Soc. (Vols. 6 and 7.)
Palmer	A. N. A History of Wrexham.
Parry	Edward Parry. Royal Visits and Progresses to Wales (1850). (Quoting many old sources but badly arranged.)
Peacock	E. Army List of Roundheads and Cavaliers (1874).
Pedigrees	J. E. Griffith. Pedigrees of the Anglesey & Caernarvonshire families (1914).

Pennant	Thomas Pennant. Tours in Wales (1883 ed.).
Phil.	J. Roland Phillips. The Civil War in Wales and the Marches (1874).
Powys Fadog	A History of Powys Fadog. J. Y. W. Lloyd.
Q.S.R.	Quarter Sessions Records.
UNV. OF N.W.	University of North Wales.
Warburton	Eliot Warburton. Memoirs of Rupert and the Cavaliers. (Paris ed. 1849.)
Williams	J Williams. Ancient & Modern Denbigh; also Records of Denbigh.
Wms, Parlt. Hist.	W. R, Williams. Parliamentary Hist. of the Principality of Wales.

Gloddaeth Hall at the time of the Civil War consisted of the old stone frontage visible here. Note the culverin cannon thought to date from the Civil War. John Williams, Archbishop of York, died here.

Acknowledgment

My particular thanks are due to Brigadier Peter Young, D.S.O., M.C., M.A., F.S.A., of the Royal Military Academy, Sandhurst, who has, from his vast store of Civil War material, given me numerous names and much general information. His kindness is greatly appreciated. Mr. B. G. Owens, M.A., Keeper of Manuscripts and Records at the National Library of Wales has kindly made selections for me and checked my transcripts. I am grateful to Mr. J. Gwynn Williams, M.A., lecturer in history at the University of North Wales for augmenting this index with names from his own note-book, thereby relieving me of much tedious copying.

Again I would like to express my thanks to the Governors of the University of North Wales, and to the Librarian (Mr. Emyr Gwynne Jones, M.A.) in particular, for use of the history research room, and to the Governors of the National Library of Wales, and to the Librarian, Mr. E. D. Jones, B.A., F.S.A., for facilities willingly provided. I wish to acknowledge my indebtedness to the Public Record Office, British Museum and Bodleian Library for extracts from their records. At the Caernarvonshire County Record Office, the archivist (Mr. Keith Williams-Jones) has readily assisted me in searching the files. To Librarians, too numerous to specify, my gratitude is due for their courteous answers to many inquiries.

During the compiling of this list, Professor Emeritus A. H. Dodd was in the U.S.A., and I was unable to turn to him for advice. Since his return he has been kind enough to look at the proofs and I greatly appreciate his generous comments.

Norman Tucker

Ruddlan Castle & Church, showing the river realigned when the castle was built

Foreword

This list is incomplete; it could not be otherwise. It is, nevertheless, an attempt to save something from oblivion. The loyalty of North Wales to King Charles has never been adequately recognised. Here is evidence that the squires and their kin raised more than a score of regiments; no mean achievement for six remote counties.

There must, inevitably, be many names unrecorded; a number of John Lloyds and Robert Wynnes have defied identification. At times it has been impossible to allocate well-known officers a regiment – Major David and Major Hugh Pennant are an example. Even when facts have been preserved by a family, an ancestor's war record may be succinctly dismissed in a phrase as, 'he was an officer in the royal army'.

If men of quality like Sir Richard Lloyd or Sir Evan Lloyd could raise regiments and then vanish, as it were, into the blue, what hope is there of finding out what happened to Cornet Hughes or Ensign Evans?

No one could be more aware of the inadequacy of this work than the compiler yet this provisional list may prove of assistance to students until the time when a more complete record is possible. This effort seems little better than a mark of interrogation! So much remains undiscovered.

Who was the Colonel Owen slain in the attempt to relieve Beeston Castle? Who was the Colonel Thomas killed at Naseby? Which Lieutenant Ellis climbed the glacis at Bristol? Who was Captain John Wynn? Came he from Denbigh or Nerquis? Such queries are endless. Other searchers, more persevering, may continue the quest. It is in this faith that I have laboured. Ironically many officers owe the perpetuation of their names not to fame but to misfortune.

Much information is extracted from the official lists of indigent officers some six thousand of whom applied for grants from the £60,000 set aside for their relief. It was a commendable gesture on the part of Charles II, but pitifully inadequate. If the officers' portion was meagre, what of the rank and file? Many a broken private soldier, having appealed to the magistrates who distributed the maimed soldiers' mize, considered himself fortunate if their worships allowed him a pension of twenty shillings a year!

Sacrifice is speedily forgotten. Sympathy becomes diluted with each passing year. There is a time limit to compassion. The injustice cannot now be rectified; at least let some of these men be honoured by recording their names in print.

1

The devotion accorded the Stuarts by the leading families of North Wales resulted in the royal army being increased by a remarkable number of regiments. This loyalist ardour was inspired by groups of gentry whose families for generations dominated public affairs. In many instances a justice of the peace automatically became a commissioner of array. Baronets and knights were few; no great personage dominated the scene. It was from the homes of the squirearchy that the swordsmen came; usually inexperienced amateurs whose qualification was zeal.

Around each small but ancient town clustered an irregular ring of manor houses whose names were part of the county history. Wrexham boasted the greatest number. It was then a small, unprotected place whose dwellings fringed the modest river Gwenfro or sheltered beneath the majestic tower of St. Giles' Church. Its great house, Bryn-y-ffynnon (whose gate-house still hides its mellow brick amid commercial property), was then set amid broad lawns and stately trees. Denbighshire's commissioners of array conferred in Wrexham; later it became a garrison town and several times changed hands. From this neighbourhood King Charles was served by the Broughtons of Marchwiel, the Manleys and Salusburys of Erbistock, Lloyd of Esculus, Puleston of Hafod-y-wern, Roberts of Hafod-y-bwch, Ellice of Gwasnewydd, Robinson and Sutton of Gwersyllt and others of lesser renown.

From Denbigh there rallied to the standard the Salusbury clan, the numerous Dolbens of Segrwyd, Chambers of Plas Chambres, the Vaughans, Lloyds, Griffiths and Heatons. In Flintshire leadership emanated from the Mostyns, the Pennants and the ardent Whitleys of Aston Hall. Caernarvonshire produced such doughty warriors as Sir John Owen of Clenennau, Col. Hugh Wynne of Bodysgallen, Lieut-Colonel Hugh Hookes of Conwy, and Major Richard Griffith of Llanfair-Isgaer. Anglesey drew its inspiration from the Bulkeleys of Baron Hill. Colonel William Price of Rhiwlas near Bala (youthful M.P. until disabled) and the scholar Rowland Vaughan of Caer Gai, high sheriff in 1643, were prominent in Merionethshire. From Montgomeryshire there came the Hon. Richard Herbert of Cherbury and Sir Arthur Blayney of Gregynog.

These amateur warriors rode far and wide across the English countryside. They gathered around the King at Oxford. Their names are linked with many a famous field. Rupert led Salusbury's Welshmen over the Brentford barricades. It was at the head of Broughton's and Ellice's Foot that the Prince stormed Bolton. During the attack on Bristol's forts, Sir John Owen was shot through the throat. Col. Mark Trevor is said to have wounded Cromwell at Marston Moor. Broughton's and Owen's regiments were virtually wiped out at Naseby.

Battle honours of the North Wales regiments would include Edgehill, Cirencester, Birmingham, Newbury, Newark, Cropredy Bridge, Leicester, Bolton, Marston Moor, Lostwithiel, and many a siege and skirmish.

These honourable ranks were reluctantly joined by a few lukewarm malcontents whose homes were environed by royalists. When the tide turned they hastened to don the orange-tawny scarf of the Parliamentarians – Colonel Thomas Ravenscroft of Pickhill, Sir William Williams, Bart., of Vaynol, Colonel Thomas Glynne of Glynllifon and his lieutenant-colonel, William Lloyd of Plashen who later lost his life when captured by his former colleague, Sir John Owen.

Many a comfortable dwelling suffered for the devotion of its occupants. Mostyn Hall, Manley House, Gwysaney and Downing were all taken by assault. The Broughtons and the Eytons were

NOTE: *A list of squires in England and Wales in Charles I's reign shows the following distribution: Montgomery, 32; Denbigh, 28; Merioneth, 25; Flint, 20; Anglesey and Caernarfon, 15 each. Total 135. (Harleian MS. 255 f. 25b.).*

kidnapped from beneath the family rooftree. In Merionethshire, Mathafarn and Caer Gai were attacked and burnt, while Corbett's home, Ynysymaengwyn, which Sir Marmaduke Langdale fortified, went up in flames, destroyed by its own people to save its falling into enemy hands. Rhual, the Mold home of 'Baron' Evan Edwards was pillaged. Many another domestic hearth was violated but their fate is obscured by the dispassionate silence of the centuries.

Many officers followed Charles II on his continental wanderings – Roger Whitley, John Robinson, Sir Richard Lloyd, John Bodvel, Richard Bulkeley, to name some of his colonels in exile.

Kinsmen and neighbours fought shoulder to shoulder. The degree in which county families intermarried would afford an interesting study; it is also a source of bewilderment to a collector of names!

The compilation of regimental lists is not without its difficulties. Such names as 'Lieut. Wynn', 'Ensign Morgan', or 'Captain Morris' signify little and are retained merely because of possible identification. By assembling facts it is hoped that a recognisable person will emerge. Here is an illustration: Prisoners captured at Middlewich in March, 1643, include a ' Capt. Lloyd '.[1] The list of Knights of the Royal Oak has a ' –Lloyd Esq.'[2]. Powys Fadog'[3] unites these by stating that a John Lloyd was a captain in the regiment of Colonel Robert Ellice (all captured at Middlewich), that he came from Plas Madoc, Ruabon, and was nominated a Knight of the Royal Oak. Unhappily this fortunate coincidence is infrequent.

There are instances where the colonel of a regiment is known but not the name of a single officer serving under him, yet all the while there is a waiting list of officers whose regiments cannot be found. David and Hugh Pennant are a case in point. Both are majors but their learned descendant, Thomas Pennant, when writing about them, mentions no regiments. Colonel Roger Mostyn had serving under him a Captain Peter Mostyn – a relation, surely, yet he awaits identification.

Another problem is how to treat Welsh officers serving in English units, such as Major Bevis Lloyd of Llanrhaeadr, or English officers in Welsh regiments.

When war broke out there were in the vicinity of Wrexham a Captain John Edwards of Stansty, a Captain John Edwards of Cristionedd, and a Captain John Edwards of Chirkland. One had a son and heir (named 'John Edwards, gent.') who was in the Booth revolt of 1659. One can sympathise with the sequestrators who lament: 'John Edwards of Chirkland Esquire has been put down as a delinquent instead of John Edwards of the same place, gentleman. He is not to be troubled.'[4]

Those were the happy days when there was no such thing as bad spelling. Each writer was a law unto himself. Accordingly Lloyd might become Floyd, Wynne get shortened into Win, and Prys changed to Price. It is a possibility to be borne in mind.

Before the first Civil War broke out there were sundry preliminary rehearsals in the shape of the two wars against Scotland, known as the Bishops' Wars, and the campaign of 1641-1643 against the rebels in Ireland. These, though insignificant in the light of subsequent events, provided some practical training which otherwise was limited to the volunteers who crossed the seas to serve under Gustavus Adolphus, or the King of Denmark. The names of a few men of experience have come to light. One source is 'A list of officers and gentlemen that had served in forraine parts and are now selected for his Majesty's service'.[5] In this list are the names of Captain John Edwards, Captain Robert Broughton, Captain James Broughton, Lieut.-Col. Trafford, Serg.-Major Thelwall, Captain John Dutton, Captain Robert Wynne, Lieut. Ellice Price, also John, Roger and Richard Powell.

The list of officers prepared by Peacock contains several familiar names. In the Earl of Northumberland's regiment in 1640 is Captain John Edwards, apparently of Cristionedd, and Captain Charles Lloyd, later Sir Charles Lloyd, who succeeded Sir Thomas Salusbury. In Lord Grandison's regiment is a Captain Thomas Ellis and a Lieut. Daniel Broughton (of Staffs.). The Earl of Barrymore's regiment includes Captain Tom Trafford who might be a brother of Lieut.-Col. Francis Trafford.

[1] *Phillips, ii, p.62.* [2] *Parry p.404.* [3] *Vol. ii, p.196.* [4] *H.M.C. Report, ii. p.67.* [5] *N.L.W., Chirk Castle, MS. 7442.*

Lieut. Robert Roberts and Ensign Edward Roberts are in Colonel Henry Wentworth's regiment.

During the Irish expedition in the spring of 1642, Ensign Robert Davies served under Colonel Thomas Ballard. There is nothing, however, to prove that this was the squire of Gwysaney.

Another list of 1642 shows a 'Captain Floyd' in the 2nd regiment under Colonel Lord Taffe. The 6th (Lord Grandison's) has a 'Captain Morgan'. Particular interest attaches to the 7th regiment under Colonel Endymion Porter as the 'Captain Owen' in it might be the future Sir John. Other names are Captain Thomas (in Viscount Kilmurrey's), Sergeant-Major Powell under Sir George Gotherick, and a Captain Jones in the 14th regiment. Some officers, of course, joined the Parliamentarians.

Place must be found for the 'gentleman volunteer'. He appears in most articles of surrender. It was the lawyer, Eubule Thelwall, who carried Colonel William Salesbury's message to King Charles at Newcastle. No rank is accorded him, but he was considered worthy to be nominated a Knight of the Royal Oak.

It should be borne in mind that commissions did not always come from the King. For instance, Charles issued the commission to Sir Thomas Hanmer to raise 200 dragoons,[6] and that of Wm. Owen to be a lieut.-col. in Col. R. Villiers' Shropshire regiment,[7] but it was Prince Maurice who made Sir John Owen a major-general.

The petitions of maimed soldiers to the Justices for relief (usually it represented a 'pension' of 20s. a year!) proved a source of information. Unfortunately only two North Wales lists survive: that of Caernarvonshire in the County Record Office, and Denbighshire's in the Chirk Castle collection in the National Library of Wales. The names of a number of field officers and company commanders incidentally emerge from these pathetic recitals of the woes of men to whom the wars brought wounds and destitution. Had the Quarter Sessions records of the remaining four counties survived this list could have been appreciably increased.

During the search over two dozen colonels have come to light, representing more than twenty-four regiments in the royal army.

When nearly eight hundred names of officers and volunteers are obtained as a result of this inadequate search, what might be the total of royalist officers from North Wales were the roll complete?

---

[6] *N.L.W. Bettisfield MS. 111.* [7] *Clenennau MS. 537.*

NOTE: *Brief reference only is made in the instance of well-known figures such as Lord Capell, Sir Marmaduke Langdale or Sir Faithful Fortescue, as information is available elsewhere.*

Colonels of North Wales Regiments (Volunteers and Trained Band)

BLAYNEY, John	Montgomeryshire	Dragoons.
BLAYNEY, Sir Arthur, Gregynog	Montgomeryshire	Horse.
BODVEL, John, Bodvel Castle	Caernarvonshire	Dragoon & Foot.
BROUGHTON, Robert, Marchwiel	Denbighshire	Foot.
BULKELEY, Thos., Viscount, Baron Hill	Anglesey	Foot.
BULKELEY, Hon. Richard, Baron Hill	Anglesey	Horse.
DAVIES, Thomas, Gwysaney	Flintshire	Dragoon & Foot.
ELLICE, Robert, Gwasnewydd	Denbighshire	Foot.
* GLYNNE, Thomas, Glynllifon	Caernarvonshire	Foot.
HERBERT, Hon. Richard, Cherbury	Montgomeryshire	Foot & Troop of Horse.
LLOYD, Sir Charles, Moel-y-Garth	Montgomeryshire	Foot.
LLOYD, Sir Evan, Bodidris	Denbighshire	Foot.
LLOYD, Sir Richard, Esclus	Denbighshire	Horse.
LLOYD, Sir Richard, Esclus	Denbighshire	Dragoons.
* MADRYN, Thos, Madryn (Doubtful)	Caernarvonshire	Foot.
MOSTYN, Roger, Mostyn	Flintshire	Foot.
MOSTYN, William, Rhyd	Flintshire	Unknown.
OWEN, Hugh, Bodeon	Anglesey	Foot.
OWEN, Sir John, Clenennau	Caernarvonshire	Foot.
OWEN, Sir John, Clenennau	Caernarvonshire	Foot.
OWEN, William, Brogyntyn (Salop)	Merioneth	Foot.
PRICE, William, Rhiwlas	Merioneth	Foot.
* RAVENSCROFT, Thomas, Pickhill	Denbighshire	Foot.
ROBINSON, John, Gwersyllt Ucha	Denbighshire	Foot.
SALESBURY, William, Bachymbyd	Denbighshire	Foot & Troop.
SALUSBURY, Sir Thos., Bart., Lleweni	Denbighshire	Foot & Troop.
SANDYS, Thomas, Amersley	Worcester	Dept. Govr. of Beaumaris.
(Nephew of Lard Bulkeley)		
SONTLEY, Robert, Sonlle, Wrexham	Flintshire	
THELWALL, John, Plas Coch	Denbighshire	Foot.
THOMAS, Sir William, Aber	Caernarvonshire	Foot.
TRAFFORD, Francis, formerly Esclus	Denbighshire	Horse.
TREVOR, Mark, Brynkinallt	Denbighshire	Horse.
(Originally Lord Capell's Horse)		
WHITLEY, Roger, Aston, Hawarden	Flintshire	Horse.
WHITLEY, Roger, Aston, Hawarden	Flintshire	Foot.
* WILLIAMS, Sir William, Bart., Vaynol	Caernarvonshire	Foot.
WYNNE, Hugh, Bodysgallen	Caernarvonshire	Foot.
WYNNE, William, Melai	Denbighshire	Foot.

* Turned Parliamentarian.

Regiments were not necessarily raised in their Colonel's home county, but a summary may give a rough guide to the respective contributions of the shires: Denbighshire 13; Caernarvonshire 8; Flintshire 5; Montgomery 3; Anglesey 3; Merionethshire 2; Total 34. This includes Trained-band regiments. Sir Iohn Owen appears to have had two regiments of foot. Colonel Roger Whitley's younger brother, who was killed in Conwy, 1646, is referred to as Colonel John Whitley, but no trace of his regiment has been encountered.

ALCOCK, Captain –. Mentioned in Caernarfon articles.   Phil. ii. p.311.
ALDERSAY, Lieutenant –. Captured at Montgomery, 1644.   Phil. ii. p.207.
ALDERSEY, Colonel John, of Daniels Ash, Hawarden.   Morris. p.35.
     Subscribed to Chester levy for defences. In November,   Ibid. p.47.
     1643, supported Colonel Ravenscroft when Hawarden
     Castle was betrayed to Brereton. Turned Parliamentarian.
ANDREWS, Cornet John, of Flintshire.   I.O.
ANWYL, Richard of Park, Esq., Merioneth, nominated   Parry. p.404.
     Knight of the Royal Oak.
ARTHUR, Lieutenant Roger, of Salop. In Colonel Robert   Phil. ii. p.334
     Werden's Horse; in Captain Jones' troop. A defender of
     Harlech Castle.
ARTHUR, Thomas. In Harlech siege; 'the Governor's man'.   Ibid.
ARUNDELL, Captain John. Parliamentary registrar at Conwy,   Parish register.
     but turned Royalist with Sir John Carter, the governor,   Penrhos Papers.
     before the Restoration. It was a John Arundell,   Phil. ii. p.212
     Master Gunner for Sir Thomas Myddelton, who blew
     open Powys Castle gate, 1644.

BAGNALL, Captain Nicholas, of Plas Newydd, Anglesey. A recusant. In   UNV. OF N.W.
     Conwy plot, 1655, with Bayly. Pardoned.   Penrhos Papers.
         v.212.
BAKER, Captain Thomas, of Wrexham. Married daughter of   A. N. Palmer.
     Edwards of Stansty; thus a nephew of Captain John   Ottley Papers.
     Edwards. Baker acted as Sir Richard Lloyd's messenger.   D.M.S.
     Was in Lord Byron's Foot in Chester siege. In Booth   Chirk Castle Accts.
     revolt of 1659. Died at Wrexham, 1672.
BALL, Richard, of Denbighshire. Lieutenant to Captain Hugh   I.O.
     Morris. Horse.
BARRON, Captain –. In Denbigh Castle, possibly in Colonel   W. J. Smith in
William Salesbury's Foot.   Salusbury
         Correspondence.
BARTLETT, Captains John and Thomas, brothers, who   Phil. ii. p.89.
     commanded the royal ships *Swan* and *Confidence* in Irish seas.
BAYLIE, Captain in Colonel W. Wynne's Foot.   Crosse. 1123.
BAYLY. 'One Bayly' was in the plot to seize Conwy Castle   Penrhos Papers.
     in 1655. Confessed and was pardoned. (See next.)   v.212.
BAYLY, Captain Nicholas, son of Dr. Lewys Bayly, Bishop   Griffith's Pedigrees.
     of Bangor, was governor of Galway. 'Colonel of a   51.
     regiment he raised for Charles I.' Gentleman of Bed-chamber to
     Charles II.
BELLAY, John. Signed Aberystwyth articles.   Phil. ii. p.305.
BENBOW, Captain John. Parliamentarian, wounded at   Parry. p.389.
     Beaumaris, turned Royalist. Captured 1651, and shot at   Grave in old church-
     Shrewsbury Castle. Buried old St. Chad's. A Captain   yard.
     Benbow was at Worcester, 1651 (Boscobel).
BENNET, Captain –. Mentioned in Caernarfon articles.   Phil. ii. p.311.

BERKELEY, Quartermaster, of Brymbo. In Booth revolt, 1659.　　　　P.R.O. SP. 25/29. fos. 36/7.

BERKQUT. Captain-Lieutenant to Lord Byron at Conwy.　　　　Clenennau 610.

BESWICK, Ensign Roger. Aided in attempt to rescue Sir J. Owen from Denbigh, 1648.　　　　P.R.O. SP. 23-4 & 5.

BLAYNEY, Captain Andrew, Montgomery. In Herbert, Lord Cherbury's Foot. Spelt 'Blayny'.　　　　I.O.

BLAYNEY, Sir Arthur, of Gregynog, Montgomery. Colonel of Horse. Defender of Harlech; acted as commissioner. Knighted 9 November, 1643. King passed his house, September, 1645. Was at Y Dalar Hir and Beaumaris fights. Badly wounded. Died 1655; buried Tregynon.　　　　Phil. ii. p.334. Mont. Collection. vol. 8. p. 342. Parry. p.388/91.

BLANEY, Cornet Edward. In Lieutenant-Colonel Price's troop of Lord Gerard's Horse.

BLAYNEY, John (no rank, but probably Colonel), of Montgomery. Dragoons. Had two indigent officers under him. Commissioner of Array　　　　I.O.

BLODWELL, Captain John. In Colonel Richard Herbert's regiment.　　　　D.M.S.

BLODWELL, Ensign Nathaniel, to Captain John Blodwell, Montgomeryshire, in Herbert, Lord Cherbury's regiment.　　　　I.O.

BLODWELL, Ensign Richard. In Colonel R. Ellice's Foot. In Major Gillmore's company. Of Denbighshire.　　　　I.O.

BLODWST, Captain –. With Sir John Owen in 1648 at Dolgellau.　　　　Parry. p.390.

BOASSE, Major –. In Ruthin in 1645.　　　　Council Minute Book.

BODDEN, – ., Esq., of Anglesey. Nominated Knight of the Royal Oak.　　　　Parry. p.404.

BODVEL, Colonel John, of Bodvel Castle, Caernarvonshire. Had King's commission, 1 August, 1643, to raise 1,200 Foot and Dragoons for defence of Caernarvonshire and Anglesey. Made governor of Caernarfon Castle, 1645. Signed for Anglesey revolt, 1648. Compounded under both Beaumaris and Anglesey articles of surrender. Was in company with Charles Stuart 'the late pretended King of Scots' in Holland and elsewhere. References to domestic troubles in C.W.P. Was M.P. for Anglesey until 'disabled'.　　　　Wms. Parliamentary History. Black's Oxford Docquets, p.68. C.W.P. 1768. Parry. p.387. C.C.C. p.1599.

BODWRDA, Hugh. Captured at Y Dalar Hir, 1648.　　　　Phil. ii. p.384.

BODWRDA, John. A Caernarvonshire Commissioner of Array. Died 1648.　　　　Clenennau 535. Parry. p.390.

BOLD, William, of Tre'r ddol. H.S. Anglesey. Signed Anglesey articles. Nominated Knight of the Royal Oak.　　　　Phil. ii. p.400.

BONCLE, George. Major in Sir Thomas Salusbury's Foot. Was commissioned major, Woodstock, 29 October, 1642. (Harl. 6804/221). Sir Thomas refers to him as 'his sergeant-major who is a stranger'. According to John Gwynn:　　　　C.W.P. 1711. Harleian MS. 1802/ 221.

was with Salusbury's Foot at Brentford.
Later made lieutenant-colonel of Sir Arthur Aston's Horse. Signed articles of surrender for Reading, 1643. Fought at first Bristol and the relief of Basing. Knighted 7 Nov., 1644. Deputy Governor of Oxford. Captured at Naseby, and died in captivity of 'hard usage' (Lloyd).

Memoirs. Gwynn

BOSTOCKE, Lieutenant-Colonel Edward (possibly also named George). In Sir John Owen's Foot. Probably from Holt where a George B. was H.S.Denb. in 1636. A 'George Bostock' was captain in Sir John Owen's regiment. Survived the war but died, according to the Reverend Philip Henry of drink after acting as a J.P. at Llanrwst Quarter Sessions, 1663. A J.P.'s signature appears as 'G. E. (?) Bostocke'.

D.M.S.
Arch.Camb. 1906 p.102.
Denb. H.S.T. Vol.9.p.186,

P.R.O.-W.O. 55/459.

BOWEN, Griffith, of Carmarthen. Lieutenant to Captain Floyd in R. Ellice's Foot.

D.M.S.

BOWEN, Cornet John, Montgomeryshire. Cornet to Captain Edward Floyd, in Lord Capell's regiment.

I.O.

BOWEN, Lieutenant. Captured at Montgomery.

Phil. ii. p.207.

BREAD, Captain. Wounded at Wem, 1643.

H.M.C. i. p.143.

BRETT, Owen, Esq., of Rowney, Bedfordshire and London. Son of Sir John Brett. 'Lived in several garrisons.' Was commissioner for Sir Richard Lloyd arranging the surrender of Holt Castle, January, 1646-7. Fined £1,396.

C.C.C. 1804.
P.R.O. SP. 23/208.

BROUGHTON, Sir Edward, of Plas Isa and Marchwiel, County Denbigh. A Commissioner of Array, Father of Lieutenant-Colonel Sir Edward. Captured in raid on Marchwiel, October, 1643, with two sons.

Parry. p.337.

BROUGHTON, Lieutenant-Colonel [Sir] Edward. Went to Ireland as captain of Foot under his uncle, Colonel Robert B. but returned as major to Woodhouse in 1643. Was wounded at Wem. Some reports say, Major Robert (Junior). Captured at Rowton Moor, 1645; captured at Worcester, 1651. Probably served in Royal Guards. Gwynn mentions a Broughton serving at Ypres in Spanish service. Captured at Chirk, 1659, and nearly lost his life breaking parole. Imprisoned in Gatehouse where he wooed and wed the keeper's daughter. Pennant prints the amazing 'imprecation' he swore to prove his good intentions. Knighted in 1663. Died of wounds sustained in sea fight against the Dutch, 1665. Buried in Westminster Abbey. Described in C.C.C. as a 'bloody delinquent'.

D.M.S.
Phil. ii. p.88.
C.W.P. 2193.
Llanfair 50.
Memoirs.
Palmer: 'The Broughton's of Marchwiel'.
Morris. p.116.
C.C.C. 2453.

BROUGHTON, Major. Captured at Naseby.

Whitelocke's Memorials. i. p.450.

BROUGHTON, Captain James. Served in 'forraine parts'.

BROUGHTON, Captain Oliver, of Flintshire. In Sir Michael Woodhouse's Foot. In 1655 uprising.

I.O.

BROUGHTON, Major Richard, of Isycoed. In Booth revolt
of 1659.

P.R.O. SP. 25/29. fos.
36/7.

BROUGHTON, Colonel [Major-General] Robert, brother
of Sir Edward (Senior). Served 'in forraine parts'; in
1640 led Denbigh levies against Scots. As colonel in 1641
led 1,000 Denbighshire men to Ireland. Returned February,
1644, to Chester. Followed Rupert to relieve Newark;
then to Liverpool siege. Led attack on Bolton. Fought at
Marston Moor. Made governor of Shrewsbury. As major-
general was at Montgomery where he was wounded and
captured. His regiment suffered severely at Naseby.
Compounded under Oxford articles. Fined £77. In Booth
revolt of 1659. Captured in Chirk Castle.

Crosse.
D.M.S.
Warburton.
Phil. ii. p.206.
    and p.125.
C.C.C. p.761.

BROUGHTON, Major Robert. Apparently nephew of above.

C.C.C. 1437.

BROUGHTON, Captain Thomas. Low Country soldier.

Palmer:'The
Broughton's
of Marchwiel'.
p.3.

BROUGHTON, Captain William, 'of Bersham' near
Wrexham. Another brother of Sir Edw. Led Denbighshire
levies to Selby, 1639. A Low Country soldier. In Sir
Thomas Salusbury's original regiment, but transferred to
the dragoons of Sir Richard Lloyd. Was in Harlech siege.
Compounded for £90.

Ibid.
I.O. & D.M.S.
C.C.C. 1220.

BROWNE, Captain. In Sir John Owen's Foot.

P.R.O. W.O. 55
    (1661).

BRYNKIR, James. Commissioner of Array for Caernarfonshire. 'A Great Sufferer for his Royal Master.' Died
1644; buried Penmorfa.

Mitre & Musket.
Epitaph.

BRYNKIR, Captain John. Younger brother. In Sir John
Owen's Foot. Captured at Conwy, 1646, but exchanged.
Escaped from Y Dalar Hir, 1648.

C.M.S. and
Clenennau 619.
Parry.p.391.
C.M.S.

BRYNKIR, Captain William, of Brynkir. Brother. Cousin of Sir John
Owen in whose regiment he served. Killed at Newbury.

BULKELEY, Honourable Richard, heir of Viscount Bulkeley.
Aged 16 in 1642. By 1646 was colonel and governor of
Beaumaris Castle, which he surrendered to Mytton. Helped
in Harlech siege, and fought at Y Dalar Hir. Headed
1648 Anglesey revolt as Com.-in-Chief. Captured in
Beaumaris Castle, September, 1648. Exiled. In 1649 he
returned and was killed by Major Rd. Cheadle in a chance
encounter on Lavan Sands. Cheadle was executed at Conwy.

Phil. ii. p.312.
C.W.P. 1799 & 1910.
P.R.O. SP. 23/4 & 5.
A.A.S.T. 1948. p.76.

BULKELEY, Thomas, 1st Viscount of Baron Hill, Anglesey.
D.L. and Commissioner of Array. Colonel of Trained
Band of Tyndaethwy and Menai. Prisoner 1646. Was at
Y Dalar Hir. Sponsored 1618 Anglesey revolt. 'Had it
not been for Thomas and Rich. Bulkeley, there had been

Baron Hill. MS.
    5370.
C.W.P. 1910.
P.R.O. SP. 23/4 & 5.
C.A.M. 1163.

no revolt in Anglesey.' Born 1585, died 1659.

BULKELEY, Lieutenant John. In Beaumaris garrison. — C.W.P. 1874.

BULKELEY, Roland, of Porthamel. Son of William. Signed
articles. — C.W.P. 1768. Phil. ii. p.401.

BULKELEY, William. Constable of Beaumaris, 1643. Signed
Anglesey articles of surrender, 1648. — Ibid.

BURGES, Lieutenant-Colonel Roger. In Sir John Owen's
Foot. Was in attack on Bristol. Defied Cromwell at
Farringdon House. Commanded Owen's regiment at
Naseby and was captured. Held Castle Cornet, Gurnsey,
until December, 1651. — Warburton. Burne & Young. p.195.

BURTON, Quartermaster Roger, Salop. Q.M. to Sir Richard
Crane. Was in charge of 'new wall' at Harlech Castle. — I.O. Phil. ii. p.334.

BUSHELL, Captain Thomas (F.). In Irish expedition, June, 1642. — B.M. 109. g.13. p.209.

BUSHELL, Captain Walter. In Colonel R. Whitley's Horse. — I.O.

BYRON, Sir Nicholas. Governor of Chester until captured at
Ellesmere, January, 1644. Commanded a brigade at
Edgehill. Colonel of the first regiment of Horse.
Distinguished himself at Roundway Down. Uncle of Lord Byron. — Phil. ii. p.124.

BYRON, Sir John. 1st Lord Byron. Governor of Chester after
his uncle. Defeated at Nantwich, January, 1644. Commanded
right wing at Marston Moor. Led N.W. troops to Montgomery
and was defeated, 1644. Welcomed Charles to Chester, 23
September, 1645, and after Rowton promised to hold city for
eight days. He resisted until 3 February, 1646. Marched to
Conwy, and then to Caernarfon which he defended until 4 June,
1646. Tried to raise N.W. in 1648, but when Richard Bulkeley was
made Com.-in-Chief Anglesey, Byron withdrew in chagrin. Died in
France, 1652. Eldest of seven brothers. — D.N.B.

BYRON, Sir Richard. Governor Newark. Captured with Sir Robert,
April, 1645. Succeeded to title. — Morris. p.81.

BYRON, Sir Robert. Returned from Ireland, January, 1644.
Was in Nantwich fight, 25 January, 1644. Governor of
Liverpool where captured. Regiment at Naseby. — Phil. ii. p.130.

BYRON, Sir Thomas. Wounded dangerously at Hopton
Heath. Stabbed in brawl in Oxford, and died there, 1644.
Commanded Prince of Wales' Horse. — Burne & Young. p.69.

BYRON, Sir William. Captured near Wem. Was in Caer-
narfon Castle siege. Said to have died at sea. — Phil. ii. p.311. D.N.B.

BYRON, Sir Philip. Wife and child died during Chester siege.
Was killed defending York, 16 June, 1644. — R. Morris. appenx. B.M. Royal Martyrs. 109. g.13. p.233.

BYRON, Sir Gilbert. Governor of Rhuddlan Castle. Helped
to relieve Chester. Escaped to fight at Stow-in-the-Wold.
Knighted by 1651. (Some letters in Clenennau Papers, N.L.W.) — Phil. i. p.351. C.A.M. p.1388.

NOTE: *Neither Sir Thomas nor Sir Philip appears to have served in Wales, but are included as indicating the*
remarkable record of this family.

CAPELL, Arthur, Lord. Made lieutenant-general of North
    Wales and the Border in Spring of 1643, under the boy
    Prince of Wales. Joined in Salop by Colonel W. Wynne,
    also by Mark Trevor and Edward Broughton. Ousted by
    the ambitious Lord Byron. Letters to Sir Rd. Lloyd and
    Denbighshire Commissioner of Array have been preserved.
    His commission to raise a regiment of Horse is dated 24
    November, 1642. See Life by Puckering in H.M.C.
                            Ottley Papers, Salop.
                                Ant.Soc.
                          Llanfair 50.

CARTWRIGHT, Captain –. In Colonel R. Whitley's Foot.   *D.M.S.*

CHALONER, Ensign Anthony. In Sir Charles Floyd's   *I.O.*
    (Salusbury's) Foot. L. & W.

CHALONER, Captain Robert. In Sir Charles Floyd's Foot.   *I.O.*
    Captain 1643. A Denbigh man. Great-nephew of Edward
    Chaloner, Chester Herald who sponsored the first Randle
    Holme. Made Bluemantle, 1660, and Lancaster Herald, 1666.

CHAMBERS, Captain Charles, of Plas Chambres, Denbigh.   *R. Morris. appenx.*
    Married Ellen, daughter of Lieutenant-Colonel Edward   *Parry. pp. 381 &*
    Griffith of Garn. Was in Chester siege, then Denbigh   *388.*
    siege. In June, 1648, joined in plot to rescue Sir John Owen
    from Denbigh Castle, 16 July, 1648. Discharged pistol at Denbigh
    Castle 'in a bravado', and went away. In Anglesey revolt of 1648.
    Again in Booth rebellion of 1659. Compounded on Denbigh articles.
    Fined £356/5/0.

CHAMBERS, William, of Denbigh. In attempt to rescue Sir   *P.R.O. SP. 23/4 & 5.*
    John Owen, 1648.

CHAMBERS, Lieutenant. In Colonel William Wynne's Foot.   *C.A.M. p.1245.*
    Probably lived in Essex after the Restoration.

CHEADLE, [Sir] Thomas. High Sheriff, Caernarvonshire.   *C.W.P. 1801.*
    In 1642 he executed the Commission of Array in Caer-   *C.W.P. 1873.*
    narvon, Merioneth and Anglesey, and brought armed men
    from Bangor or Caernarvonshire to assist the King. Captain
    of Beaumaris trained band. Accused of stealing a brass robinet
    from castle while constable. Fortified 'Lady Cheadle's Fort' at
    Aberlleiniog nearby and turned Parliamentarian. Family feud with
    Bulkeleys.

CHURLOCKE, Captain, in Sir Thomas Salusbury's Foot.   *D.M.S.*
    (Might be Shurlocke of Ruthin.)

CLOUGH, John. Signed Denbighshire Maimed Soldiers'   *D.M.S.*
    petition. No rank specified. Probably of Plas Clough, Denbigh.

COLE, Joshua. Captured at Y Dalar Hir, 1648.   *Phil. ii. p.384.*

CONWAY, Edward, 2nd Viscount, owner of Conwy Castle.   *D.N.B.*
    Was General of Horse in Northumberland, 1640. In 1641,   *C.S.P.D.*
    went to Ireland in that capacity, but returned and was   *C.C.C. 980.*
    involved in Waller's plot to raise London for the King. Imprisoned

for a short time, 1643, but later joined the King at Oxford. For
some reason he soon forsook the King and appears to have lived
henceforth abroad. Fined £3,000. Died in France 1655. 'Had two
sons in arms for Parliament.' Home, Ragley Hall, Warwickshire.

CONWAY, Frederick. Captured at Chirk, 1659.   Mercurius Politicus.

CONWAY, Henry. Heir of William of Bodrhyddan. H.S.
    Flint in 1657, but made baronet by King, 1660, so may have
    worked for the Restoration.

CONWAY, John, gent., of Llanrhaeadr. Suspect of Booth   P.R.O. SP. 25, 36/7.
    revolt of 1659.

CONWAY, 'Mr.' Samuel. Captured at Y Dalar Hir.   Phil. ii. p.384.

CONWAY, Lieutenant Will, of Flintshire.   I.O.

CONWAY, William. Succeeded Sir John as squire of Bodrhyddan.   UNV. OF N.W.
    A Commissioner of Array. Was authorised to   Bodrhyddan
    impress soldiers. Obtained lease of Rhuddlan Castle.   Papers.
    Tradition in family that he surrendered Rhuddlan Castle   C.C.C. 1632.
    (July, 1646). Compounded by Deputy being weak and old.

CONWAY, Captain Robert. Captured at Dartmouth, January,   Rylands Library.
    1645.   Battles, etc. p.136.

CONWAY, 'Mr.' Captured on Bardsey Island, 1649.   Parry. p.385.

COOPER, Quartermaster William, of Montgomeryshire. To   I.O.
    Major Thomas Nanfan in Colonel Henry Grady's regiment.

CORBETT, Sir Thomas, of Salop. Served as major in Mark   Puckering.
    Trevor's Horse.*

CORBETT, Robert. Owner of Ynys-y-Maengwyn, Merioneth.   Arch.Camb. 1875.
    House fortified by Sir Marm. Langdale, but burnt to   p.207.
    prevent its capture.

COTTINGHAM, Captain. Killed in sortie from Holt Castle,   Phil. ii. p.302.
    1647.

CUNNINGHAM, Quartermaster Thomas. Involved in fracas   Caern. Q.S. records.
    in Llannor Churchyard, 1646.   Rec. Office.

CUTLER. See Rutter.

DAMPORT, Captain. Captured after Wem. (Probably   Phil. ii. p.88.
    Thomas Davenport.)

DANIEL, (?) John, Colonel. In Ruthin in 1645.   Council Book.

DARRENFIELD, Lieutenant. In Colonel R. Broughton's   Peacock.
    Foot. Captured at Naseby.

DAVENPORT, Ensign. Captured at Middlewich.   Phil. ii. p.62.

---

* Brigadier Young writes: "Sir Thomas Corbett, Bart., of Sprewston, Norfolk, left London for York at the beginning of
the war and became captain of a troop for the King (C.C.C. 1193). I have no doubt that this troop was in Lord
Capel's regiment of horse as he was Capel's nephew. He probably served at Edgehill, but like Capel and 'Puckering',
as a gentleman in the King's Lifeguard. In 1643, he was a field officer in Capel's horse, and he was a ward and
probably younger than [LieutenantColonel?] Sir Henry Newton (Puckering), I presume he was Major. He almost
certainly fought at Marston Moor under Trevor, and at Torrington (1646), by which time Trevor's had been merged
into Prince Charles' Horse. He compounded on Truro Articles, and even after reduction his fine was £1,247/17/8
(C.C.C. 1193), so he was not exactly hard up."

DAVENPORT, Captain Thomas. Captured at Middlewich. 'Of Woodford' (states Phillips).	Ibid.
DAVENPORT, Lieutenant. Captured at Oswestry.	Phil. ii. p.176.
DAVENPORT, Captain Thomas. In the Foot regiment of Sir Henry Vaughan of Golden Grove.	I.O.
DAVENPORT, Lieutenant. In Colonel Vaughan's regiment of Foot. Captured at Naseby.	Rylands Library. Civil War Collection. vi-vii. p.116.
DAVENPORT, Captain Thomas. In Colonel R. Whitley's Foot. Of Flintshire. Spelt Whittly.	I.O.
DAVENPORT, Captain Thomas. Captured at Middlewich. He broke out of Nantwich but was recaptured at Aldford.	Hall. p.156.
DAVENPORT, Thomas, of Flintshire. In 1648 Anglesey revolt.	Parry. p.388.
DAVIES, Captain –. Wounded at Wem. Probably in Colonel William Wynne's Foot.	Phil. ii. p.88.
DAVIES, 'Mr.' Peter, gentleman volunteer, slain at Denbigh.	B.M. Royal Martyrs. 109. g.13. p.233.
DAVIES, Lieutenant Robert. In Captain Peter Runford's firelocks in Colonel T. Ballard's regiment. Irish expedition 1641-2.	B.M. 109. g.13. p.208.
DAVIES, Captain Robert (1616-1666), squire of Gwysaney, Mold, H.S. Flint, 1660. Home captured by Brereton, April, 1645 after a fortnight's siege, about 27 officers and men taken prisoner. Was in Denbigh siege. Took part in Booth revolt, 1659, and was captured. Nominated Knight of the Royal Oak. Fined £645.	Morris. p.80. C.C.C. 1717. Parry. p.404.
DAVIES, Captain Mytton (or Mutton Davies). Son and heir of above. (1634-1684). Aged 11 when he helped to defend Gwysaney, Married Elizabeth Wilbraham of Woodhey, County Cheshire. Captain of Horse under Colonel Roger Whitley in 1659. Captured in Booth revolt. Released to visit wife by Colonel T. Croxton, governor of Chester Castle.	C.C.C. 1717. Gwysaney Ltrs. & Papers. No.3.
DAVIES. A Captain in the royal garrison of Bristol, captured at the surrender, September, 1645.	Rylands Library. Civil War Collection. vi-vii. p.116.
DAVIES, Captain Thomas. Captured in Chirk Castle, 1659; probably a younger brother of Mytton.	Chirk Castle Accounts.
DAVIES, Colonel Thomas, uncle of Robert Davies. Served in Thirty Years War under King Christian IV of Denmark. Letters in N.L.W. Commissioned to raise 500 Foot and Dragoons under Capell in 1643, and appointed to chief command of Flint and Denbigh. Made constable of Flint Castle but probably never took charge. His regiment was	Gwysaney Ltrs. No. 1. R. Morris. p.47. C.C.C. 1718.

scattered by Brereton, November, 1643, but rallied and
helped to recapture Hawarden Castle. Helped to defend
Denbigh Castle. Fined for delinquency in arms, £51. Later
in ill health. Buried Mold Church, 1655.

DAVIS, Colonel Sir Charles. Treasurer of Ireland. Mentioned   D.M.S.
in Denbigh maimed soldiers' petition.

DAVIS, (Captain?) Raphael, of Whitford, County Flint.   C.A.M. p.1113.
Helped Thomas Mostyn to defend Flint Castle. Concealed
£1,000 with Lord Windsor, and £200 with Lady Mary Mostyn
or Colonel Roger Mostyn.

DAVIS, Lieutenant Owen, of Anglesey. In Earl of Derby's regiment   I.O.
as lieutenant of Horse to Colonel Standish.

DAVYES, Captain. 'Mortally wounded and taken at Wem,'   H.M.C. i. p.143.
1643.

DAWSON, Captain Stephen. In Colonel Sir Thomas Salus-   I.O.
bury's troop of Horse.

DIGBY, Lord. Was at Denbigh Castle with King after Rowton
for four days only.

DISNEY, Lieutenant-Colonel. Signed Caernarfon articles,   Phil. ii. p.311.
1646.

DOLBEN, Captain David. In attempt to rescue Sir J. Owen   P.R.O. SP. 23/4 & 5.
from Denbigh Castle, 1648. Possibly the officer in Ellice's   Phil. ii. p.62.
Foot; if so, captured at Middlewich, 1643.

DOLBEN, Ensign Hugh, of Denbigh, ensign to Captain   I.O.
Dolben in Sir Thomas Salusbury's Foot. Both spelt Daulben
in original also Dolehn at Montgomery.

DOLBEN, Captain Hugh. Killed in Ireland.   Pedigrees.

DOLBEN, John. Future Archbishop of York (1625-1686), a   D.W.B.
great nephew of Archbishop J. Williams. Served in
the royalist army, 1642-6.

DOLBEN, Lieutenant-Colonel John, of Segrwyd, near   D.M.S.
Denbigh. A captain in Sir Thomas Salusbury's original   Parry. p.357.
regiment. A Captain Dolben was captured at Montgomery,   C.C.C. p.207.
1644. Led attempt to rescue Sir John Owen from Denbigh,
1648. As a major served under Colonel R. Bulkeley in Anglesey,
1648. Taken in Chirk Castle, 1659. Twice sequestered. Buried in
Llanrhaeadr Church. Epitaph in Williams' Ancient and Modern
Denbigh. Fined £107.

DOLBEN, Robert. Ordered by Commissioner of Array to   C.W.P. 1723.
manufacture gunpowder for North Wales.

DUPPEY, Lieutenant, in Colonel R. Broughton's Foot.   Peacock.
Captured at Naseby.

DUTTEN, Ensign. Captured at Montgomery, 1644.   Phil. ii. p.207 and
    Parry. p.357.

DUTTON, Captain. In Booth revolt, 1659.

DUTTON, Captain. 'Capt. Dutton gott into Chestr very safe   Clenennau 598.
with ye money and Ammucon'(Sir W. Neale to Colonel

Gilbert Byron), 1645.

DUTTON, Captain Richard, Cefn-y-Wern, near Chirk, 'In   Chirk Cast. Ac.
    Tower more than once'. Fined £185.   C.C.C.

DUTTON, Richard, of Cefn-y-Wern. Compounded on   Chirk Castle MSS.
    Oxford articles. 'Never took arms.' Fined at 1/10 £185.   445 & 468.

Probably father of above – both have same name.   C.C.C. 1679.

DYER, Captain, Sir Thomas Salusbury's Foot.

DYMOKE, Edward. Signed with Captain Ellis Sutton a   D.M.S.
    Denbigh maimed soldiers' application for mize.

DYMOKE, Humphrey. 'Captain-ensign' in Irish expedition,   B.M. 109. g.13.
    16 June, 1642.   p.209.

DYMOKE (Dimmock), Humphrey (and his son), 'of   Parry. p.349.
    Millington' (sic) captured at Sir Gerard Eyton's house in
    February, 1644, by Colonel Mytton.

DYMOCK, Captain William of Flintshire. In Lord Byron's   I.O.
    regiment. Horse.

EATON, Lieutenant John. In Viscount Grandison's troop   Peacock. Appen.
    during 1640 expedition against Scots. (From Leeswood?)

EDDOW, Captain Thomas. Of Flintshire. Horse.   I.O.

EDDOW, Lieutenant Richard. Of Flintshire. Horse.   I.O.

EDISBURY, John, of Pentre'r Clawdd. Prothonotary of   C.A.M. p.1480.
    Denbighshire and Montgomeryshire, taken prisoner in
    pursuit from Bangor-on-Dee, after its capture by Myddelton
    in November, 1643. Carried to Blechfield but exchanged.
    Returned to 'the King's quarters'. A Commissioner of Array.
    Later became Myddelton's steward for Chirk.

EDWARDS, Ensign David, of Denbighshire. Ensign to   I.O.
    Captain Geo. Hosyer in Colonel R. Ellice's Foot.

EDWARDS, Evan. Of Rhual, Mold. 'Baron' Edwards of the   C.C.C. 1605.
    Exchequer, Chester. Commissioner of Array, Flintshire.
    Had house pillaged.* Compounded for £157.

EDWARDS, John, of Flintshire. Quartermaster of Horse to   I.O.
    Captain Edward Morgan (Golden Grove).

EDWARDS, Major John, of Cristionedd (now Pen-y-Cae),   Chirk Castle MS.
    near Wrexham. Probably the J.E. who served in 'forraine   7442.
    parts'. In Earl of Northumberland's regiment with Captain   D.M.S.
    Charles Lloyd in 1640. A captain in Sir Thomas Salus-   C.C.C. 3128 &
    bury's regiment at Culham. Captured at Winnington   P.R.O. S.P. 25/59.
    bridge, 1659. Compounded.   pp.36/7.

EDWARDS, Captain John of Plas Newydd, Chirkland. A   C.C.C. 1720.
    Commissioner of Array and trained band captain. Was in
    Denbigh siege and then at Harlech where he died.
    Compounded under Denbigh articles for £80.

EDWARDS, Captain John, of Stansty, near Wrexham. Of   Palmer.
    old Welsh family descended from Edwin of Tegiengle.   P.R.O. S.P. 25/29,

---

*   *See North Wales in the Civil War.*

Born 1619, buried Wrexham, 1673. Married Frances,   36/37.
widow of Edward Norrys of Speke. Captured in Holt   I.O.
Castle; was one of Sir Richard Lloyd's commissioners
negotiating surrender. Probably the Captain John Edwards
in Ellice's Foot. Taken in Booth revolt, 1659.

EDWARDS, John, gentleman, of Isycoed. Captured in Booth revolt.   Ibid.

EDWARDS, Randle, gentleman, of Isycoed. Taken in Booth revolt.   Ibid.

EDWARDS, Rice. Lieutenant to Major Morgan in Ellice's   I.O.
    Foot. From Merioneth.

EDWARDS, Lieutenant Roger. Of Flintshire. Horse.   I.O.

EDWARDS, William, of Cefn-y-Wern. In Harlech siege.   Phil. ii. p.334.

EDWARDS, Captain William. Son of Captain John Edwards.   D.M.S. & I.O.
    In Colonel William Wynne's Foot. Served in Denbigh   Phil. ii. p.334.
    siege and Harlech siege, acting as a commissioner in   Caerns. Record
    latter. Was in fracas in Llannor churchyard in 1646,   Office
    and was hit on head by stone. In Booth Rebellion, 1659.

ELLICE, Ensign Richard, of Wrexham. In Booth revolt, 1659.

ELLICE, Colonel Robert, of Croesnewydd (formerly Gwas-   Palmer.
    newydd), near Wrexham. Trained under Gustavus   Arch.Camb. i. p.34.
    Adolphus. Captured Chirk Castle, January, 1643, and   Phil. ii. p.62.
    used money to equip regiment of Foot. Helped to design   Warburton.
    Chester's mud walls. Captured with his whole regiment   C.C.C. 1499 &1550
    of 600 men at Middlewich, March, 1643; exchanged in   C.W.P. 1746.
    September. Defended Holt Bridge with new regiment   D.W.B.
    but this too was scattered by Brereton, 9 November, 1643.
    Formed a third regiment which operated with Sir William
    Vaughan in Shropshire. His regiment present at Montgomery battle.
    Under Rupert, fought at Liverpool and led the attack on Bolton.
    Captured Apley House, 24 March, 1644. Compounded under
    Oxford articles 'of Ruabon'. Fined £150. Might be the 'Ellis'
    referred to by Archbishop Williams as being in Conwy. A
    connection of the Lloyds of Bodidris.

ELLICE, Thomas. Younger brother of Colonel Robert Ellice.   D.W.B.

ELLIS, Griffith, of Eivionedd (Caernarvonshire), gent, who   Caerns. Record Office
    drew the maimed soldiers' mize of £2 p.a.   file 1669.

ELLIS, Ensign John. Ensign to Captain [Charles] Cotterell   I.O.
    in Lord Gerard's regiment. Foot.

ELLIS, Lieutenant Owen, of Gwtherin. In Captain H. Lloyd's   D.M.S.
    coy in Sir Thomas Salusbury's Foot.

ELLIS, Lieutenant. Distinguished himself in assault on   Warburton.
    Bristol.

ELLIS, Captain. Slain at Wem. Might be the Captain Ellys   Phil. ii. p.88.
    'sore hurt and wounded at Wem' while serving in Ellice's   H.M.C. i. p.143.
    regiment.

ELLIS, Richard, of Bodychain. Suspected in 1648 revolt.   Arch.Camb. ii. p.3.

ELLIS, Captain Thomas. In same troop. Might be the brother   Ibid.
    of Colonel R. Ellice. Probably killed at Wem.

ELLIS, Captain Thomas, in Lord Grandison's regiment in 1640.   Peacock. p.77.

EVANS, Lieutenant Austin, of Montgomery. In Colonel
Samuel Sandys' regiment. Foot. — I.O.

EVANS, Lewis, of Montgomeryshire, Captain of Foot. — I.O.

EVANS, Reverend Michael. Lord Bulkeley's chaplain who
helped to draw up Anglesey's protestation of 1648. — Phil. ii. p.400.

EVANS, Ensign Roger, of Flintshire. In Roger Whitley's Foot. — I.O.

EVANS, Robert. Captured in Chirk Castle, 1659.

EVANS, William. In Captain Goodman's coy. Sir Thomas
Salusbury's Foot. — D.M.S.

EVET, Major –. 'Some 100 horse under the conduct of Major
Evet, put in the last supply of meal and powder' (to
Chester). Archbishop Williams to Ormonde, January,
1646. A mayor of Worcester was named Evett. — Phil. ii. p.288.

EYTON, Sir Gerard, of Eyton, near Wrexham. Professor A.
H. Dodd describes the Eytons of Eyton as 'the biggest
landowners in Ruabon and Iscoed, with estates extending
to almost every corner of the lordship'. A Commissioner
of Array. Recommended to succeed John Thelwall as
High Sheriff, 1643. Father of Kenrick. He was captured
by a parliamentary raiding party under Mytton in
Eyton House, 15 February, 1644. Was in Denbigh siege.
Signed articles. Compounded for £457. Buried at
Bangor-on-Dee, 23 June, 1652. — Arch.Camb. i. p.36. / Parry. p.337. / C.C.C. 1236. / C.W.P. 1985. / Parry. p.349.

EYTON, John (Senior), of Leeswood, Flintshire. Compounded
for £172/15/0. 'Of Dring.' Signed Denbigh articles. — C.C.C. 1224.

EYTON, Captain John. Son of above. A captain in the
Royalist army. Fined £42. Might be the Captain Eyton
taken at Middlewich, 13 March, 1643. — C.C.C. 1220. / Hall. p.147. / Phil. ii. p.62.

EYTON. A 'Captain Eaton' served with Captain Richard
Gruffith in the seige of Chester. — Llanfair. Bundle 94.

EYTON, (Sir) Kenrick. Son of Sir Gerard, later a judge.
Captured with his father. Was in Denbigh siege.
Married daughter and co-heiress of Sir Peter Mutton
of Llannerch; also brother-in-law to Captain R. Davies of
Gwysaney. Probably a captain. Acted as commissioner for
Salusbury at surrender of Denbigh. Knighted 1675. — Wms. A. & M.Denb. p.234.

EYTON, Sir Robert, of Pentre Madoc, Salop. Taken prisoner
in Sir Gerard Eyton's house. A Commissioner of Array
for Salop, but not enthusiastic. A kinsman of the Bulkeleys,
he found his way to Anglesey where he was accused, by Byron,
of playing the spy. For certificate by Humphrey Mackworth
see Arch.Camb. 1875, pp.322/3. — C.C.C. 1599. / C.W.P. 1771.

EYTON, Sir Thomas, of Eyton-in-the-Wild-Moors, Salop.
Ancient family. Was in Conwy siege and is specially
mentioned in the articles. Allowed to go home for his
health he returned as promised but was prevented by the leaguer
from re-entering the castle. Was allowed to compound on articles.
'His activity and zeal' cost him £976. Later in Harlech siege. — C.C.C. 1674. / Clenennau ii. p.16.

Was buried at Wellington, 1648.

EYTON, Captain William, of Denbighshire, in Anglesey, 1648   Parry. p.388.
    Was at Wrexham in 1655 uprising.

FLOYD. The numerous officers under this name are included with
    LLOYD.

FORTESCUE, Colonel Sir Faithful. Joined Anglesey   Parry. p.388.
    insurrection, 1648.

FOULKES, Captain John, of Vaynol, Flintshire. Killed in   Arch.Camb. 1887.
    Chester in 1645.   p.43.

FOULKES, (Fulkes) Mr. Robert. Died at end of Harlech siege.   Phil. ii. p.334.

FREESTONE, Captain. Prisoner at Naseby. In Colonel R.   Peacock.
    Broughton's Foot.

FRYER, Captain Jeremy, of Lord Byron's Horse. In Chester   Clenennau 620.
    during siege. Followed Byron to Conwy, and there remained
    under Owen. Was captured when outside the walls. Exchanged
    for Major Cheadle.

FOX, Captain Gilbert. Captured at Y Dalar Hir, 1648.   Phil. ii. p.384.

FULKES, Lieutenant Llowarch, of Denbighshire. In Captain   I.O.
    Price's company of Colonel W. Price's Foot.

GARROWAY, Captain. In Sir Thomas Salusbury's Foot   Gwynn. p.64.
    (then Sir C. Lloyd) at Devizes.

GARROWAY, Ensign Will(iam), in same company   I.O. L. & W. Sir
    (brother?). Spelt Garaway.   Charles Floyd.

GAWTHOP, Ensign John, of Nottinghamshire. In Colonel   I.O.
    Whittly's Foot. Captain Cartwright's company.

GERARD, Sir William, Bart., County Lancashire. 'Lived in   C.C.C. 1720.
    the King's garrisons.' Captured at Denbigh Castle and
    compounded under Denbigh articles.

GERRARD, Colonel. Captured at Bardsey Island, 1649.   Parry. p.385.

GETHIN, Lieutenant Humphrey. In Sir John Owen's Foot.   I.O.
    (Might come from Holt.) Denbighshire.

GETHIN, Captain Robert. In Colonel Hugh Wynne's Foot.   D.M.S.

GLYNN, Captain Wm., of 'Llyar'. Caernarvonshire, marched   C.A.M. p.1102.
    to join Prince Maurice, February, 1645. Also at Y Dalar   P.R.O. S.P. 23/4 & 5.
    Hir, described as 'of Glyn Llair'.

GLYN, of Penchanog, at Y Dalar Hir.

GLYNNE, Edward of Montgomery, Captain of Dragoons.   I.O.

GLYNNE, Colonel Thomas, of Glynllifon, Caernarvonshire.
    Colonel of trained band and Commissioner of Array.
    Turned Parliamentarian in 1646, and made governor of
    Caernarfon Castle. Elder brother of Sergeant John
    Glynne, Parliamentary Chief Justice.

GOODMAN, Edward, of Nantglyn, County Denbighshire.   C.C.C. 1718.

NOTE: *Sir Richard Lloyd writing Colonel Thomas Davies refers to Llanfair MS. 32a.*
    'Cosyn Eyton' at Oxford, Christmas, 1643.

Compounded on Denbigh articles. Fined £48/10/8.

GOODMAN, Captain –. In Sir Thomas Salusbury's Foot. — D.M.S. & I.O.

GOODMAN, Charles and John (no rank given), both signed — D.M.S.
    Denbighshire maimed soldiers' appeal.

GREGORY, Lieutenant John, of Salop. In Colonel R. Ellice's Foot. — I.O.

GRIFFITH, Lieutenant-Colonel Edward, of Gain (Henllan), — C.C.C. 1964.
    near Denbigh. (1589-1671.) In Denbigh during siege and
    compounded on Denbigh articles for £159/8/9.

GRIFFITH, Captain Hugh, of Anglesey. Might be son of — N.L.W. Garreglwyd
    Dr. William Griffith, Chancellor of Bangor. Signed for — Papers 232.
    bullets &c. for Talybolion (Anglesey) Coy. 1645.
    Apparently was killed.

GRIFFITH, John, of Cefnamlwch, County Caernarfonshire. — Williams Parlt. Hist.
    (1591-1643.) An ardent Commissioner of Array and — D.W.B. p.288.
    veteran M.P. Left the House to join King at Oxford and
    died there, August, 1643, apparently of plague. Vice-Admiral
    of N.W. and H.S. Caernarvonshire, 1618.

GRIFFITH, Captain John, of Flintshire (Foot). — I.O.

GRIFFITH, Lieutenant. Captured at Montgomery. — Phil. ii. p.206.

GRIFFITH, Lieutenant-Colonel Peter, of Plas Issa, Caerwys, — R. Morris. p.195.
    County Flint. As captain he first served in Chester. — C.C.C. 1722.
    Promoted. Served through siege and was one of Byron's
    commissioners for surrender. Then went to Denbigh
    where he acted as one of Salesbury's commissioners.
    Compounded under Denbigh articles for £113.

GRIFFITH, Ensign Richard, of Flintshire, in Colonel Roger — I.O.
    Mostyn's Foot.

GRIFFITH, Major Richard, of Llanfair Isgaer, near Bangor. — C.M.S.
    Was trained-band captain before the war. Commissioned in 1639.
    Served early in Chester. Might have been the Major Richard
    Griffith at Bristol. See correspondence in Llanfair and Bryn Odol
    Papers, N.L.W. In 1648 he went for service in Ireland against
    rebels. Survived the wars.

GRIFFITH, Lieutenant Robert, of Chester, in Lord Kilmurry's — I.O.
    troop in Colonel Mark Trevor's Horse.

GRIFFITH, Captain Robert. In Sir John Owen's Foot. He — D.M.S.
    might be the 'Captaine Gruffith' sent by Sir John to — C.W.P. 2096.
    Gwydir to arrest Sir Owen Wynn.

GRIFFITH, Ro., of Henllan, at Y Dalar Hir. Might be a — P.R.O. SP. 23/4 & 5.
    Griffith of Garn.

GRIFFITH, Lieutenant Thomas, of Flintshire, in Colonel R. — I.O.
    Bulkeley's regiment. Horse. Spelt: Richard Buckly (sic).

GRIFFITH, Lieutenant William, of Caernarfon. Horse. — I.O.

GRIFFITH, Lieutenant. Stationed at Ruthin in 1645. Entry
    in Ruthin minutes reads: 'paid to leute Griffith to
    p'vide a horse to fetch powder for his Mat[s] especiall service'.

GRIFFITH, Lieutenant. Of Colonel Bunkley's Horse. — Peacock.
    Captured at Naseby.

GRUFFYDD, Dr. William, of Craiglwyd, Chancellor of Bangor.
    Anglesey Commissioner of Array. Signed Anglesey articles, 1648.
    Master of the Rolls, born 1598, died 1648.

GRUFFYTH, Captain Francis. Sir John Owen's Foot.   C.M.S. Culham.

GWYNNE, Captain John (later of the Royal Guards). In
    Salusbury's original Foot. Joined in time to fight at Brentford
    and was made ensign. Remained with regiment until it finally
    surrendered at Devizes, 23 September, 1645. Many adventures at
    home and on continent which he describes in his Military Memoirs,
    ed. by Sir Walter Scott (rare).

GWYNNE, John, Captain of Foot in the Earl of Holland's   I.O.
    regiment. Must be the same man as he refers to his share
    in Holland's abortive revolt. Of Trelydan, Montgomeryshire.

HANMER, John, son of Richard H. of Pentre Pant. In   Parry. p.385.
    Harlech siege.

HANMER, John, Esq. Captain of Foot. Commission dated   Bettisfield. MS. 112.
    8 August, 1642, for 'one company of soldiers'. Nominated   Parry. p.404.
    Knight of the Royal Oak.

HANMER, Sir John, knight and baronet, son of Sir Thomas.   Progress.
    Visited by Duke of Beaufort, 1684. Described by Dineley as
    'an excellent horse officer'.

HANMER, Sir Thomas, of Hanmer, 2nd Bart. Warrant by King at
    Nottinghamshire, 7 February, 1642-3, to raise 200 dragooners.   Bettisfield. MS. 111.
    Already commanded a troop of Horse. After   Ottley Papers.
    capture of Chirk Castle was made governor for a short while
    and then moved to Chester. In 1644, asked for leave
    to go overseas. See C.C.C. p.943.

HANMER, William, of Fenns, Esq. Had his house raided.   C.C.C. 1040.
    Compounded for £1,370. Asked leave to go with his   Parry. p.404.
    cousin, Sir Thomas, overseas. Nominated Knight of the Royal Oak.

HASSAL, Captain –. Mentioned in the Caernarfon articles.   Phil. ii. p.311.

HAUGHTLEY, Charles. Signed Aberystwyth articles.   Phil. ii. p.305.

HERBERT, Honourable Richard, Colonel (later 2nd Lord   Williams Parl.Hist.
    Herbert of Cherbury). M.P. Montgomeryshire, until   D.W.B.
    disabled. Commissioner of Array for Salop. Raised 1,200   C.C.C. 1682.
    foot soldiers and a troop of Horse. Served in campaign
    against Scots. Performed 'prodigies of valour' at Newburn,
    according to Professor A. H. Dodd. Took his troop to Ireland,
    1642. Had Foot regiment at Culham Camp, May, 1643. Was
    successively governor of Bridgnorth, Ludlow, Aberystwyth and
    Newport, Monmouthshire. Succeeded father in 1648, and died
    1655. He compounded for £1,000.

HERBERT, Mr. Morgan, in Sir John Owen's revolt, 1648.   Parry. p.390.

HERBERT, Captain Edward, his son.   Ibid.

HIDE, William, of Cheshire, gentleman volunteer. Captured at Y Dalar Hir.

HILL, Ensign John, of Denbighshire. Ensign to Captain Pine in Sir Thomas Lunsford's regiment. Foot. — I.O.

HOLLAND, Lieutenant-Colonel Edward, of Conwy. (No local record.) — Wms. Records of Denbigh. p.31n.

HOLLAND, Ensign. An officer who served 'in forraine parts.' — Chirk MS. 7442.

HOLLAND, Owen. Anglesey Commissioner of Array, who took little active part.

HOOKES, Lieutenant-Colonel Hugh, of Conwy. Was a lieutenant in 1632, according to wife's tablet in Conwy church. Captain in Sir John Owen's Foot. Promoted. At siege of Bristol. Took charge in Merionethshire, 1645. Fought in Anglesey revolt. Survived and signed maimed soldiers' petition. His niece, Jane Hookes, married a Captain Pettris. — Register. p.367. Parry. p.388. Caern.Rec.Off. Conwy Register. Culham.

HOOKES, Captain Hugh. Nephew of Colonel Hugh Hookes. Was killed in Ireland. — Pedigrees. p.293.

HOOKE(S), Lieutenant Nicholas [of Conwy?] captured at Oswestry. — Phil. ii. p.175.

HOOKES, Captain Robert. In Colonel Sir J. Owen's Foot.

HOOKES, William, of Conwy. Captain of Caernarvonshire Light Horse, 1640. Served Archbishop J. Williams when Bishop of Lincoln and later acted as his executor. A Commissioner of Array. Sided with Sir John Owen, and remained loyal when Archbishop forsook royal cause. In Conwy siege, then went to Harlech. Was Alderman of Conwy. — Llanfair. Bundle 94. C.W.P. 1764. Arch.Camb. 1875. p.204. and 317.

HOSYER, Captain George. In Colonel R. Ellice's Foot. — I.O.

HUES, Charles. Captured at Winnington Bridge, 1659. — Merc. Politicus.

HUGHES, Lieutenant-Colonel. At Y Dalar Hir fight, 1648. — Parry. p.391.

HUGHES, Major Charles. — D.M.S.

HUGHES, Major –. Mentioned in Denbigh maimed soldiers' mize. — D.M.S.

HUGHES, Lieutenant Edward. Low Country Soldier. Killed. In Sir Thomas Salusbury's Foot. — D.M.S.

HUGHES, Humphrey, of Merioneth. Commissioner of Array. Fought at Y Dalar Hir. Of 'Querckle' (Gwerclas). Compounded for £333/1/9, at one-sixth. — C.C.C. 57. P.R.O. S.P. 23/4 & 5.

HUGHES, Cornet John, of Flintshire. In Sir Arthur Slingsby's regiment. Horse. — I.O.

HUGHES, Captain John, of Bronbuckle. In Booth Revolt. — P.R.O. S.P. 25/59, 36/37.

HUGHES, Captain, of Brombagle (sic), of Keven Llanvair. In attempt to rescue Sir J. Owen from Denbigh Castle. — P.R.O. S.P. 23/4, 4/5.

HUGHES, Major John. In Colonel R. Gerard's regiment. Queen's Life Guard. L. & W. At Oxford, 1646. Foot. — I.O.

Dugdale's Diary.

HUGHES, Captain John. Order of 20 July, 1648: 'That
    Captain John Hughes, now in the Gatehouse, be discharged'.
    C.S.P.D. 1648.
    p.201.

HUGHES, Captain Robert of Denbigh. In Anglesey revolt, 1648.   Parry. p.388.

HUGHES, Ensign Robert. In General Lord Wharton's
    regiment, Irish expedition, 1641-2.
    B.M. 109. g.13.
    p.208.

HUGHES, Captain –. Captured at Hunstett, Yorkshire, in 1644.
    Fairfax Corr. Vol. I.
    p.94.

HUGHES, Lieutenant Robert, in Captain W. Broughton's
    company, of Sir Richard Lloyd's dragoons. Denbighshire.
    I.O.

HUGHES, Captain Robert, Denbighshire, in Sir William
    Russell's Foot.
    I.O.

HUGHES, Thomas of Potfari. Captured after Y Dalar Hir.   P.R.O. SP. 23/4 & 5.

HUGHES, Thomas. In 1643, sued by William Salusbury,
    gentleman, for £200. Stayed on judge's order upon
    Governor of Worcester's certificate that defendant was a
    soldier at Worcester.
    Arch.Camb. 1888.
    John Lloyd's note-
    book.

HUMPHRYES, Ensign Gabriel, of Merioneth. In Sir John
    Owen's Foot. In Captain Humphryes' company.
    I.O.

HUMPHREYS, Captain. In Sir John Owen's Foot.

HUMPHREYS, Captain. In Sir Thomas Salusbury's Foot.   Culham.

HUMPHREYS, Richard, of Hendre, Penrhyndeudraeth,
    Merioneth. Father of Dr. Humphrey Humphreys,
    Bishop of Bangor and later of Hereford. He was a
    Royalist Officer.
    D.W.B.

HUMPHREYS, Quartermaster Richard Humphreys, of
    Merioneth, in Lord Gerard's regiment. Horse.
    I.O.

HUMPHREYS, Captain Theodore. In Colonel [James]
    Usher's Dragoon's. L. & W.
    I.O.

HUNCKES, Sir Fulke. Landed from Ireland, November,
    1643, with first English-Irish contingent. At Middlewich
    victory, 9 January, 1644. Governor of Shrewsbury. For
    a short time governor of Wrexham. Was connected by
    marriage with Reverend Richard Baxter.
    Phil. ii. p.98.
    Ibid. p.117.
    Ibid. p.194.

JEFFREYS, Captain Edward. In Sir J. Owen's Foot. Second
    son of John Jeffreys of Acton, Wrexham. Survived war
    and dwelt at Broughton. Died 1680.
    D.M.S.
    Palmer.

JEEFREYS, John, of Wrexham. Captured near Sir Gerard
    Eyton's house by Colonel Mytton, 1643. Fought for
    Charles I. Father of Judge Jeffreys.
    Parry. p.349.
    D.W.B.

JENKINS, Captain, in Sir John Owen's Foot.   D.M.S.

JOHNSON, Ensign Thomas, in Captain Freestone's company
    of Colonel Robert Broughton's Foot. L. & W.
    I.O.

JOHNES, Captain. Captured at Holt Bridge, November, 1643.   Hall. p.157.

JONES, Captain Daniel, of Anglesey. In Sir John Owen's   C.M.S. and I.O.

    Foot. Signed maimed soldiers' application.

JONES, Lieutenant Edward, of Wrexham. In 1659 revolt.   P.R.O. SP. 25/59.
     pp.36/7.

JONES, Cornet Edward, Montgomeryshire. In Colonel James   I.O.
     Long's Horse.

JONES, Lieutenant Evan, Denbighshire, lieutenant to   I.O.
     Lieutenant-Colonel William Walton in Lord Byron's Horse.

JONES, Captain-Ensign Francis. In Irish expedition, 12 June,   B.M. 109. g.13.
     1642. Might be Parliamentarian.   p.233.

JONES, Captain Hugh, of Sir Thomas Salusbury's Foot.   Gwynne.
     Killed at Devizes, when serving under Sir Charles Lloyd.

JONES, Henry. Anglesey negotiating commissioner, 1648.   Parry. p.387.

JONES, Humffrey, of Penrhyn (near Bangor), Archbishop   C.W.P. 1882.
     Williams home. J.P. and Commissioner of Array. King's   Parry. p.386.
     receiver. Helped to raise 50 men in August, 1645. House   Arch.Camb. 1875.
     raided. Jones invited soldiers to cellar to drink while   p.312.
     neighbours fetched Royalists and captured thirty-six of   C.C.C. 3055.
     Colonel J. Jones men.

JONES, Lieutenant Ithel, of Flintshire. In Colonel R. Mostyn's   I.O.
     Foot. Captain James Llewellyn's company. Spelt 'Ithell'.

JONES, John, gentleman. Caernarvonshire Commissioner of   Clenennau 535.
     Array.

JONES, John (Senior), of Halkyn. Compounded for £156 on   C.C.C. 1723.
     Denbigh articles for delinquency in arms. Might be J.J.   C.W.P. 2047.
     of 'Llys'.

JONES, John, gentleman. Captured at Shrewsbury.

JONES, 'Mr. Jones, of Caus. Commissioner of Flint, now a   Symonds Diary.
     prisoner in Chester Castle' (1645). (Might Caus be Llys?)   p.276

JONES, Lieutenant Mathew, 'of Oxford', in Sir Thomas   I.O.
     Salusbury's Foot.

JONES, Lieutenant Nathaniel. Captured at Ormskirk,   Cheetham Soc.
     20 August, 1644. Probably of Hendwr, Merionethshire.   Tracts, 1844.
     A Nathaniel Jones was High Sheriff in 1672.   p.204.

JONES, Quartermaster Owen, taken prisoner at Duddleston,   Phil. ii. p.172.
     19 June, 1644.

JONES, Major Richard, in Sir Evan Lloyd's Foot. Denbigh-   I.O.
     shire.

JONES, Major Richard, in Sir John Owen's Foot.   D.M.S.

JONES, Lieutenant Richard, Montgomeryshire. Lieutenant to   I.O.
     Captain John Pierce in regiment of Herbert, Lord Cherbury. Foot.

JONES, Ensign Robert, Denbighshire. In Colonel William   I.O.
     Salesbury's Foot.

JONES, Ensign Robert, Montgomeryshire. In Sir Charles
    Floyd's Foot, ensign to Captain Hugh Jones.   I.O.

JONES, Richard. Colonel's captain. Irish expedition, June,   B.M. 109. g.13.
    1642. (Royalist?)   p.209

JONES, Lieutenant Thomas, Flintshire. In Sir Richard   I.O.
    Lloyd's Horse.

JONES, Captain. Captured at Middlewich, March, 1643;   Phil. ii. p.62.
    same as Captain Johnes, in Colonel R. Ellice's Foot,   Hall. p.147.
    captured at Middlewich.

JONES, (Johnes). Captured at Holt Bridge, November, 1643.   Hall. p.157.

JONES, Lieutenant-Colonel. Killed at Bridgewater, Somerset.   B.M. Royal Martyrs.
                                                  109.
                                                  g.13. p.233.

JONES, Colonel. Archbishop Williams to Digby: 'Coronel   Phil. ii. p.243.
    Jones can tell you howe I sett him out from this countye   Black's Oxford
    to drive the rebels out of Denbighshyre'. He might be   Docquets.
    Sheriff Robert Jones who was commissioned with Sir Win.   p.222.
    Williams, Bart., to raise Horse and Foot, June, 1644.

KAY, Cornet Dennis, of Lancaster. In Colonel Roger Whitley's Horse.   I.O.

KILMURRY, Lord. Captain in Colonel Mark Trevor's   I.O.
    Horse. Viscount Kilmorey was captured at Winnington Bridge.   Chirk Cast.
                                                    Accounts.

KILVERT, Cornet Robert, of Mortlake, Surrey. In Sir   Ottley Papers, clxix
    Thomas Corbett's troop in Colonel Trevor's Horse.   & C.C.C. 2111.

KYNASTON, Captain James, at Y Dalar Hir, 1648. (Of Plas   Parry. p.390-1.
    Kynaston, near Wrexham?).

KYNASTON, Captain –. Killed near Drayton, May, 1643.   Hall. p.150.

KYNASTON, Lieutenant Thomas, of Salop. Carter's deputy   Penrhos Papers. Vol.
    governor at Conwy Castle, May, 1655, during plot.   v. 202.
    Apparently turned Royalist with Carter in 1660.

LANGFORD, Quartermaster John, Montgomeryshire. In   I.O. and Arch.Camb.
    Colonel Roger Whitley's Horse.   1906.
                                                      p.166.

LEDSAM, Lieutenant Edward, of Denbighshire (a Holt   I.O.
    family). In Sir Richard Lloyd's dragoons.

LEE, Colonel. Was with Sir John Owen in 1648 revolt.   Parry. p.390.

LEWIS, Captain Anthony, Burton Hall. Buried Gresford,   Powys Fadog, 3.
    1643.   p.229.

LEWIS, Ensign David. Lieutenant-Colonel Robert Wynne's   I.O.
    company of Colonel Hugh Wynne's Foot. Denbighshire.

LEWIS, Lieutenant David, of Denbighshire. In Captain   I.O. and D.M.S.
    Dolben's company of Colonel R. Ellice's Foot.

LEWIS, Lieutenant Edward, in Captain Walter Bushell's   I.O.
    troop of Colonel Roger Whitley's Horse. L. & W.

LEWIS, Howell, gentleman. Signed Anglesey articles, 1648.   Phil. ii. p.401.

LEWIS, Major Richard. Under Sir Nicholas Kemys, in South Wales.	I.O.
LEWIS, Lieutenant Richard, Caernarvonshire. In Sir John Owen's Foot.	I.O.
LEWIS, Lieutenant. Captured at Montgomery, 1644.	Phil. ii. p.207.
LEWIS, Ensign. Captured Nantwich, January, 1644.	Hall. p.170.
LILL, Major. In Colonel R. Broughton's Foot.	I.O.
LILE or LISLE, Captain, in Colonel R. Broughton's Foot. Captured at Naseby. (Presumably all one man called Lisle.)	Peacock.
LITLE, Colonel. Byron to Sir John Owen in Conwy Castle: 'By case you have part of Litles men all ready I shall send the rest to you & likewise some horse.' (Writing indistinct; might be 'Littes' or 'Lisle'; not identified.)	Clenennau 611.
LLEWELLIN, Captain James. In Colonel R. Mostyn's Foot.	I.O.
LLONG, Captain Denys, of Mold. In Booth revolt, 1659. (Llong is on outskirts of Mold.)	P.R.O. SP. 25/29. fos. 36/7.
LLOYD, Major Bevis, of Llanrhaeadr, near Denbigh. As a captain he was captured by Waller at Alton, December, 1643, when under Colonel R. Bolle in Lord Paget's regiment. Captured in Booth revolt, 1659. Nominated Knight of the Royal Oak.	D.M.S. Harl. 6802/94. P.R.O. SP. 25/29, 36/37. Parry. p.404.

NOTE: *Brigadier Young writes of Major Bevis Lloyd: "He was a Captain in Bolle's regiment at Culham, 23 May, 1643, and was captured at Alton. Was still a prisoner of war on 15 April, 1644 (Harl. 6802 / 94) and still a Captain. Yet under Bolles, Richard–who was killed at Alton, and whose regiment (what remained of it) became George Liles'–we find–[L. & W.] Heron, Will., Lieut. to M. Bevis Floyd. Who was he Major to? I don't doubt he was exchanged, or perhaps escaped, sometime in 1644. There is no evidence that he was Major to Lisle, whose Major Fowler, was a prisoner of war at Naseby. I am tempted to think that Bevis Lloyd returned to N. Wales and became Major of some regiment there. Owen or Ellice might well have welcomed an experienced officer."*

LLOYD, Colonel Sir Charles, son of soldier-of-fortune Captain Brochwell Lloyd, of Moelygarth, Montgomeryshire. In Dutch pay then under Earl of Northumberland, 1640. Fortified Berwick. Quartermaster-General and Engineer-General to royal army. In 1643, took over Foot from Sir Thomas Salusbury. Knighted at Oxford. Was at Lostwithiel. Fortified Farringdon and Devizes. Was governor of Devizes, which he surrendered to Cromwell, 23 September, 1645. Symonds mentioned that in October, sixty of Sir Charles Lloyd's men reached Bridgnorth from Devizes. Others went to Farringdon, including John Gwynn. Died 1661.	D.N.B. Diary. p.252. Buchan. p.222.
FLOYD, Quartermaster Charles, of Montgomeryshire. In Sir Robert Howard's regiment. Dragoons.	I.O.
LLOYD, David, of Wickwar (i.e. Wigfair), County Denbigh, 'bore arms in the King's army at the siege of Nantwich'. Lent the King £1,000.	C.A.M. p.1091.

LLOYD, Major David. Former Mayor of Beaumaris. Signed   Phil. ii. p.312.
    Beaumaris articles. Suspected by Byron of being a spy.   C.W.P. 1768.

FLOYD, Captain David. In Sir Richard Lloyd's Dragoons.   I.O.
    Merioneth.

FLOYD, Lieutenant David, Merioneth. In Captain Hum-   I.O.
    phrey's company of Sir J. Owen's Foot.

LLOYD, Colonel Edward, of Llanvorda. Made governor of   C.C.C. 2030.
    Oswestry by Capell. Nearly kidnapped by Mytton through
    an invitation to dine. Shipman replaced him as being less
    convivial. An ardent royalist, Lloyd sacrificed his own property
    to prevent giving cover to enemies. Raised company of
    dragoons at his own cost. Compounded for f300.

LLOYD, Sir Edward, of Berthlwyd, Montgomeryshire.   C.C.C. 1724.
    Commissioner of Array. He married Ursula, sister of Sir   Parry. p.404.
    Thomas Salusbury. Compounded for £520. Nominated
    Knight of the Royal Oak.

FLOYD, Captain Edward. In Sir Richard Lloyd's Dragoons.   I.O.

FLOYD, Captain Edward, Salop. In Sir J. Owen's Foot. Might   I.O.
    be a son of Colonel Richard Lloyd, Llwyn y Maen.   Arch.Camb. 1876.
                           p.117.

LLOYD, Captain Edward. Foot. Probably in Sir J. Owen's   D.M.S.
    regiment.

FLOYD, Captain Edward. In Lord Capell's regiment. Horse.   I.O.

LLOYD, Sir Godfrey. Younger brother of Sir Charles. He   D.W.B.
    also trained as engineer under the Dutch. Conspired when
    in exile and was knighted by Charles II in Brussels.

FLOYD, Captain Edward, of Flintshire. Foot. In Colonel   I.O.
    Thomas Davies' regiment.

LLOYD, Captain Edward. Possibly the same man.   D.M.S.

LLOYD, Ellis. Brother-in-law of Major Richard Griffith,   Studies in Stuart
    Llanfair Isgaer. 'Ellis,' writes Professor Dodd, 'as a very   Wales. p.101.
    young man, left his studies at Barnard's Inn to serve
    under Hopton in the west.'

LLOYD, Lieutenant Eubule. Colonel William Wynne's Foot.
    Might also have served under Colonel Charles Gerard.

LLOYD, Sir Evan, of Bodidris, County Denbighshire. High   D.M.S.
    Sheriff Denbighshire, 1643-5. Raised regiment of Foot, and   C.C.C. 1272.
    fought in England. Created Bart., May 1645. Fined   Vol. ii. p.196.
    £1,000. Pennant states, 'a considerable sum was ordered   Pedigrees.
    for his apprehension'. According to Powys Fadog, he was   D.W.B.
    killed in London after the war. Son also called 'Sir Evan'.*

LLOYD, Edward, Herseth, gentleman. 'Was at surrender   C.C.C. 1718.
    of Denbigh' and was fined under articles £64.

FLOYD, Humphrey. Captain of Foot. Flintshire.   I.O.

FLOYD, Captain Hugh of Merioneth. Captain of Horse in   I.O.
    Sir John Girlington's regiment.

---

*   *Sir Evan Lloyd's mother was Margaret, daughter of Sir Bevis Thelwall. Might Major Bevis Lloyd be Sir Evan's son? Or his brother?*

FLOYD, Cornet Hugh, of Merioneth. In Captain Edward   I.O.
     Lloyd's troop of Sir Richard Lloyd's Dragoons.

LLOYD, Captain Harry, of Fox Hall, near Denbigh. Probably   C.M.S.
     in Trevor's Horse. Might be the Captain Lloyd killed at
     Montgomery 'in a tyrranous manner'.

LLOYD, Captain Henry, of Penhwnllys. Captain of Tin-   A.A.S.T. 1915.
     daethwy trained-band. At battle of Beaumaris he locked   p.51.
     his men in the church and ran away, being henceforth   Parry. p.389.
     known as 'Captain Church'.

LLOYD, Captain Harry, of Hafodunos, County Denbighshire.   D.M.S.
     In Colonel Hugh Wynne's Foot. (This might be the Henry
     Lloyd of Chester siege.) MS. damaged.

LLOYD, Henry. Signed in Chester with Hugh Wynne,   R. Morris. p.131.
     Robert Wynne &c.

LLOYD, Captain Henry Lloyd. In Sir Thomas Salusbury's   D.M.S.
     Foot.

LLOYD, Cornet (Ancient) Hugh. Captured at Oswestry,   Phil. ii. p.174.
     1644.

LLOYD, Humphrey, gentleman, of Lower Berse, Wrexham.   P.R.O. SP. 23/208.
     In Holt Castle during siege and signed articles of   Palmer.
     surrender. Said to be cousin of Colonel R. Ellice. Epitaph   Chirk Castle MS. i.
     in Wrexham Church says he was one of the Masters in   p.247.
     Chancery. Churchwarden, 1661-2. Became for a while   Crosse 1107.
     Myddelton's steward for Chirk. Might be a Commissioner
     of Array.

LLOYD, Captain John. In charge of company in Ruthin   Minutes.
     castle in 1645.

LLOYD, John, of Plas Llanynys. Portrait in buff coat at   N.M.W. Portraits in
     Wigfair. (1620-1663). Mentioned by J. Steegman.   Welsh Houses.

LLOYD, Captain John. In Colonel J. Robinson's Foot.   D.M.S.

LLOYD, Captain John. In Colonel Hugh Wynne's Foot in   D.M.S.
     Chester.

FLOYD, Captain John of Denbigh in Lord Hopton's   I.O.
     regiment. Horse.

FLOYD, Ensign John, of Denbighshirc. In Colonel William   I.O.
     Salesbury's Foot.

LLOYD, Captain John, of Plas Madoc, Ruabon. A captain in the   Powys Fadog. ii.
     royal army in the regiment commanded by Colonel   p.196.
     Robert Ellis of Y Groes Newydd. Captured at Middle-   Parry. p.404.
     wich, 1643. Was in attempt to relieve Beeston Castle, 1645.
     Was living in 1667 'but was killed in London with Sir Evan
     Lloyd of Bodidris'. Nominated Knight of the Royal Oak.

FLOYD, Ensign John, of Merioneth. In Captain John Pugh's   I.O.
     company of Sir J. Owen's Foot.

FLOYD, Ensign Lewis. Ensign to Captain Blodwell in Lord   I.O.
     Gerard's regiment. Merioneth.

LLOYD, Captain Lewis, of Maes-y-Porth. Captain of Menai   A.A.S.T. 1915. p.51.

trained band.

LLOYD, Lewis, 'of Rhiwaedog', Esq., Merioneth. A
    prisoner in Chester Castle with Sir John Owen, 1651.
                          Parry, p.399.

FLOYD or LLOYD, Cornet Meredith, of Llanfair Caereinion,   I.O.
    Montgomeryshire. Served in Lord Grandison's Horse and   Phil. i. p.196.
    was probably at Edgehill. The regiment was destroyed at   Phil. ii. p.334.
    Winchester, December, 1642. Floyd was a cornet in the
    troop of 'Major Willy'(i.e. Sir Richard Willis) who later
    became a colonel of Horse. Floyd doubtless followed Willis
    to Shropshire but may have escaped when Willis was captured
    (with Sir Nicholas Byron) at Ellesmere by Mytton, 12 January,
    1644. Later he joined Colonel William Owen in Harlech
    Castle and survived the siege of 1646-7.

LLOYD, Captain Mathias. Taken at Y Dalar Hir, 1648.

LLOYD, Captain Nanney, of The Rofft, Wrexham. In   D.M.S.
    Colonel Sir Thomas Salusbury's Foot (original). In Booth   P.R.O. SP. 25/59,
    revolt 1659. Buried Wrexham, 1670. Described as Nanny   36/7.
    Floyd in Culham list.

FLOYD, Cornet Peter, of Denbighshire. In Colonel Trevor's   I.O.
    Horse.

LLOYD, Pierce. Signed Anglesey articles, 1648.   Parry. p.389.

FLOYD, Lieutenant Richard. In Captain Richard Vaughan's   C.M.S. and I.O.
    company of Col. Lord Gerard's Foot. Of Denbighshire.

LLOYD, Major Richard. In Sir Charles Lloyd's Foot at 2nd   Gwynn's Memoirs.
    Newbury: 'my worthy friend Major Richard Lloyd'.   p.42.

LLOYD, Colonel Richard, of Llwyn-y-Maen, Salop, 'delin-   Parry. p.391.
    quent in both wars'. Joined Sir John Owen. Was at   C.C.C. 1500 and
    Dolgellau, May, 1648. Captured at Y Dalar Hir, 1648,   2030
    and at Chirk, 1659. Had regiment of dragoons. Fined
    £480. Died 1663.

LLOYD, Corp. [sic] Richard. Sir John Owen's senior   Clenennau 16.
    commissioner negotiating the surrender of Conwy Castle,
    November, 1646.

LLOYD, Colonel Sir Richard, of Esclus. Attorney General   D.M.S.
    for N. Wales. Denbighshire Commissioner of Array.   Ottley Papers.
    Delivered loyal protestation to King at York, August,   R. Morris. p.110.
    1642. Knighted by Charles, October, 1642, at Wrexham.   C.C.C. 2030.
    Raised regiments of Horse and Dragoons. Went to Oxford,
    spring 1643. Governor of Holt Castle, 1645. Surrendered 13
    January, 1647. Not allowed to compound. Exiled and was
    'excepted from pardon'. Rewarded with Judgeship.
    Epitaph in Wrexham Church. Daughter Mary married Sir Henry
    Conwy, Bart, Bodrhyddan.

LLOYD, Lieutenant Richard. In Captain Windebanke's   D.M.S.
    company in Colonel William Wynne's Foot.

FLOYD, Ensign Robert, of Denbighshire, to Captain Somes,   I.O.
    in Lord Gerard's regiment. Foot.

LLOYD, Robert, gentleman, of Chirk. In Booth revolt, 1659.

LLOYD, Lieutenant Thomas. Captured at Y Dalar Hir.   Phil. ii. p.384.

LLOYD, Thomas. Of Llanwnda. Was at Y Dalar Hir.   P.R.O. SP. 23/4 & 5.

LLOYD, Captain Thomas, Salop. In Colonel R. Villiers' Foot.   D.M.S.

LLOYD, Captain Thomas, of Plas Engian, County Denbigh.   D.M.S.

LLOYD, Thomas, of Plas Engion, County Denbighshire.   Crosse 377.
    Died 19 April, 1648.

FLOYD, Captain Thomas. In Sir John Owen's Foot. Signed   Clenennau. ii. 16.
    Conwy articles as commissioner. Salop.   I.O.

LLOYD, Tristram, of Hanmer, 'a delinquent in arms', was   C.C.C. 1719 and
    killed during Denbigh siege. Son Thomas compounded   2845.
    for his father's estate.

LLOYD, Captain William, of 'Llan y ynene' (Llanynys). In   P.R.O. SP. 25/59.
    Booth revolt, 1659.   f.36/7.

LLOYD, Lieutenant-Colonel William, of Plashen. In Colonel   C.C.C. 1828.
    Thomas Glynne's Foot. Turned Parliamentarian. Mortally
    wounded in clash with Sir J. Owen's before Y Dalar Hir.

FLOYD, Major. Foot. Might be Major Mathias Floyd, Salop,   I.O.
    who served under Sir Aubyn Thomas.

LLOYD, Captain. In Sir John Owen's Foot.   C.M.S.

LLOYD, Captain. Taken at Middlewich. (Thomas of
    Ruabon or possibly Edward.)

LLOYD, Captain. In Trevor's Horse. Was served by Sir J.   C.W.P. 1746.
    Owen with a warrant. (Archbishop Williams to Owen
    Wynn.) Might be Edward.

LLOYD, Captain. 'One Captain Lloyd' taken by Twisleton   Parry. p.390.
    at Llwyn-gwril, 1648.

FLOYD, Captain. In Ellice's Foot.   I.O.

FLOYD, Lieutenant. Captured at Montgomery, 1644.   Phil. ii. p.207.

FLOYD, Captain. Captured at Montgomery, 1644.   Ibid.

LLOYD, Lieutenant. Fought at Tilston Heath (near   C.M.S.
    Tarporley) and Middlewich.

LOVE, Captain Thomas of Flintshire. Foot.   I.O.

MADOCKS, Edward (no rank) of Bodfari. Slain at Edgehill.   Pedigrees. p.315.

MADDOCKS, John, gentleman, of Wrexham. Assisted the   C.C.C. 1220.
    King. Fined £96.

MADRIN, Captain. Slain at Y Dalar Hir.   Dispatch.

MADRYN, Captain John. Captured at Oswestry.   Phil. ii. p.176

MADRYN, Colonel Thomas, of Madryn, Caernarvonshire.   Clenennau 61.
    High Sheriff, and a Commissioner of Array when war   C.W.P. 1724.
    broke out. Probably a Royalist officer before he became a   Pedigrees. p.242.
    Parliamentarian. Colonel in 1646. Admitted to St John's
    College, Cantab, 1631, aged 18. His mother, Sydney, daughter
    of Robert Wynne of Conwy, builder of Plas Mawr. He had a
    younger brother John.

MALLERY, Captain Edward, of Cambridge. In Colonel   I.O.
    Robert Broughton's Foot.

MANLEY, Major Francis, of Manley House, Erbistock,   Phil. ii. p.183.
    County Denbighshire. Captain in Colonel William   Ruthin Council
    Wynne's original Foot. Wounded at Wem, 1643; Byron   Book.
    made him major and governor of Bangor-on-Dee; captured
    near Shrewsbury by Earl of Denbigh, July, 1644. Home taken by   C.C.C. 1675.
    Brereton, April, 1645. Helped to defend Denbigh, and acted as a
    negotiating commissioner for Salesbury. Made peace with
    Parliament in 1655. After Restoration was knighted and made a
    judge. Myddelton's steward of Chirk for a while. Fined £75 on
    Denbigh articles. Younger brother Major John a prominent
    Parliamentarian.

MANLY, Captain Roger, Denbighshire. In Lord Byron's Foot.   I.O.

MARTIN, James, Captain. Selected by Archbishop Williams to bear   Hacket.
    his remonstrance to the King.

MARTYN, Captain. Chosen by Lord Bulkeley as messenger   C.W.P. 1910.
    to negotiate with Prince Charles about 1648 revolt, but
    was distrusted.

MASON, Lieutenant Francis. Naval. In Harlech garrison.   Phil. ii. p.334.
    Also involved in fracas in Llannor Churchyard.   Caern. Record
    Served in the frigate *Michell*.   Office.

MATHEWS, Captain Humphrey. Irish expedition, June, 1642.   B.M. 109. g.13.
    p.209.

MATHEWS, Lieutenant John, of Flintshire. In Captain   I.O.
    Ravenscroft's troop. Roger Whittly's (sic) Horse.

MATTHEWS, Captain of Mold. In Booth revolt.   P.R.O. SP. 25/29,
    ('Mathewes')   36/37.

MATTHEWS, Ensign. Had service 'in forraine parts'.   Chirk Castle. MS.

MATTHEWS, Thomas (lieutenant). In Sir J. Owen's Foot.   I.O.
    Denbigh. Captain Brunker's company.

MATTHEWS, Lieutenant Richard, Montgomeryshire. In Sir   I.O.
    J. Owen's Foot.

MAURICE, Major John. In Colonel R. Ellice's Foot.   D.M.S.

MAURICE, Lieutenant-Colonel John. In Colonel R. Ellice's   D.M.S.
    Foot.

MAURICE, Captain William, Treborth Ucha. Buried in   Hyde Hall. A
    Bangor Cathedral, 1668. Married Jane Jones, Castellmarch.   Description
    of Caerns.
    p.157.

MENNES, Sir John. Captain of the *Victory*. Sent by Rupert   Phil. ii. pp. 136/7;
    in 1644, to be governor of North Wales. Not popular.   168.
    Clashed with Archbishop Williams. Governor of Beau-   D.N.B.
    maris, 1644.

MEIRICKE. Commissary with Lord Byron's Horse at Ruthin,   Ruthin Council
    1645.   Book.

MERRICK, Captain. In Sir J. Owen's Foot.   I.O.

MEYRICK, Captain John, of Trefri, Anglesey. Buried 1677.   Pedigrees.

MEYRICK, Edmund, of Ucheldre. Merionethshire Com-   Clenennau 538.
    missioner of Array. Imprisoned in Chester Castle with   Parry. p.399.

Sir J. Owen, 1651.

MIDDLETON, Richard, of Llansilin, son of Foulk Middleton. Crosse, 1112.
  A Commissioner of Array for County Denbighshire; H.S. Parry. p.404.
  1650. Nominated Knight of the Royal Oak.

MIDDLETON, Captain Hugh, of Flintshire. Foot. I.O.

MILTON, Quartermaster Randolph, of Flintshire. Horse. I.O.

MOLYNEAUX, Cornet Adam. A commissioner for Sir P.R.O. SP. 23/208.
  Richard Lloyd at surrender of Holt Castle, January, 1647.

MORGAN, Captain Edward, son of Robert Morgan, Esq., Newcome. p.75.
  of Golden Grove (Gwlgre), Flintshire. Captured near
  Denbigh, April, 1646. Horse. Killed trying to prevent rout
  at Winnington Bridge, Northwich, 1659. Son's epitaph in Stoke
  Church, Cheshire. Edward's first wife was a sister of Colonel
  Roger Whitley.

MORGAN, Ensign. Captured at Nantwich, January, 1644. Hall. p.170.

MORGAN, Captain –. Participated in relief of Beeston Phil. ii. p.227.
  Castle, 18 January, 1645, and was taken prisoner.

MORGAN, Captain John, Carmarthen. In Colonel Robert I.O.
  Broughton's Foot.

MORGAN, Captain John. In Anglesey revolt, 1648. Parry. p.388.
  Merioneth.

MORGANS, Captain John Morgans. In Harlech garrison Clenennau 542 and
  under Colonel William Owen. H.S. Merioneth, 1644.   Warburton.

MORGAN, Captain John, Merioneth. In Colonel R. Ellice's I.O.
  Foot.

MORGAN, Captain John Morgans, of Gelli Iorwerth, in the Arch.Camb. Vol. i.
  parish of Trawsfynydd.   p.260.

MORGAN, Ensign Lewis. Captured at Oswestry. Phil. ii. pp.175/6.

MORGAN, Lieutenant Ellis, Montgomeryshire. Lieutenant to I.O.
  Captain Cotterell in Lord Gerard's regiment. Foot.

MORGAN, Captain. Captured at Montgomery. Phil. ii. p.207.

MORGAN, Lieutenant. Captured at Montgomery. Ibid.

MORGAN, Major. In Colonel R. Ellice's Foot. I.O. and D.M.S.

MORGAN, Captain William, of Golden Grove. Younger brother
  of Robert, and uncle of Captain Edward Morgan. In Chester
  siege. Morgan's Mount is probably named after them.

MORRIS, Major. Captured at Rowton Heath, 1645. Morris. p.116.

MORRIS, Lieutenant Griffith, of Caernarfon. Foot. I.O.

MORRIS, Lieutenant Henry. Lieutenant to Lieutenant- I.O.
  Colonel Morgan. London and Westminster at time of
  application. In Colonel William Pretty's Foot.

MORRIS, Captain Hugh. From Denbigh garrison. Horse. Newcome. p.75.
  Captured April, 1646.

MORRIS, Hugh of Weston, Salop. Compounded under C.C.C. 1720.
  Denbigh articles for £40. 6. 8d.

*MORRIS, Major Theodore. In Sir Fulk Hunks' Foot. I.O.

---

* *His Ensign, Lewis Roberts, was from Montgomeryshire, but there is no other evidence that he was from N. Wales.*

MORRIS, Thomas. In list of additional compounders.   C.C.C. Vol. i. pp.57/8.

MORRIS, Captain Thomas. Was made free burgess of   Borough Minutes.
    Denbigh with Whitley and Rogers in 1644.

MORRIS, Captain –. In Colonel W. Wynne's regiment. Also   Crosse, 1118.
    mentioned in Commissioner of Array's report.

MORRIS, Captain. Captured at Middlewich, 13 March, 1643.   Phil. ii. p.62.
    Hall. p.147.

MORRIS, Ensign. Captured at Middlewich.   Ibid.

MORRIS, Major. Wounded at Dodleston, May, 1645. Was he   Morris. p.84
    John Maurice?

MORRIS, Captain William. Foot. Caernarvonshire.   I.O.

MORRIS, Lieutenant-Colonel. Had drum beaten for   C.A.M. p.1094.
    volunteers in 1648. (Probably of Ellice's regiment. See 'Maurice'.)

MORRIS, Colonel John. Governor of Pontefract. One of   Gardiner, iv. p.146.
    Langdale's officers who siezed castle, 1648. Tried 1649,   B.M. Royal Martyrs.
    and executed.   109. g.13. p.233.

MOSTYN, Sir Edward. Nominated Knight of the Royal Oak.   Parry. p.404.

MOSTYN, John, of Maesmynan, County Flintshire. Uncle   C.C.C. 1200.
    of Colonel Roger. M.P. Flint until disabled. Compounded
    under Beaumaris and Anglesey Articles. Served in the siege of
    Flint and mentioned in articles. Buried at Bodfari.

MOSTYN, Peter. Captain in Colonel (Sir) Roger Mostyn's   I.O. Flint.
    Foot. Flintshire.

MOSTYN, Robert. Captain in 1640.   C.M.S.

MOSTYN, Colonel Roger. Grandson of Sir Roger, knight.   Whitelocke quoted
    He inherited the estate in 1642, when 18. Fought at   in Taylor's 'Flint'
    Edgehill as captain of Volunteer coy.; was Colonel by   p.136.
    1643. Raised 1,500 men at own expense in 12 hours. Helped
    to recapture Hawarden Castle, November, 1643.   C.C.C. 1632 and 1666.
    Assisted in siege of Chester. Helped to bring provisions through
    blockade. Disagreed with Byron. Went to Ireland to raise men but
    arrived too late to save city. Governor of Flint, which he defended
    until August, 1646. Nephew of Bulstrode Whitelocke. Arrested in
    Conwy in 1658, but released on parole. Knighted in May, 1660,
    and made a baronet soon after. Entertained Duke of Beaufort, 1684.
    Died at Mostyn, 4 October, 1690.

MOSTYN, Thomas. A Papist. Helped to defend Flint Castle.   C.A.M. p.1113.

MOSTYN, Colonel William, of Rhyd, County Flintshire.   C.C.C. 1634.
    Compounded by deputy 'being weak and infirm'. Does
    not seem to have played any active part.

MOSTYN, Captain. Mentioned in siege of Chester. Probably   Morris. p.24l.
    Peter Mostyn.

MYDDELTON, Captain Roger, of Plas Cadwgan, near   Palmer. 'Thirteen
    Wrexham. Mentioned in Peter Ellice's Will of 1637. Local   Townships of
    tradition makes Plas Cadwgan a Royalist head quarters.   Wrexham.' p.85.

NANNEY, Captain-Lieutenant John. In Sir John Owen's Foot. L. & W.	I.O.
NANNEY, Captain John. Captured at Dolgellau, December 1645, with his lieutenant, David Lloyd. Probably in Sir John Owen's Foot.	Parry. p.369 and 382.
NANNEY, Hugh (Captain?). A Merioneth Commissioner of Array.	Clenennau 543.
NANNEY, Captain-Lieutenant Robert, Merioneth. In Lord Capell's Horse.	I.O.
NEALE, Sir William. Rupert's Scoutmaster who saved Prince's life at Newark. Rupert made him governor of Hawarden which he held, helped by his wife, Lady Helen Neale, until the spring of 1646. Entertained King for three hours, 25 September, after Rowton defeat. Was captured in Booth revolt, 1659. For Lady Neale's brave letter during husband's absence see: R. Morris, p.85. Aubrey has a 'Brief Life' of him. He lived long after the Civil War.	Burne and Young. p.141. Symonds Diary. D.N.B.
NEWTON, Sir Henry, Salop. Later known as Puckering. Served under Lieutenant-Colonel Mark Trevor as 'field officer' of Horse. Volunteer company.	H.M.C.
NICOLL, Dr. The Dean of Chester. Captured in Denbigh Castle. Had 'acted much against Parliament'.	Phil. ii. p.329.
NORRIS, Captain, of Denbigh. Mentioned in Ancient and Modern Denbigh as a sworn burgess and 'a captain in the royalist army'.	Williams. p.312.
OLIVER, Lieutenant. In Colonel R. Broughton's Foot. Prisoner at Naseby.	Peacock.
OWEN, Colonel. Killed in attempt to relieve Beeston Castle. February, 1645, serving under Colonel J. Robinson.	R. Morris. p.74.
OWEN, Colonel Hugh, Bodeon, Anglesey. In 1648 revolt. Monument in Llangadwaladr Church. Brother of Henry Owen. High Sheriff, 1654.	
OWEN, Henry, of Mosoglan. Anglesey commissioner. Brother of Hugh. High Sheriff, 1652.	
OWEN, Sir John, of Clenennau (1600-1666). Major-general, vice-admiral of North Wales, High Sheriff, Caernarfon-shire. Captain in Colonel Endymion Porter's Foot. Irish expedition, 1642. Ordered by Charles, September, 1642, to raise a regiment of Foot in Caernarvonshire, intended to be life-guard for the Prince of Wales, but Owen failed to get to Edgehill. Was at Hereford by Christmas. Helped to capture Cirencester on his way to the King. Said to have taken part in seven battles, nine sieges and thirty-two actions. Was at Culham Camp with regiment in May, 1643. Distinguished himself in assault on Bristol, seriously wounded in neck. Saw attempt to relieve Gloucester and 1st Newbury. In 1644 was deputy governor of Reading.	D.N.B. Peacock. Lloyd's Memoirs. Arch.Camb. 1875. p.205.

Knighted at Oxford, 17 December, 1644, and appointed
governor of Conwy. Made major-general by Maurice,
February, 1645, and marched Caernarvonshire troops to
drive Roundheads out of Denbigh operating nr. Wrexham.
On his return he turned Archbishop Williams (9 May) out
of Conwy Castle, thereby starting a feud which harmed
the cause. His regiment at Naseby was commanded by
Lieutenant-Colonel R. Burges. A second regiment under
Lieutenant-Colonel Hugh Hookes operated in Merioneth.
Owen was active in sending supplies to beleaguered
Chester. Co-operated with Byron. Conwy town captured
9 August, 1646, but Owen defied Mytton and held castle
until 18 November. Headed revolt, 1648. Captured at Y
Dalar Hir, near Bangor, and imprisoned in Denbigh.
Rescue attempted in July, and he was removed to Windsor.
Tried with Hamilton, Capell, Holland and Goring, and
condemned to be executed but reprieved. Imprisoned
Chester, 1651; again in 1655, and captured in Booth
uprising, 1659. Married Janet, daughter of Griffith
Vaughan of Corsygedol, Merioneth. Buried Penmorfa
Church. Epitaph quoted in *Mitre and Musket*.

OWEN, William. Son of Sir John. Married Catherine,
    daughter of Lewis Anwyl, of Park, Merioneth. Was with
    Sir John at Y Dalar Hir, and in attempted rescue.
    Nominated Knight of the Royal Oak. — Parry. p.404. P.R.O. SP. 23/4 & 5.

OWEN, Colonel William, of Brogyntyn (sometimes called
    Porkington), Salop. Brother of Sir John. Made lieutenant-
    colonel in Colonel Robert Villiers' Foot, 15 June, 1643.
    Appointed governor of Harlech by Rupert, 1644. Resisted
    attacks from Spring of 1646 to 16 March, 1647 – the last castle
    to surrender. Taken after Preston, 1648. Imprisoned
    at Nottingham. — Rylands Library. Battles, Sieges, etc. p.136. Clenennau 537. Warburton.

OWENS, Captain Hugh. — Phil. ii. p.334. C.M.S.

PARREY, Captain, 'slain at Denbigh'. — B.M. Royal Martyrs. 109. g.13. p.233.

PARRY, Ensign David, of Anglesey. In Colonel R. Brough-
    ton's Foot. Prisoner at Naseby. — I.O. Peacock.

*PARRY, Lieutenant-Colonel. Foot. — I.O.

PARRY, Lieutenant-Colonel Owen, 'in actual arms against
    Parliament'. — C.A.M. p.544.

PARRY, Jo, of 'Potfari'. At Y Dalar Hir. — P.R.O. SP. 23/4 & 5.

PARRY, 'Mr.' Richard, of Denbighshire, 1648. In Anglesey revolt. — Parry. p.388.

PARRY, Henry. Signed Denbighshire maimed soldiers'
    petition–that of Griffith ap Rees, of Henllan, near Denbigh. — D.M.S.

---

* Is this Owen Parry, Foot. L. & W. (Sir Henry Cary?) If so, his lieutenant, also L. & W., was Will Parry,
  probably his son.

PARRY, Robert, of Denbigh (Lleweni). Compounded on
    Denbigh articles. Fined £28.

C.C.C. 1703.

PARRY, Captain. Attempted to rescue Sir John Owen from
    Denbigh Castle, July, 1648.

Wms. A. and M.
    Denb.
    p.241.

PARRY, Captain, of Plas Llanrhaeadr. In attempt to rescue
    Sir John Owen from Denbigh. Was a descendant of
    Bishop Parry of St. Asaph who translated Bible into
    Welsh, 1620. (These three entries the same.)

Parry. p.381n.

PARRY. Sent by Sir John Owen to Gwydir to gather
    contributions, 1646.

Clenennau 612.

PEETERS, George. Prisoner in Anglesey. In list for com-
    pounders.

C.W.P. 1815.
C.C.C. Vol. i. p. 57/8.

PETTRIS, Captain. Wife, Jane Hookes, niece of Lieutenant-
    Colonel Hugh Hookes. She was buried at Conwy,
    25 September, 1664. (Peters?)

Register. p.144.
Pedigrees. p.293.

PENNANT, Major David, of Bychtyn, Flintshire. H.S., 1642.
    Ancestor of Thomas Pennant who writes: 'He was an
    officer in the garrison of Denbigh when it was besieged.'
    Was imprisoned there and was only kept from starving by his
    wife walking from Whitford with oatmeal. Compounded for
    £197. Portrait painted with wife and son, is at Nantlys,
    County Flintshire.

A. and M. Denb.
p.243 quoting
C.C.C. 1719.

PENNANT, Major Hugh, of Plas Ucha, younger brother of John. Pennant
    states he defended Harlech Castle until he was deserted by his
    men and then he surrendered to the Parliamentarian forces.
    Nothing else has come to light yet about this 'siege'. Pennant
    fought at Beaumaris, September, 1648, having
    first disputed Mytton's landing at Cadnant. The next day
    'Major Pennant and his troop charged the enemy, and was like
    to take Colonel Louthian prisoner'. Also participated in Booth
    revolt, 1659.

Wm. Wms, quoted
by Parry. p.389.

C.C.C. 3254.

PENNANT, Robert, of Downing. Pennant states Downing
    was attacked when a Parliamentary patrol was fired on.
    Robert was heavily fined – £298. Pennant compounded under
    Denbigh articles for delinquency 'in taking up arms for the King'.
    Fine according to C.C.C. was £40/6/8.

C.C.C. 1720.

PHILLIPS, Ensign. Captured at Nantwich, January, 1644.

Hall. p.170.

PHILLIPS, Captain Edward, of Flintshire. In Lord Byron's
    regiment.

I.O.

PHILLIPS, Captain –. In Sir J. Owen's revolt, 1648.

Parry. p.390.

PHILLIPS, Major. Sent by Lord Bulkeley to Prince of Wales
    with news of proposed Anglesey revolt.

C.W.P. 1910.

PHILLIPS, Edward of Worthenbury (Wrexham). Com-
    pounded for £24.

C.C.C. 1526.

PHILLIPS, William, of Gwernhayled, gentleman. In Booth
    revolt, 1659.

P.R.O. S.P. 25/59,
    ff. 36/7.

PICKERING, Francis, of Holt. Served in Holt Castle garrison. Fined £10. — Palmer in Arch.Camb. 1906

PICKERING, Captain. Captured by Mytton's troopers near Ruthin during raid, April, 1646. Horse. Served in Holt Castle and at Wrexham in 1655 conspiracy. — Newcome. p.75.

PIERCE, Ensign John. In Colonel R. Mostyn's Foot. Flint. In Captain Peter Mostyn's company. — I.O.

PEIRCE, Captain John. In regiment of Herbert, Lord Cherbury. Foot. — I.O.

PLOT, James. Signed Aberystwyth articles. — Phil. ii. p.305.

POLDEN, Captain. In Colonel R. Broughton's Foot. Prisoner at Naseby. — Peacock.

POLKINHO, ap Edward [sic]. Captain of Pioneers from Caernarfon. — I.O.

PORTER, Ensign. In Colonel R. Broughton's Foot. Prisoner at Naseby. — Peacock.

POWELL, James. Captain of Foot. Irish expedition, June. 1642. — B.M. 190. g.13. p.209.

POWELL, Jo. Captain of Foot. Irish expedition, June, 1642. — Ibid.

POWELL, Lieutenant John. Served 'in forraine parts'. — Chirk Castle. MS. 7442.

POWELL, Sir Thomas, of Plas Horsli (Horsley), near Wrexham. Prominent Royalist. Denbighshire Commissioner of Array. Taken in Chirk Castle, Booth revolt, 1659. Carried helmet and crest at Colonel J. Robinson's funeral. — C.W.P. 2195.

POWELL, Lieutenant Thomas, Denbighshire. In Captain Jones' company of Sir J. Owen's Foot. — I.O. P.R.O. SP. 29/68.

POWELL, Ensign Thomas. In Colonel R. Mostyn's Foot. — I.O.

POWELL, Captain Thomas. In Colonel R. Ellice's Foot. Denbigh. — I.O.

POWELL, Captain [Thomas]. In Sir John Owen's Foot in 1643. Christian name not given. — Culham.

POWELL, Captain Thomas. Wife gave paten to Wrexham Church. 'The gift of Christian Powell the wife of Capt. Thos. Powell of Gouines (Gofynys, Brymbo), the daughter of John Edwards of Kuienawern (Kefn-y-Wern) Esq., 1689.'* — Country Quest, Spring. 1961. p.47.

POWELL, Lieutenant Richard. Served 'in forraine parts'.

POWELL, Lieutenant Roger. Served 'in forraine parts'.

POWELL, Walter. Captain's-ensign Irish expedition, 1642. — B.M. 109. g.13. p.209.

POWELL, Lieutenant William, Denbighshire. In Lord Byron's regiment. Foot. Captain Ellis Sutton's company. — I.O.

PREECE, Captain. Taken at Holt Bridge, November, 1643. — Hall. p.147.

PRICE, Captain (Edward). In Colonel Richard Herbert's Foot at Culham. Denbigh. — Culham.

* *Article by Canon D. E. M. Glynne Jones, Vicar of Wrexham.*

PRICE, Lieutenant Ellis. Captured in Chirk Castle.	C.W.P. 2193.
PRICE, Lieutenant Ellice. Had served 'in forraine parts'.	Chirk. MS. 7442.
PRICE, Captain Ellis. Grandson of Captain Thomas Price (Prys), of Plas Iolyn, poet and seaman, described as 'Lord of the manor of Yspytty Ifan'.	Pedigrees.
PRIS, Captain Ellis, Denbighshire. In Sir Charles Floyd's Foot (i.e. Salusbury's regiment). Probably Price of Plas Iolyn.	I.O.
PRICE, Major –. Killed defending Bristol, 1645.	B.M. 109. g.13. p.233.
PRICE, Sir John, of Newtown, Montgomeryshire. An unreliable leader who changed sides. At the outset he seems to have been royalist and 'Sr Jo. Price & 2 men' appears in a List of Strangers in Oxford, January, 1644. By late summer he sided with Myddleton. After Montgomery battle Brereton wrote: 'Sir John Price is already come in.' Made governor of Montgomery Castle. Another writer states he was always 'a Parlt. man . . . but was so overmastered by the enemy that he durst not appear.' In December brought prisoners to Newtown.	Bodleian MS. Add. p.114. St. Aldate's list. Phil. ii. p.203. Parry. p.356.
PRICE, Captain Robert, of Denbigh. Horse. Under Colonel Richard Bulkeley. (Buckly.)	I.O.
PRICE, Robert, of Gilar, near Pentrevoelas. Concerned in 1659 revolt.	C.W.P. 2193.
PRICE, Robert, of Plas Yollin (Iolyn) nearby. Was 'engaged in late wars' but no fine imposed.	C.C.C. 1890.
PRICE, Robert. Signed several Denbighshire maimed soldiers' petitions with Robinson, Manley and Puleston, as though he dwelt in Wrexham vicinity.	D.M.S.
PRICE, Reverend Richard, M.A. Vicar of Betws-yn-Rhos. Killed in Beaumaris battle, 1648.	Parry. p.389.
PRICE, Captain Thomas. In Colonel William Salesbury's regiment.	D.M.S. and I.O.
PRICE, Captain Thomas, of Skeibien, near Llanynys. In Colonel William Wynne's Foot. (Transferred?)	D.M.S.
PRICE, Captain Thomas. In Colonel R. Mostyn's Foot. Flint.	I.O.
PRICE, Captain Samuel. In Colonel W. Bamfield's regiment. Irish Expedition, Spring, 1642.	Peacock.
PRICE, Colonel William, of Rhiwlas (Bala). M.P. for Merioneth until 'disabled', 1644. Left House in time to join the King at Brentford. Epitaph in St. Asaph cathedral states he raised soldiers whom he commanded. A Commissioner of Array for Merioneth. He married Mary co-heiress of Kinmel, County Denbighshire, and spent much time in this area. Nominated Knight of the Royal Oak. Received Duke of Beaufort in 1684, at Rhiwlas. Parliament charged him with 'deserting the service of the house, being in the King's quarters and adhering to that body'. Died 31 Oct, 1691 aged 72 years.	H.C. Journal. C.C.C. 3286.
PRICE, Captain. In Colonel W. Price's regiment. Probably	I.O.

a relative. Foot. His Lieutenant Edward Fulkes, from Denbigh.

PRICE, Dr. Robert. Commissioner for Colonel R. Bulkeley   Phil. ii. p.312.
    negotiating surrender of Beaumaris Castle.

PRICE, Archdeacon. Captured in Caernarfon Castle, 1646.   Phil. ii. p.311.

PRICHARD, Captain. With the Earl of Derby's force at   Anderton Papers.
    Wigan in 1651.   Wigan Ref. Library.

PRITCHARD, Ensign. In Colonel R. Broughton's Foot.   I.O.
    Captured at Naseby. Applied from 'London and Westminster'.
    Major Lills company.

PRITCHARD, Philip, Captain. In attempt to relieve Beeston Castle.   Phil. ii. p.227.

PRYTHERCH, Richard. Anglesey revolt, 1648. Signed   Phil. ii. p.401.
    articles of surrender.

PUGH, Captain John. In Sir John Owen's Foot. Probably   C.M.S.
    his cousin. (See Brynkir pedigree.)

PUGH, John, Esq., of Montgomeryshire. Nominated Knight   Pedigrees.
    of the Royal Oak.   Parry. p.404.

PUGH, Captain Gwilym or William. Younger brother of   Phil. ii. p.323.
    Captain Robert Pugh of Penrhyn Creuddyn. Served
    Marquis of Worcester, and was captured at Raglan Castle.

PUGH, Lieutenant-Colonel. In Llannor churchyard fracas, 1646.   Caern. County
    Record Office.

PUGH, Captain Robert, of Caernarvonshire. In Colonel   C.M.S.
    William Salesbury's Foot.

PUGH, Captain Robert, of Penrhyn Creuddyn. Captain of   C.W.P. 1758.
    one hundred men. '£10 for maintenance, and to provide   I.O.
    drum and colours.' (October, 1645.) Followed Colonel   Mont. Collection.
    Twisleton with one hundred men when latter   Vol. 8
    marched to Y Dalar Hir. Probably Jesuit priest who was
    later chaplain to Queen Henrietta Maria.

PUGH, Captain Robert, of Montgomeryshire. In Marquess of   I.O.
    Worcester's regiment. Horse.

PUGH, Major. Prisoner at Naseby.   Peacock. p.94.

PUGH, Major Rice. Foot.   I.O.

PUGH (Pue), Thomas. Commissioner of Array for Caer-   C.W.P. 1764.
    narvonshire.

PUGH, Ensign Thomas. In Sir Charles Floyd's Foot. Living   I.O.
    in London and Westminster area. Captain Garaway's
    company.

PUGH, Lieutenant William, of Merioneth. In Sir John Owen's   I.O.
    Foot, in Lieutenant-Colonel Roger Burges' company.

PULFORD, Thomas, of Wrexham, gentleman. Captured in   C.C.C. 1928.
    Holt Castle. Compounded for £96.

RAVENSCROFT, Captain. In Colonel R. Whitley's Horse.   I.O.

RAVENSCROFT, Captain. Captured in effort to relieve   Phil. ii. p.227
    Beeston Castle, January, 1645.

RAVENSCROFT, Captain. In Sir Thomas Salusbury's   Culham.

original regiment. Might be the Ravenscroft who betrayed
    Hawarden Castle. If so, of Pickhill, near Wrexham.

RAVENSCROFT, Captain George. Signed Conwy Castle   Brogyntyn ii.
    articles as commissioner for Sir J. Owen.   Appenx 16.

RAIGNOLDS, John. Deputy Governor of Ruthin. Signed   Phil. ii. p.304.
    articles of surrender, 12 April, 1646.

REYNALDS, Major. Signed Denbigh Castle articles.   Wins. A. and M.
        Denb. p.234.

REYNOLDS, Lieutenant. In Denbigh Castle.   W. J. Smith.
        Salusbury Cor.
        p.169.

RICKABY, Lieutenant James. In Colonel Sir Charles Floyd's   I.O.
    troop (H). Durham. Under Captain Stephen Dawson.

ROBERTS, Major Hugh, of Hafod-y-bwch, Wrexham. Was   C.C.C. 1407.
    in siege of Exeter, and compounded under Exeter articles.   D.M.S.
    Signed Denbighshire maimed soldiers' applications. A   Palmer.
    Wrexham churchwarden. Armiger.

ROBERTS, Major –. In Colonel Roger Whitley's regiment.   D.M.S.

ROBERTS, Lieutenant John, of Anglesey. In Sir J. Owen's   C.M.S.
    Foot. A former ensign to Captain Merrick.   P.R.O. SP. 29/68.

ROBERTS, Lieutenant John, of Salop. In Colonel William   I.O.
    Owen's Foot. Was in Harlech during siege.   Phil. ii. p.334.

ROBERTS, Ensign Lewis, of Montgomeryshire. Ensign to   I.O.
    Major Theodore Morris in Sir Fulk Hunckes' Foot.

ROBERTS, Lieutenant Peter, of Denbigh. In Colonel William   I.O.
    Wynne's Foot.

ROBERTS, Richard. Drum Major to Sir Edward Norris   D.M.S.
    (Cheshire).

ROBERTS, Lieutenant Robert. In Colonel H. Wentworth's   Peacock.
    regiment, 1640.

ROBERTS, Ensign Edward. In Colonel H. Wentworth's   Peacock.
    regiment, 1640.

ROBERTS, Gabriel, of Segrwyd, County Denbighshire.   C.C.C. 1685.
    Compounded under Denbigh articles for being 'in arms'.

ROBERTS, Captain William. In Colonel Charles Essex's   Peacock.
    regiment in Irish expedition of spring, 1642.

ROBERTS, William, of Bangor. Order to seize estate for   C.C.C. 399.
    non-payment of fine.

ROBERT ap Edward, of Esclusham. Went to Ireland in   D.M.S.
    company of Captain Edward Broughton, later Sir
    Edward. Came back to England and continued under
    Colonel Robert Broughton. Was at the relief of Newark,
    the taking of Liverpool (11 April, 1644), Bolton capture,
    and the battle near York [Marston Moor] where he was
    wounded.

ROBINS, Lieutenant Herbert, of Caernarvonshire.   I.O.

ROBINSON, Lieutenant Jo. In list of officers for Ireland,   B.M. 190. g.13.
    16 June, 1642. Foot.   p.209.

ROBINSON, Colonel John, of Gwersyllt Ucha, near Wrexham, eldest son of Captain William Robinson and grandson of Bishop Nicholas Robinson, Bishop of Bangor. Defended Holt Castle against Brereton, November, 1643, then helped, as lieutenant-colonel, to recapture Hawarden, in December. Posted to Ellice's Foot, 12 January, 1644. Served throughout Chester siege, possibly as lieutenant-colonel to Byron's Foot. Acted as a commissioner of surrender. Found Gwersyllt pillaged and fled in disguise. Joined Byron in Caernarfon Castle, which he helped to defend. Acted as Byron's commissioner for surrender of Beaumaris. About this period he captured 'Lady Cheadle' Fort, near Beaumaris. Was at Y Dalar Hir fight, and later marched to Beaumaris fight, 1648, but arrived too late. Fled from his home, Monachdy, to Ireland. Planned to capture Bardsey Island the next year but was frustrated. Landed with Earl of Derby's forces 1651, and was taken at Wigan. Apparently obtained freedom and went overseas until Restoration. Made vice-admiral of N.W. (1661-1679). M.P. for Anglesey. Nominated Knight of the Royal Oak. Died March, 1681, aged 65, 'worn out as well as ennobled by honourable wounds', according to his epitaph in Gresford Church.

D.M.S.
R. Morris. p.52.
Harl. 6851/67.
D.N.B.
Pennant.
D.H.S.T. p.124
Parry. pp. 385 & 389

ROBINSON, Major Nicholas. Younger brother of John.

ROBINSON, Captain William, of Gwersyllt, father of the two. Served as captain in Salusbury's Foot, 1642. A Commissioner of Array. Died 1644.

Pedigrees.
Culham.

RODEN, Captain John, of Iscoed. In Booth revolt, 1659.

ROGERS, Captain Robert. Made free burgess of Denbigh, 1644.

P.R.O. SP. 25/29, Minutes.

ROGER, Captain. Mentioned by Colonel R. Mostyn, 1649.

C.W.P. 1876. 36/37.

ROYDEN, Lieut.-Col. John. Of Is-y-Coed, until he married the Maurice heiress of Lloran Isa. Was captain of Chirk-land light horse in 1640. Salusbury's lieutenant-colonel in August, 1642. Not in regiment in 1643. Survived war. Died 23 March, 1665, and buried at Holt, aged 81.

ROYDEN, Captain Roger, of Iscoed. 'A Captain in the Royal Army.' Of Roden Hall. Father (? brother) of John.

RUTTER, Captain Reynold. In Colonel William Salesbury's Foot. Denbigh. He helped Dolben and Chambres in attcmpt to rescue Sir J. Owen from Denbigh Castle. Parry spells name 'Cutler'. The Rutters were a Denbigh family. *Records of Denbigh* give Reynauld R. a councilman in 1619.

D.M.S.
Chirk Castle. MS. f.166.
Palmer.
C.C.C. 1220.
Powys Fadog, ii. p.113.
Denbigh I.O.
Williams. p.128.

SALESBURY, Charles, second son of Colonel William. Helped in defence of Denbigh Castle. No rank. Was nominated

Knight of the Royal Oak. Inherited Bachymbyd. High
Sheriff of Denbighshire, 1661.

SALESBURY, Captain Owen, of Rhug, near Corwen,
Merioneth. Eldest son of Colonel William. At outset was
a Royalist Commissioner of Array for Merioneth. Was
estranged from his father over Owen's marriage. Turned
Parliamentarian and was captain of horse militia. Died
1657.

Clenennau 538.

SALESBURY, Colonel William, of Bachymbyd and Rhug.
Had served in Low Countries and sailed to East Indies.
Accepted King's commission, September, 1643, when he
and kinsfolk repaired Denbigh Castle. Defied Myddelton,
November, 1643, when summoned to surrender. Enter-
tained Charles, 25 to 28 September, 1645, after Rowton.
Saw Sir William Vaughan defeated on Denbigh Green,
November, was besieged April, 1646. Surrendered 28
October, after receiving King's permission. Compounded
under Denbigh articles. Lived in seclusion, in ill health. Died
before Restoration. Fined £781.

Symonds.
Williams A. & M.
Denbigh. p.255n.
Newcome. pp. 65/103.
C.C.C. 1723.
D.W.B. p.901.

SALUSBURY, Lieutenant. Captured at Holt Bridge,
9 November, 1643.

Hall. p.157.

SALUSBURY. Commanded a trained band which paraded
for King at Chester, September, 1642.

Phil. i. p.112.

SALUSBURY, Captain. Was 'Lieutenant of Militia' for
Caernarvonshire at Restoration.

C.W.P. 2389, 2409.

SALISBURY, Captain H. (John?) In Sir Thomas Salusbury's
regiment of Foot.

Culham.

SALUSBURY, John, of Erbistock Hall. Wrote Sir John
Salusbury of Lleweni, 1662, asking support for
Denbighshire maimed soldier. Signed 'your loving
cousin' – apparently a real cousin.

D.M.S.

SALUSBURY, John (Junior), of Bachygraig, County Flint-
shire. Was Borough M.P. until disabled. (Was he a
Captain?) In Chirk Castle, 1659. Assessed at £1,200.
Nominated Knight of the Royal Oak.

Wms. Parlt.Hist.
C.W.P. 2193.
C.A.M. p.432.
Parry. p.404.

SALUSBURY, Captain John. Sworn burgess of Denbigh,
1664.

Wms. Records of
Denbigh. p.136.

SALUSBURY, Captain John. In Colonel William Salesbury's
Foot.

D.M.S.

SALISBURY, Captain John, of Denbighshire. In Prince Maurice's
regiment. Horse.

I.O.

SALUSBURY, Colonel Sir Thomas, Bart., of Lleweni, County
Denbighshire. Colonel of first Denbigh-Flint regiment of
1,200 Foot raised August, 1642. Also troop of Horse.
Fought at Edgehill. Made D.C.L. at Oxford for services.
Regiment led the charge at Brentford, November, 1642.
Went into garrison at Reading. By May, 1643, he had left
regiment, and by August he was dead. Grave unknown.

C.W.P. 1711.
Crosse, 1118.
Warburton.

SALUSBURY, Captain Thomas. March 1, 1661, 'killed one
     Thomson of the general guard in a duel'.   C.W.P. 2288.

SALISBURY, Captain Thomas, of Flintshire. In Lord   I.O.
     Molyneaux's regiment. Horse.

SANDERS, Captain. In Beaumaris fight, 1648, 'enemy were   Parry. p.388.
     stoutly repulsed by Captain Sanders and the towne's company'.

SANDERS, Edward. Captain-lieutenant in Irish expedition,   B.M. 109. g.13.
     June, 1642.   p.209.

SANDERSON, Captain. Killed at Y Dalar Hir.   Parry. p.391.

SANDYS, Colonel Thomas. 'Saunds' was deputy constable   C.W.P. 1917.
     of Beaumaris under his uncle, Lord Bulkeley. Of a
     Worcester family.

SCRIVEN, Lieutenant-Colonel Sir Thomas, of Frodesley,   H.M.C. Vol. ii.
     Salop. At Wem, mortally wounded when Wynne was   p.143.
     slain. Was governor of Whitchurch. Died 21 January,
     1644.

SCRIVEN, Lieutenant-Colonel Richard. His brother. 'In both   Parry. p.391.
     wars.' Led Sir J. Owen's forlorn hope at Y Dalar Hir   C.C.C. 1859.
     and escaped after battle. Compounded for £100 and
     £162.

SHAKERLEY, Colonel Sir Jeffrey, of Holme, Cheshire. In   Pennant.
     Chester siege. Carried message from Rowton Moor to   Phil. ii. p.311.
     Charles in Chester by crossing Dee in a tub. In Caernarfon   C.C.C. 1446.
     siege. Created bart. Bought Gwersyllt Isa from Captain
     E. Sutton to dwell next to Colonel Robinson, his comrade in-
     arms. Compounded for £784.

SIMON, Peter. In Harlech siege, 1647.   Phil. ii. p.334.

SINGLETON, Samuel. In Anglesey revolt, 1648.   Parry. p.388.

SMITH, Captain John. Captain of Pioneers of Caernarfon.   I.O.
     Captured 1659 at Chirk.

SMITH, Will (no rank). Signed Denbighshire maimed   D.M.S.
     soldiers' petition for R. Wynne, Wrexham. Might be
     vicar of Whitford.

SPICER, Major William, of Caernarfon. A captain in 1641.   Parry. p.362.
     When Mytton appeared in 1646 before Caernarfon   C.W.P. 2258.
     'Byron . . . sent Mr. Spicer with a company of soldiers   Caerns. Q.S.
     for provision . . . but Spicer was taken'. In 1660 Sir   Records.
     Richard Grosvenor refers to him as his 'old fellow   C.C.C. 399 & 2010.
     prisoner'. Appeals for Spicer to be again made Clerk of the
     Peace for Caernarfon. Was chairman of County Maimed
     Soldiers' Committee. Order for his estate to be seized for
     non-payment of fine.

STAPLETON, Cornet Arthur. Prisoner at Y Dalar Hir.   Phil. ii. p.384.
     Order for his release from Denbigh Castle.   Brogyntyn. MS.
                                1998.

ST. POL, Count. Byron's general-of-horse at Chester. Escaped   Bodleian MS. ADD.
     to Rhuddlan to bring relief during siege. Might be of   d.14.
     ducal house of Lorraine. At time of Oxford Parliament,   Warburton.

January, 1644, non-residents included 'Monsieur de Ste
Paule a ffrench Lo: And his brother with two servants'.
He was captured after the Stow-in-the-Wold surrender.
The brother was killed at Marston Moor.

SUTTON, Captain John. Served 'in forraine parts'.   Chirk Castle.

SUTTON, Captain Ellis, of Gwersyllt Isa. In Lord Byron's   D.M.S.
    Foot. Commanded Colonel J. Robinson's own company.   C.C.C. 1256.
    Was in Chester siege. Impoverished after war he had to
    sell home. Fined £75.

SWORD, Captain. Governor Ruthin Castle under Colonel   Phil. ii. p.215.
    Mark Trevor. He repulsed attack by Myddelton, October,
    1644, with stones and shot, 'the place but in repairing'.
    (Archbishop Williams to Ormonde)

SWORDS, Captain. 'Slain at Denbigh.' The same.   B.M. Royal Martyrs.
    190, g. 13. p.233.

SYDENHAM, Major Humphrey. Fought in Chester siege   Clenennau 608/9.
    and then went to Beaumaris. Brought arms to Byron in
    Caernarfon.

SYMKIES, Captain Thomas. Mytton's own captain of Horse.
    Turned Royalist in 1648 when governor of Beaumaris.

TAYLOR, Captain Anthony, Kent. In Col. Roger Whitley's   I.O.
    Foot.

THELWALL, Colonel Anthony. In command (as lieutenant-   Warburton.
    colonel) of Sir Edward Fitton's Cheshire Foot at   Powys Fadog.
    Bristol. A member of the Thelwalls of Plas-y-ward,
    near Ruthin. Succeeded in command on death of Fitton.
    Mentioned by Clarendon for his bravery at Cropredy
    Bridge. Met death heroically at 2nd Newbury.
    However he may have been alive in 1648, see C. S. P. D.

THELWALL, Andrew, called 'The Captain', buried   Palmer. History of
    Wrexham, 1705.   Wrexham. p.49.

THELWALL, Eubule. Took Colonel William Salesbury's
    message to the King asking for permission to surrender
    Denbigh. Nominated Knight of the Royal Oak.

THELWALL, Edward (no rank). Signed maimed soldiers'   D.M.S.
    petition for T. Lloyd, Llanrhaeadr.

THELWALL, Colonel John, of Plas Coch, near Ruthin. Son   C.W.P.
    of John Thelwall, H.S. Flintshire, 1643. As Colonel of   Clenennau 581.
    Foot, co-operated with Sir J. Owen. After Naseby, Rupert   C.C.C. 1124.
    ordered 'Byron to speed away Colonel Thelwall with
    800 men'. Owen suggested Thelwall should establish a
    bridgehead at Llanrwst. Helped to defend Denbigh and
    signed articles of surrender, acting as Salesbury's com-
    missioner. Compounded for £117. Died 1686.

THELWALL, Captain –. In Colonel W. Wynne's original Foot.   Crosse 1118.
    (?) Col. John Thelwall before promotion.

THELWALL, Captain Maurice. In siege of Chester.   Arch.Camb. 1869.

Died 1645.

THOMAS, Colonel –. Killed at Naseby, 'a Welsh officer'.

THOMAS, Edward Morris (Captain?), of Montgomeryshire. Raised men in markets and fairs for Lieutenant-Colonel Morris in 1648. Took oath in Llanrhaydr Church. Active in raising money for the King in Montgomeryshire.

THOMAS, Lieutenant-Colonel. A papist, prisoner at Naseby.

THOMAS, Ensign. Captured at Nantwich, January, 1644.

THOMAS, Major. In Sir Charles Vavasour's Regiment

THOMAS, John, of Montgomery. Quartermaster to Lieutenant-Colonel Bridgman. Sir Thomas Aston's Horse.

THOMAS, Cornet William, Montgomery. In Harlech garrison, 1647.

THOMAS, William, gentleman. Received Caernarfon mize of 30/- per annum.

THOMAS, Sir William, of Aber. Eldest son of Sir William Thomas. Was High Sheriff, Caernarfon in 1638. M.P. for Caernarfon Borough until disabled in 1644. Colonel of 1,200 foot volunteers he was commissioned to raise, 14 October, 1643. Assessed at £800 per annum. Compounded under Anglesey articles. ' Volu(n)tiers from Sir Wm Thomas & my selfe marched over the Foryd' (Archbishop Williams, 1645).

THORNTON, Captain –. Sent by Byron to Gwydir, 15 April, 1646.

THOROLD, Ensign John. In Colonel Sir Charles Floyd's Foot. L. & W. Lieutenant-Colonel Edward Tyrwhyt's company.

TIRWHITT, Lieutenant-Colonel Edward. Succeeded Royden in Sir Thomas Salusbury's Foot, May, 1643. He led regiment in assault on Bristol, and still with it in 1645.

TRAFFORD, Captain Thomas. In Earl Barrymore's regiment, 1640. Ormonde letters mention a Tom Trafford.

TRAFFORD, Lieutenant-Colonel Francis. Might be of Esclus, Wrexham. Served under Earl of Northumberland in 1640. Had experience in 'forraine parts' as major. Went to Maryland [he was Catholic] and fought against Red Indians. Returned in 1643 to Ireland, and was sent by Ormonde to Wales, with three hundred 'good well-armed men' with ordnance, but parliamentary warships hampered his departure. Crossed later and joined with Colonel Trevor in defence of Ruthin against Myddelton in October. Returned to Ireland. Went over the sea and died in poverty. (See Professor A. H. Dodd's article, Board of Celtic Studies, part iv, May, 1652.) Was a Colonel of Horse under Northumberland.

p.101.

Angl. Rediviva (Sprigge). p.51.
C.A.M. p.1094.

Ibid.

Hall. p.170.

D.M.S.

I.O.

Phil. ii. p.334.

C.M.S. (1669).

Wms. Parlt. History.
Arch.Camb. 1875.
p.312.
C.A.M. p.434.
Clenennau 592 and 597.
C.C.C. 2740.
Black's Oxford Docquets.
Clenennau 612.

I.O.

Warburton.

Peacock. p.78.

Phil. ii. p.161.
C.S.P.D. 1644/5.
p.80.
I.O.

TREVOR, Arthur. Half-brother of Mark Trevor. A noted correspondent for Rupert and Ormonde.	C.S.P.D. 1644/5. p.80. C.C.C. 1589.
TREVOR, Captain John. In Booth revolt, 1659. 'Of Trevour.'	P.R.O. SP. 25/29. f.36/ 7.
TREVOR, Captain John, of Llys Trevor and Valle Crucis Abbey, 'a captain in the royal army'. He died in gaol at Wrexham for debt and was buried in Wrexham church. Married Mary, daughter of John Eyton, of Leeswood.	Powys Fadog. ii. p.113.
TREVOR, Captain. 'Troopers busy looking for Captain Trevor', in Conwy Valley, 1646.	C.W.P. 1802.
TREVOR, Colonel Mark (Marcus) who became Viscount Dungannon. Son of Sir Edward Trevor, born on his Irish estate, but of Brynkinallt ancestry. Came from Ireland in 1643 to join Lord Capell in Salop, and was made major of Horse. At Holt Bridge, November, 1643. Succeeded Capell as colonel of what was merged into Prince of Wales' Horse. At relief of Newark. Followed Rupert to Marston Moor where, it is alleged, he fired the pistol* which wounded Cromwell. Defeated at Malpas, August 26, 1644. At Montgomery battle, 18 September, 1644, where his horse, Bay Squire, was killed. In border fights in Salop and Chester. Captured 12 men at Alford. Made Governor of Ruthin by Rupert, was driven out of town by Myddelton, October, 1644. Surrendered in Cornwall in Spring of 1646. Went to Ireland to fight for the Parliamentarians against the Rebels, but rejoined Royalists in 1649.	D.N.B. R. Morris. p.103. Puckering. Phil. ii. p.199, 209 and 227. C.A.M. p.1209.

* Author's copy of book endorsed ("? sword wound").

TURNBULL, Lieutenant. In Denbigh Castle. Mentioned in the Calendar Salusbury Correspondence.	W. J. Smith.
TUTCHELL, Lieutenant-Colonel. Was given a pass for Ireland, December, 1645.	Arch.Camb. 1875, p.314.
VALLET, Captain. In Byron's Horse. Governor of Beeston Castle. On its surrender he marched some of his men to Flint and Conwy.	C.W.P. 1763.
VANE, Colonel John. Served in Ireland. Sent by Byron into Merioneth. At Dolgellau. 'I have sent orders to Coll. Vane to march back out of Merioneth.' (Byron to Owen.) Signed Caernarfon articles.	Phil. ii. p.226n. Arch.Camb. 1875, p.315. Parry. p.362. Phil. ii. p.309.
VAUGHAN, Quartermaster Alban. Under Major Roberts in Colonel Roger Whitley's Horse.	I.O.
VAUGHAN, Captain Bithell. In Colonel William Pretty's regiment. Of Flintshire. Foot.	I.O.
VAUGHAN, Lieutenant Evan, of Denbigh. Lieutenant to Lieutenant-Colonel Robert Wynne in Colonel Hugh Wynne's Foot.	I.O.

VAUGHAN, Ensign. In Colonel R. Broughton's Foot.   Peacock.
    Captured at Naseby.

VAUGHAN, Major Henry. Believed to be of Pant Glas.   Parry. p.349.
    Killed in assault on Hopton Castle. In Sir Michael Wood-   D.M.S.
    house's Foot.

VAUGHAN, Captain Henry. In Colonel Edward Norris   D.M.S.
    (Cheshire) Foot. He may be the Henry Vaughan, church-
    warden, whose name is on Llandrillo-yn-Rhos lychgate as
    he signed maimed soldiers' petition for Henry Merton,
    yeoman of Llandrillo.

VAUGHAN, Herbert, of 'Lloydiart'. Delinquent in 1648.   P.R.O. SP. 23/4 & 5.
    He escaped from Y Dalar Hir.   Parry. p.391.

VAUGHAN, 'Halbert' (sic) (Herbert?). In Harlech siege.   Brogyntyn.

VAUGHAN, Howell, Esq., Merioneth. Nominated Knight   Parry. p.404.
    of the Royal Oak.

VAUGHAN, Lieutenant Hugh, of Ruthin, 'a Lieutenant in   C.H.S.T. Vol. x.
    the wars' married a Lloyd of Hafod Unos.   p.16.

VAUGHAN, Captain John, of Denbighshire. In Sir Evan   I.O.
    Lloyd's Foot.

VAUGHAN, Captain John. Perhaps of Pant Glas. Husband   C.W.P. 2247.
    of Joan, daughter of Sir Henry Townshend of Cound,
    Salop. Justice of Chester.

VAUGHAN, Lieutenant John. In Captain Robert Chaloner's   I.O.
    company in Sir Charles Floyd's Foot. Denbigh.

VAUGHAN, Captain–. Captured at Rowton Heath,   Phil. ii. p.272.
    September, 1645.

VAUGHAN, John, of Henllan. In Denbigh siege. Received   C.S.P.D. (1647).
    pass from Mytton, 27 October, 1646, 'to be protected   p.545.
    in his person and goods'. He 'took up arms against Parlt'.   Records of Denb.
    John Vaughan, gentleman, was made burgess, 1638.   p.131.

VAUGHAN, Captain Richard, of Pant Glas, Denbigh. In Col.   I.O.
    Lord Gerard's regiment. Wounded in jaw and blinded.   C.M.S.
    Petitioned Caernarvonshire justices for relief and was
    pensioned as 'lieut', until 1663, when he was made a Poor
    Knight of Windsor, where he died in 1700, aged 80. Brass
    in St. George's cloisters. Gave almshouses to six poor men
    at Yspytty Ifan. Inscriptions in *The Heart of Northern Wales*,
    Vol. ii. W. Bezant Lowe. Also see articles by Dr. R. T. Jenkins,
    Caern.H.S.Trans. Vol. x, *Vaughans of Pant Glas* (Denbighshire).

VAUGHAN, Lieutenant Robert, of Denbighshire. In Sir   I.O.
    Michael Woodhouse's Foot. Prince of Wales' regiment.

VAUGHAN, Quartermaster Roger, of Chester. In Colonel   I.O.
    Mark Trevor's Horse, in Lord Kilmurry's troop.

VAUGHAN, Captain Rowland, of Caer Gai, Merioneth.   Clenennau 538.
    High Sheriff in 1643, and Commissioner of Array. Made   Parry. p.392.
    captain of one hundred musketeers in November, 1643.   Parry. pp. 357 &
    Said to have fought at Naseby. Caer Gai was burnt by   399.
    Myddelton's troops in Aug 1645. In March, 1651, Vaughan

was imprisoned in Chester Castle with Sir John Owen as suspect. Captured (with others) in Merionethshire.

VAUGHAN, Captain Thomas. In Ireland with Sir Michael Ernley. — D.M.S.

VAUGHAN, Captain Thomas, brother to Lord Vaughan, sworn burgess of Denbigh, 21 October, 1623. — Ibid. p.129.

VAUGHAN, Captain Thomas, of Pant Glas, County Denbigh. In June, 1660, 'Cousin Vaughan of Pantglas is returned from travel'. He appears to have served in Flint Castle. — C.W.P. 2240.

VAUGHAN, Thomas. Begs to compound, being in Flint Castle. — C.C.C. 1653.

VAUGHAN, Captain Thomas, of Plas Thomas, Dudleston and Burton Hall, Salop. Killed at Hopton Castle. — Powys Fadog. i. p.95.

VAUGHAN, Captain –. Henry Vaughan's son (of Golden Grove, Carmarthenshire) captured by Colonel Twisleton, near Penal, 1648. — Parry. p.390.

VAUGHAN, Major-General Sir William, of Herefordshire. Returned from Ireland, November, 1643, with six troops of Horse. After Rowton Moor, the King made him General-of-Horse for Wales and Border, October, 1645. Defeated at Denbigh Green, 1 November, 1645. Fled to Llanrwst and pillaged Gwydir. As governor of Shrawardine Castle, his troopers got an evil name. Captured Hopton Castle and Apley House. Pillaged Dolgellau drapers. He was killed at Rathmines, 1649. — Symonds. Parry. p.370. Quoting Symonds. C.W.P. 1810. D.N.B.

VAUGHAN, William, Esq., Merioneth. Nominated Knight of the Royal Oak. — Parry. p.404.

VAUGHAN, Willi. Colonel William Owen's 'guard' in Harlech Castle. He might be the Colonel's nephew, son of Sir John's daughter Elizabeth who married Robert Vaughan of Cors y Gedol. — Brogyntyn. Arch.Camb. 1875. p.12.

VAUGHAN, Major. In Colonel William Wynne's Foot, 'his Major wounded in the ribs' at Wem (wrote Richard Baxter). — Shrop. during the C.W. p.82.

VAUX, Quartermaster Gilbert, of Denbighshire. In Sir Richard Lloyd's Horse. — I.O.

VERE, Colonel Edward. Signed Caernarvonshire articles for Byron. — Phil. ii. p.309.

VERNEY, Sir Edmund. With Byron in Chester. Appointed commander in Flintshire and Denbighshire in 1645. 'The forces of theise two Counties are for the psent comitted to the order of Sr Edmund Verney Knight Colonell of foote.' — Clenennau 547.

WAKE, Captain Sir Baldwyn. Commodore of royalist fleet at Beaumaris, winter, 1643-4. — Barn Hill, MS. 5367 and C.W.P. 1768.

WALL, Lieutenant. Temporarily in charge of Chirk, May, 1645.

WATTS, Colonel Sir John, son of Sir John of Mardocks, Ware, Herts. Governor of Chirk Castle. Beat off attack by Sir Thomas Myddelton, Christmas, 1644. Knighted by Charles, — Symonds. Harl. MS. 944. Arch.Camb. Vol. i.

September, 1645. Betrayed castle to Mytton for £200, February, 1646. Was captured at Churchstoke, 1 March (William Maurice's diary). Fined at £100.

C.C.C. 1865.

WALLY, Randolph. Signed Anglesey articles.

Phil. ii. p.401.

WALTON, Lieutenant-Colonel. Taken prisoner in Anglesey.

C.W.P. 1815.

WANTON, Mr. Captured at Y Dalar Hir.

Phil. ii. P.384.

WAREINGE, Edmund, Esq., Montgomeryshire. Nominated Knight of the Royal Oak.

Parry. p.404.

WHITLEY, Lieutenant-Colonel John. Fourth son of Thomas Whitley of Aston Hall. Lieutenant in 1644, made free burgess of Denbigh. Probably helped in defence of Aberystwyth; thence to Caernarfon and sent to Conwy where he was killed. (Willett says ' Colonel of Foot'.)

Minutes.
Willett's History of Hawarden. p.ll9.
B.M. Royal Martyrs.
109. g.13. p.233.

WHITLEY, Captain John, of Shotton Hall. Horse. In Booth revolt, 1659. Probably cousin of above. Flint.

I.O.
P.R.O. SP. 25/29.
f.36/37.

WHITLEY, Joseph. Signed Aberystwyth articles.

Phil. ii. p.305.

WHITLEY, Ralph. Second son of Thomas by second marriage. Served Rupert. Made constable of Flint Castle, 1664.

Taylor's Flint. p.145.

WHITLEY, Robert. Eldest son of Thomas by first marriage. Signed Aberystwyth articles as commissioner.

Phil. ii. p.305.

WHITLEY, Colonel Robert, of County Pembroke. 'He was a major for the King of Scots at Worcester, listed soldiers, sent provisions' &c. His wife was 'a Gerard'.

H.M.C. Vol. iii.
p.1468.

WHITLEY, Colonel Roger. Eldest son of Thomas by second marriage to Elizabeth Brereton. Born 1618. At Grey's Inn 1637. 'Ro. Whitley' * was a captain in Colonel Charles Gerard's Foot in 1643. In 1644 as major was made free burgess of Denbigh. Commanded regiments of both Horse and Foot. Led two hundred Horse at Denbigh Green. Made governor of Aberystwyth which he defended stubbornly until 14 April, 1646. A diarist writes: 'his men about 100 or more came to Harlech, thence to Caernarvonshire; and they went to Llanrwst. From thence they marched to Denbigh.' Some arrived at Caernarfon Castle, and Byron informed Owen, 'I have furnished most of the Aberystwyth men with musketts, the rest may esily bee supplied with pikes or brown bills, they are very good men, and carried themselves with great fidelity and courage during that seege.' In 1648, Roger joined revolt, first meeting Byron in Delemere forest, then going to Anglesey to serve as second-in-command to Colonel R. Bulkeley. Both were captured in Beaumaris Castle, 30 September, 1648. Released and went overseas. Was one of Charles' principal plotters. He was captured on Bardsey Island in March 1650. In 1659, he brought King's commission to Sir George Booth. Fortified

Culham.
Minutes.
Symonds.
Phil. ii. P.305.
Arch.Camb. Vol. i.
Parry. p.362.
Clenennau 615.
Parry. p.389.
Flint. p.144.
Arch.Camb. 1875.
p.27.

* *Probably Roger, but might be Robert.*

Hawarden Castle. Escaped defeat and went overseas until
Restoration. Made a fortune farming the Post Office and
bought Peel Hall, Cheshire, where he entertained William III
on his way to Ireland. Roger devoted many years to Parliament;
turned Whig. Four times mayor of Chester. Married sister of
Gerard, later Earl of Macclesfield. Died 1697. Buried Hawarden.
Epitaph quoted by Taylor.

WHITLEY, Captain Richard. Third son of Thomas Whitley.
Killed in defence of Hawarden Castle.

Willett's of Aston.
'Hawarden.'
B.M. Royal Martyrs.
109. g.13. p.233.

WHITLEY, Thomas, of Aston Hall, near Hawarden. Father
of Colonel Roger Whitley. Compounded on Denbigh
Articles, 'for delinquency in deserting his habitation and
going into the garrison'. Fined £125. Took N.O. and N.C.,
16 June, 1648.

History of
Hawarden. p.119.

C.C.C. 1723.

WILLIAMS, Edward, of Isaph (Conwy Valley). 'appeared
in arms' with William Williams. Imprisoned in Conwy
Castle, charged with treason for 1655 conspiracy headed
by Bayly.

UNV. OF N.W.
Penrhos Papers.
v.212.

WILLIAMS, Ensign Edmund, of Caernarvonshire. Foot.

I.O.

WILLIAMS, Cornet Edward, of Montgomeryshire. In
(Captain) John Blayney's troop. (Sir Arthur Blayney's
Dragoons)

I.O.

WILLIAMS, Captain. In Colonel Endymion Porter's
regiment in Irish expedition of spring, 1642.

Peacock.

WILLIAMS, Lieutenant Edward. In Colonel R. Mostyn's
Foot. Flint.

I.O.

WILLIAMS, Major Edward. Commanded Colonel R.
Herbert's regiment in assault on Bristol.

Warburton.

WILLIAMS, Major –. Captured at Montgomery, 1644.

Phil. ii. p.206.

WILLIAMS, Major –. Captured at Rowton Heath, 1645.

Phil. ii. p.384.

WILLIAMS, Captain Edward. In Denbighshire maimed
soldiers' signing for Edward Williams of St George.

D.M.S.

WILLIAMS, Edward. Signed letter from Chester with Hugh
Wynne, Robert Wynne and Henry Lloyd.

R. Morris. p.131.

WILLIAMS, Ensign. Captured at Montgomery.

Phil. ii. p.206.

WILLIAMS, Captain Francis. In Sir Charles Floyd's Foot.
Signed from London and Westminster.

I.O.

WILLIAMS, Captain John. In Colonel Hugh Wynne's Foot.
Of Denbighshire.

I.O.

WILLIAMS, John. Signed Anglesey articles, 1648.

Phil. ii. p.400.

WILLIAMS, John of 'Llanywith, co Denbigh'. Compounded
on Denbigh articles, being 'under age'. Fined £66.

C.C.C. 1723.

WILLIAMS, John, Archbishop of York. Conwy-born. Chased
from See by Roundheads in 1642, returned to native town
and fortified castle. Attended Oxford 'parliament'. Turned
out of castle by Sir John Owen, May, 1645, he continued to

serve until c. April, 1646, when he joined victorious
Parliamentarians and helped to capture Caernarfon and
Conwy, being wounded in the neck, August, 1646. His
feud with Owen harmed the royal cause. Williams died at
Gloddaeth, 1649. (See *Mitre and Musket*) Not a
soldier, but the most conspicuous figure in North Wales.

WILLIAMS, Captain Griffith. Nephew of Archbishop. A
Caernarvonshire Commissioner of Array and Vice-Admiral
of N. Wales. In August, 1645, he was ordered (with Roger
Mostyn) to march 50 men to Conwy. 'During the Civil
War and Commonwealth period,' writes Professor Glyn
Roberts, 'he followed in general, the lead given by his uncle.'
Created bart. by Cromwell, 1658, he aided the Restoration
and was again made bart. by Charles II.
    C.W.P. 1764.
    Arch.Camb. 1875.
    p.312.
    D.W.B. p.1155.

WILLIAMS, Lieutenant-Colonel Maurice. In Colonel William
Salesbury's Foot. Signed for William Griffith ap Rhydderch
who was in Captain Peter (Piers) Williams' company in Colonel
R. Mostyn's Foot in Chester.
    D.M.S.

WILLIAMS, Lieutenant Osmond. In Irish expedition of
June, 1642.
    B.M. 109. g.13.
    p.209.

WILLIAMS. Captain Pierce Williams who also signed.
    D.M.S.

WILLIAMS, Captain Peter, of Flintshire. 'Unattached.'
    I.O.

WILLIAMS, Captain Robert. 'Robyn Williams, my Lord's
kinsman in France.' (Archbishop Williams' nephew in exile)
Sir Gruffyth Williams' son, of Conwy.
    C.W.P. 1843.

WILLIAMS, Captain Roger, Salop. In Sir Charles Lloyd's Foot.
    I.O.

WILLIAMS, Roger, of 'Yecoed', gentleman in 1659 revolt.
    P.R.O. SP. 25/59.
    pp.36/7.

WILLIAMS, Lieutenant Thomas, of 'Yecoed', served in
1659 revolt.
    Ibid.

WILLIAMS, Captain Thomas. 'A royalist', died 1667.
    Arch.Camb. ii. p.14.

WILLIAMS, Captain Thomas. 'In arms' in Anglesey, 1648.
    Ibid.

WILLIAMS, William. Muster Master in Chester.
    R. Morris. p.146.

WILLIAMS, Ancient (Ensign) William. Defender of
Harlech, died of wound, 1647.
    Phil. ii. p.334.

WILLIAMS, William, of Isaph. Promised to appear 'under
arms' with Bayly in Conwy, 1655.
    UNV. OF N.W.
    Penrhos Papers.
    v.212.

WILLIAMS, Sir William, Bart., of Vaynol, Caernarvonshire.
A Commissioner of Array. In June, 1644, 'by King's
warrant' he was appointed jointly with Sheriff Robert
Jones, to raise Horse and Foot in Caernarvonshire for the
trained band. As colonel he marched against Brereton in
the spring of 1645. A year later he turned Parliamentarian,
and 'Bart. Williams' helped to capture Caernarfon and Conwy.
He became royalist again in 1648, and fought at Y Dalar Hir.
    Llanfair 66.
    Black's Oxford
    Docquets.
    p.222.
    P.R.O. SP. 23/4 & 5.

WILLIAMS, William J., Bodfari. Y Dalar Hir delinquent.
    P.R.O. SP. 23/4 & 5.

WINCH, Robert, of Penllech. Y Dalar Hir delinquent.
    P.R.O. SP. 23/5.

WINDEBANKE, Captain Francis. Son of Secretary of State,
    Sir Francis Windebanke. Original captain in Colonel
    William Wynne's Foot. Fought at Cheriton. Transferred
    to Gerard. As governor of Bletchington House, he
    surrendered to Cromwell, 24 April, 1645, for which he was
    shot. Mentioned in Denbigh Minutes as burgess. Aided Lord
    Strange in attack on Manchester, 1642.
        Crosse. D.M.S. Burne and Young. p.195.

WINN, Ensign. Captured at Montgomery, 1644.
        Phil. ii. p.206

WOOD, Thomas, of Anglesey. Nominated Knight of the
    Royal Oak.
        Parry. p.404.

WOOD, Owen. Commissioner of Array, Anglesey. Signed articles.
        Phil. ii. p.400.

WOODHOUSE, Sir Michael. Formed Foot regiment to serve
    under Lord Capell and co-operated with Colonel Wm.
    Wynne in Salop. Was at Montgomery fight, 1644.
    Governor of Ludlow. Regiment later known as Prince of
    Wales' Foot. Numerous references.
        Phil. ii. p.202. Ottley Papers.

WYATT, Dudley. Deputy Governor of North Wales to Sir
    John Mennes.
        Clenennau 543

WYN, Captain. 'One Captayne Wyn was slayn', at Wem, 1643.
        H.M.C. i. p.143.

WYNN, Captain. In Flint Castle. Probably future Sir Richard,
    4th Bart.
        C.W.P. 1818.

WYNN, Captain –. In Sir Thomas Salusbury's original Foot.
        Culham.

WYNN, John. Later Sir John, 5th Bart. of Gwydir. Was at
    Wattstay, February, 1659. Might he be one of the 'Captain
    John Wynns'? Sir John carried 'the Coate' at the funeral of
    Colonel J. Robinson, so was probably a comrade-in-arms.

WYNNE, Lieutenant Cadwallader, of Denbigh. (Voelas?)
    In Colonel R. Broughton's Foot.
        I.O.

WYNNE, David, gentleman. Obtained Caernarvonshire
    maimed soldiers' mize.
        File 1669.

WYNNE, Captain Edward, fourth son of Edward Wynne of
    Ystrad, and grandson of Maurice Wynne of Gwydir and
    Katherine of Berain. Died of wounds received during
    siege of Denbigh. Buried in Llanrhaeadr churchyard.
    Newcome and J. Williams give accounts of his burial.
    Mentioned in Royal Martyrs as 'slain at Denbigh'.
        A. and M. Denbigh. p.228.

WYNNE, Quartermaster Ellis, of Denbigh. Quartermaster of
    Colonel William Wynne's troop of Horse.
        I.O.

WYNNE, Henry. Signed Anglesey articles.
        Phil. ii. p.401.

WYNNE, Colonel Hugh, of Bodysgallen, near Llandudno.
    Daughter's tombstone in Llanrhos church states he raised
    a regiment of Foot for the King at his own expense, and
    was a great sufferer for the royal cause. He took one
    hundred Denbighshire men to Chester early in 1643.
    Remained there almost continuously during the long siege.
    Was hostage during negotiations for surrender, February,
    1646. Went to Denbigh to continue the struggle and there
    acted as one of Salesbury's commissioners. Appears to have
        D.M.S. A. H. Dodd in D.H.S. Vol. iii. p.51. Parry. p.392.

been captured in 1650, but entry is ambiguous: 'Mr. Wynne,
Bodysgallen with 500 volunteers went to Ireland.' Compounded
as from 'Llanrwst' (the family home) and was fined £63.
Survived to be made a D.L. and J.P. Died 1674. Burial entered in
Llanrwst register.

WYNNE, Major Hugh. In Colonel William Wynne's Foot.   D.M.S.
He might be the colonel's youngest brother and a cousin
of Colonel Hugh Wynne (both named after the same grandfather,
Hugh Wynne of Berthddu). Served in Harlech Castle, 1647.

WYNNE, Writer wishes for an Act of Parliament to send Hugh   C.W.P. 2303.
Wynne home in 1660. Might refer to Major Hugh
in exile.

WYNNE, Captain Hugh, in 1645, ordered by Prince Maurice   Clenennau 560.
to lead his company to Wrexham (7 March).

WYNNE, Lieutenant Hugh, of Anglesey. Lieutenant to   I.O.
Captain William Wynne, in Colonel John Robinson's Foot.

WYNNE, Lieutenant Humphrey, of Anglesey. In Captain   I.O.
Jenkins' company of Sir John Owen's Foot.

WYNNE, George (Colonel?). Signed with Sir Michael   Phil. ii. p.102.
Ernley, Major-General Gibson and others reply to
Roundheads in Hawarden Castle, 20 November, 1643.

WYNNE, Captain John. Ordered by Prince Maurice to take   Clenennau 560.
company to Wrexham, 7 March, 1645.

WYNNE, Lieutenant John, of Denbighshire. In Colonel   I.O.
William Wynne's Foot.

WYNNE, John, Esq., of Denbighshire. Nominated Knight   Parry. p.404.
of the Royal Oak.

WYNNE, John (no rank). Signed Aberystwyth articles.   Phil. ii. p.305.

WYNNE, Lieutenant-Colonel Maurice. In Colonel William   D.M.S.
Salesbury's Foot.

WYNNE, Ensign Owen, of Denbighshire. In Colonel William   I.O.
Wynne's Foot.

WYNNE, Owen. Anglesey commissioner. Signed articles.   Phil. ii. p.401.

WYNNE, Captain Matthew. In Colonel William Wynne's   Chirk Castle. vi.477.
Foot. Was son of William Wynne of Hendregeginian,   I.O. and D.M.S.
County Denbighshire. It would seem Col. Hugh Wynne
took over Col. Wm Wynne's regiment after his death at
Wem, 1643.

WYNNE, Captain. Captured in Conwy town, 9 August,   Phil. ii. p.325.
1646. Possibly Robert Wynne of Plas Mawr.

WYNNE, Captain Robert. In Sir John Owen's Foot.   P.R.O. SP. 29/68.

WYNNE, Ensign Robert, of Caernarvonshire. In Colonel   I.O.
William Wynne's Foot.

WYNNE, Lieutenant-Colonel Robert. In Colonel Hugh   D.M.S.
Wynne's Foot. Probably of Gwydir. Was in Chester siege.

WYNNE, Robert, of Garthewin. In Colonel William Wynne's Foot.
His brother. No rank mentioned, but epitaph states he was
'with him when he was killed at Wem'. Married heiress of

Garthewin. Buried Llanfair Talhaearn Church.

WYNNE, Robert, of Voelas. Sheriff 1631. Provided a waggon train of twenty conveyances and horses in 1643. D.H.S. Vol. iii. p.53.

WYNNE, Lieutenant Robert, of Denbighshire. In Colonel William Salesbury's Foot. I.O.

WYNNE, Captain Robert. Imprisoned in Beaumaris, 1648. Exchange by Twisleton. Might be of Glyn, Meirion. Clenennau 633.

WYNNE, Captain Robert. Served 'in forraine parts'. Chirk Castle MS.

WYNN. Captain of Horse. Captured near Ruthin, April, 1646. Newcome. p.75.

WYNNE, Lieutenant. In Sir John Pawlett's Foot. Captured at Naseby. Peacock.

WYNNE, Major, of Llanvair (near Ruthin). D.M.S.

WYNNE, Richard, of Aberkynleth, County Denbighshire, marched with his men to Chester and mustered them at Wrexham. Frequented Chirk Castle. Took Capell's oath. C.A.M. p.1094.

WYNNE, Captain William. Foot. Caernarfon. I.O.

WYNNE, Lieutenant-Colonel Thomas. Mentioned in connection of application of Salop officer, Will Bishop. D.M.S.

WYNNE, Lieutenant Thomas, of Caernarfon. Lieutenant to Captain Robert Wynne in Sir J. Owen's Foot. I.O.

WYNNE, William (Junior), of Glyn, Merioneth. Captured in March, 1651. Parry. p.392.

WYNNE, Captain William. In Colonel R. Mostyn's Foot. Flint. I.O.

WYNNE, Colonel William, of Melai, County Denbigh. D.M.S.
Colonel of Denbigh trained-band which he turned into a Foot regiment and marched to Shropshire, Spring 1643, to join Capell. In 1642, Wynne and Salusbury were impeached by the House for their activities on behalf of the King. Epitaph of his son John in Llanfair Talhaearn Church states he raised a regiment of Foot and troop of Horse at his own expense. He was shot and killed while attacking Wem, 8 October, 1643, and buried in old St. Chad's, Shrewsbury. Letters in *Crosse* collection. N.L.W.

WYNNE, William. Asked by Sir Richard Lloyd and other Commissioners of Array to march armed supporters to the relief of Cholmondeley House, which was besieged, August, 1643. Descent on Wales expected. (Colonel?) Crosse 1112.

WYNNE, William, of Garthgynnan. Was fourth son of Sir John Wynne. H.S.D. 1651.

WYNN, Lieutenant Thomas, in the company of Captain Willliam Glynn of Llyar. In February, 1645, he marched to Prince Maurice near Wrexham. Joined Captain Glynn in Anglesey revolt of 1648. C.A.M. p.1102.

YALE, Captain Thomas, of Plas-in-Yale. In Sir Evan Lloyd's Foot. A kinsman. Emigrated to New Hampshire after war. Griffith states he married Dorothy, daughter of Humphrey Hughes of Gwerclas, Merioneth. Pedigrees. / I.O.

YATE, Commissary Robert, of Flintshire. I.O.

Index - Persons

Index - Places